Transforming Towns

Transforming Towns

The Economic Reach of Tourism

RAFEAL MECHLORE

WSM Publisher

CONTENTS

INDEX 1

INTRODUCTION 3

Chapter 1   21

Chapter 2   39

Chapter 3   57

Chapter 4   76

Chapter 5   94

Chapter 6   108

Chapter 7   126

Chapter 8   141

Chapter 9   154

Chapter 10   175

INDEX

Introduction

1. Definition of Tourism
2. Significance of Tourism for Towns
3. Purpose and Scope of the Book
4. Methodology and Research Approach
5. Overview of Chapters

Chapter 1: The Foundations of Tourism Economics
1.1 Historical Evolution of Tourism
1.2 Key Concepts in Tourism Economics
1.3 The Tourism Value Chain
1.4 Economic Drivers of Tourism

Chapter 2: Tourism as an Economic Engine
2.1 The Role of Tourism in Local Economies
2.2 Economic Impact Assessment Models
2.3 Challenges and Opportunities

Chapter 3: Planning and Development of Tourism Infrastructure
3.1 Infrastructure Requirements for Tourism
3.2 Public and Private Sector Involvement
3.3 Sustainable Tourism Development
3.4 Funding and Investment Sources

Chapter 4: Marketing and Promotion of Towns as Tourist Destinations
4.1 Destination Marketing Strategies
4.2 Digital and Social Media Marketing
4.3 Event and Festival Tourism

4.4 Branding and Identity

Chapter 5: Community Engagement and Tourism
5.1 Balancing Local Interests and Tourism
5.2 Involving the Community in Tourism Development
5.3 Cultural Preservation and Heritage Tourism
5.4 Managing Overtourism

Chapter 6: Hospitality and Accommodation
6.1 Types of Accommodation
6.2 Quality Standards and Regulations
6.3 Accommodation Business Models
6.4 The Airbnb Effect

Chapter 7: Food and Beverage Tourism
7.1 Culinary Tourism Trends
7.2 Restaurants and Local Cuisine
7.3 Food Festivals and Tours
7.4 Farm-to-Table Initiatives

Chapter 8: Transportation and Accessibility
8.1 The Role of Transportation in Tourism
8.2 Improving Accessibility to Towns
8.3 Sustainable Transportation Solutions

Chapter 9: Economic Diversification through Tourism
9.1 Tourism and Economic Resilience
9.2 Encouraging Entrepreneurship
9.3 Supporting Artisan and Craft Industries
9.4 Other Economic Spin-offs

Chapter 10: Measuring Success and Future Trends
10.1 Key Performance Indicators for Tourism
10.2 The Importance of Data and Analytics
10.3 Emerging Trends in Tourism Economics
10.4 Preparing for Future Challenges

INTRODUCTION

The phenomenon of tourism has emerged as a significant agent of economic transformation in the current global landscape, particularly in smaller towns and villages all over the world. This is particularly true in the modern global environment. A complex narrative has emerged as a result of the complicated interplay between tourism and the economic dynamics of towns. This narrative illustrates the enormous impact that this industry has had on local development, the upgrade of infrastructure, the preservation of cultural traditions, and the expansion of livelihoods. The transformative potential of tourism is becoming more obvious as it serves not only as a source of revenue creation but also as a catalyst for complete socio-economic improvement within these townships. Tourism serves not only as a source of revenue generation but also as a catalyst for these townships.

In its capacity as an economic driver, tourism possesses the extraordinary potential to resuscitate the fortunes of towns, so launching them onto a path that will lead them to continued growth and prosperity. Tourism becomes an essential component in the process of fostering economic diversity and reducing the issues associated with underdevelopment and unemployment as a result of its ability to create jobs, stimulate local economies, and propel the development of infrastructure. Furthermore, the influx of revenue associated with tourism into these towns not only revitalizes the commercial landscape but also strengthens the financial capacities of local administrations, enabling them to channel resources into essential areas such as education, healthcare, and sustainable infrastructure. This is because the commercial landscape is revitalized by the influx of tourism-related revenue.

The economic impact of tourism extends well beyond the domain of monetary profits; it permeates the cultural fabric of these towns, fostering a sense of identity and pride among the population of these communities. Tourism accentuates the value of conserving these priceless assets by displaying the rich tapestry of indigenous customs, historical monuments, and cultural history. This helps to ensure that these important aspects of the past are not lost. When viewed in this light, the promotion of cultural tourism becomes an important factor not only in luring tourists but also in cultivating a greater understanding for the singular histories and practices that define the character of these communities. This is especially true when it comes to enticing visitors.

However, the method of utilizing tourism for the purpose of fostering economic growth is not devoid of difficulties. The difficult balancing act that must be performed by city planners and policymakers in order to accommodate the needs of a rapidly expanding tourist population while also protecting the natural integrity of the area's ecology presents a significant challenge.

The shadow of over-commercialization, environmental degradation, and cultural dilution looms large, mandating a balanced strategy that prioritizes sustainable and responsible tourist practices. The specter of over-commercialization, environmental degradation, and cultural dilution hangs large.

In addition, the sensitivity of small towns to shifts in the volume of tourist traffic and the fragility of their economies to shocks from the outside world underline the necessity of comprehensive risk mitigation techniques and diversified economic planning. These communities can better negotiate the complexity of the global tourism landscape and insulate themselves from prospective economic downturns if they cultivate a culture of resilience and flexibility.

In light of these circumstances, it is absolutely necessary to delve deeper into the transformative potential of tourism, analyzing its impact on various aspects of town development, and investigating the best practices that enable towns to harness the full economic potential of this industry while protecting their cultural and environmental integrity. A comprehensive understanding of the intricate interplay between tourism and town economies can be gleaned by critically evaluating case studies, policy frameworks, and scholarly research. This provides insights into the mechanisms that underpin successful transformations and sustainable growth trajectories.

It is of the utmost importance that, in view of the continuous discussion that is taking place all over the world concerning sustainable development and responsible tourism, an investigation into the ways in which cities might align their economic goals with the preservation of the environment and social inclusion is carried out. The combination of environmentally friendly infrastructure development, community participation programs, and environmentally responsible tourist practices has emerged as a potentially fruitful avenue towards the goal of striking a balance between the advancement of the economy and the preservation of the natural world.

This extensive investigation aims to shed light on the intricate web of relationships that determine the economic reach of tourism in altering cities by synthesizing empirical evidence, theoretical frameworks, and practical insights. This will be accomplished by combining these three types of information. A holistic understanding of the intricate dynamics between tourism and town economies can be achieved through a nuanced analysis of the challenges, opportunities, and best practices that underpin this transformative journey. This will provide a roadmap for sustainable and inclusive development in the global tourism landscape.

1. **Definition of Tourism**

The industry of tourism is a complex and ever-changing phenomena that is extremely important to the socioeconomic environment on a global scale. It entails moving people from one location to another for a variety of reasons, including business, education, pleasure, and others. Even if the idea of tourism may appear to be simple, attempting to provide an all-encompassing definition for it is a complex undertaking. This article investigates the many facets that comprise the essence of tourism by delving into a variety of definitions and perspectives of the term. The goal of this investigation is to provide a full understanding of tourism as an important industry.

1. **The Historically Accepted Definitions of Tourism:**
   The United Nations World Tourism Organization, sometimes known as UNWTO:
   Tourism is defined by the United Nations World Tourism Organization (UNWTO) as the "activities of persons traveling to and staying in places outside their usual environment for not more than one consecutive year for leisure, business, and other purposes."
   This definition is one of the most frequently accepted ones, and it offers a comprehensive perspective on tourism. It encompasses both leisure travel and travel for business purposes, and it places an emphasis on the component "not more than one consecutive year," which differentiates tourists from long-term migrants.
   IATA stands for the International Air Transport Association and it does the following:
   According to the definition offered by the International Air Transport Association (IATA), tourism is "the activity of visiting a place for pleasure."
   This condensed definition places an emphasis on the leisure component of tourism and highlights the concept that the primary motivation for individuals to participate in tourism is for enjoyment and recreation.
2. **Changing Aspects of the Tourism Industry:**
   The Practice of Ecotourism
   Ecotourism is a subcategory of tourism that places an emphasis on natural environments and environmentally responsible behavior. It entails traveling to natural settings that have been left untouched while also taking part in conservation efforts and raising awareness about the environment. Ecotourism is a form of tourism that aims to reduce the environmental impact of traditional

tourism while simultaneously enhancing the quality of life in the communities to which it travels.

Travel within a Culture:

The pursuit of knowledge regarding the cultural history and customs of a location is at the heart of cultural tourism. To get a more in-depth comprehension of the culture of a destination, tourists often participate in activities such as going to museums and historical sites, going to local festivals, and engaging in conversation with members of the local community.

Tourism in the Medical Field

Traveling to another nation for medical treatments is referred to as "medical tourism." Patients frequently choose to do so because of the lower costs, shorter waiting times, or greater availability of specialist medical services. In recent years, it has been increasingly common for patients to travel out of the country for medical procedures such as operations, dental work, and wellness treatments.

The Adventure Tourism Industry:

Activities that fall under the category of "adventure tourism" are those that are often more taxing
on the body and have some form of danger or thrill. Activities such as hiking, mountaineering, and whitewater rafting, as well as extreme sports, come under this category. These are activities that thrill-seekers and adventure aficionados like participating in.

Tourism for business purposes:

Travel for professional or business reasons is included in the category of business tourism, which is also referred to as MICE tourism (which stands for meetings, incentives, conferences, and exhibitions). Attendance at company events, trade exhibitions, seminars, and conferences are all part of this responsibility. People who travel for business frequently combine work-related activities with opportunities for recreation.

3. **Essential Components and Identifiable Features of Tourism:**

    The act of traveling from one area to another, whether it be on the other side of the world or inside the same nation, is an essential component of tourism. This movement can take place across international borders or within a single nation. Staying in the Location for a Limited Amount of Time Tourism typically involves only a short visit to the location. Travelers who are only there temporarily, rather than looking to settle down, are considered tourists.

    Leisure or Other objectives: Although leisure is the primary driver of tourism, the industry also serves a variety of other objectives, such as those related to business, education, healthcare, and other fields.

    Experience: The search of one-of-a-kind and unforgettable experiences is frequently at the center of tourism. Discovering new cultures, landscapes, and activities is one of the main reasons people travel.

Impact on the Economy: Tourism has important economic ramifications, as it can significantly contribute to the revenue of a location through expenditures made on lodging, food, transportation, and a variety of activities.

Exchange of Cultures: Tourism acts as a catalyst for cultural exchange by bringing together individuals from a variety of different origins. It has the potential to foster appreciation and understanding between different cultures.

4. **The Problems That Tourism Causes and Its Effects:**

While tourism does have many positive aspects, it also has some negative aspects and repercussions that need to be taken into mind.

Popular travel locations frequently face the challenge of overtourism, which places a burden on local resources and infrastructure and contributes to the deterioration of the natural environment.

Environmental Impact Tourism can have a negative impact on natural surroundings by contributing to pollution, disturbing natural habitats, and consuming an excessive amount of resources.

degradation of Culture Excessive tourism can lead to the commodification and degradation of local cultures as a result of adaptations made to accommodate the expectations of tourists. This phenomenon is known as cultural erosion.

Inequalities on a Socioeconomic Scale: There is evidence that tourism might, in certain

instances, aggravate existing socioeconomic disparities, with local communities frequently failing to profit evenly from the business.

Strain on Infrastructure An increase in the number of tourists visiting a region may put a strain on its infrastructure, which includes things like transportation networks and accommodations.

The phenomena known as tourism is dynamic and multidimensional, and it continues to develop in reaction to shifting worldwide trends as well as the tastes of individual tourists. Traditional definitions of tourism provide a foundation for understanding the sector as a whole; however, the tourism business has evolved into numerous subcategories, which represent the wide range of reasons and interests that people have for traveling.

It is vital to have a solid understanding of the fundamental aspects and characteristics of tourism in order to fully appreciate its contribution to the global economy, intercultural communication, and the enhancement of individual experiences. However, it is of the utmost importance to realize the difficulties and repercussions of tourism, which call for responsible and sustainable practices to be implemented in order to ensure the long-term viability of this industry's transformative potential. Tourism will continue to undergo shifts in both its definition and its nature in tandem with the ongoing transformation of the world around it, making it a dynamic and ever-evolving force in our interconnected global society.

B. Significance of Tourism for Towns

In recent years, tourism has become an increasingly important driver of both economic and social change, particularly in the world's many rural areas and smaller cities. Beyond the simple act of drawing in tourists, the value of tourism to these communities lies in the fact that it acts as a driving force behind the expansion of a diverse range of industries. This article examines the significant role that tourism plays in the development of towns, shining a focus on the positive economic, social, and cultural consequences of tourism while also analyzing the potential and challenges that tourism presents.

1. **The Significance of Tourism to the Economy:**
   Development of Diverse Employment Opportunities:
   Towns often rely heavily on tourism as a significant employment generator. The sector encompasses a diverse array of employment opportunities, ranging from those in transportation and tour operations to those in hospitality and the food service business. The development of jobs in communities that value tourism is not restricted to huge corporations but also includes small businesses and entrepreneurial ventures. As a result, these communities offer a varied range of opportunities for local employment.
   Diversification of the Economic System:
   A town's susceptibility to economic downturns increases the more heavily it is dependent on a single economic industry or sector. The development of a more robust and diverse local economy is one of the many benefits that tourism may provide.
   It lessens the town's reliance on a single industry, which lessens the likelihood that residents may lose their jobs during times of economic instability. As a result, the town's economic stability is improved.
   Development of the Area's Businesses:
   The arrival of tourists drives up the amount of money spent inside the community. Visitors frequently support local services, including restaurants, stores, and service providers, which is beneficial to the town's economy. This increase in commercial activity is beneficial to the local business community and helps to strengthen the city's overall economic vibrancy.
   The Development of Infrastructure:
   Many cities make significant investments in the improvement of their infrastructure in order to cater to the requirements of tourists. Residents and tourists alike will reap the benefits of an improved road network, airports, public transportation, and utility services. A higher general quality of life, increased tourism, and increased local investment all contribute to a virtuous

cycle of sustainable economic development when better infrastructure is present.

Benefits to the Budget:

Cities and towns can reap monetary benefits from tourism. The numerous tourism-related endeavors provide cash for the local governments in the form of taxation, permits, and fees that must be paid. This additional revenue can be reinvested in public services, education, healthcare, and other critical areas, which will ultimately improve the well-being of citizens and reduce the burden of taxation.

2. **The Contribution of Tourism to Society:**

The Protection and Advancement of Cultural Practices:

Tourists are frequently drawn to a town's specific cultural and historical features due to their rarity. The tourism industry has the potential to play a crucial part in the maintenance and development of these features. When municipalities see the potential for their culture and legacy to contribute to the local economy, they are encouraged to preserve and promote it. This not only helps keep traditions alive but also results in increased revenue for cultural events, museums, and other heritage institutions.

Exchanges Between Different Cultures:

People from all different walks of life are brought together thanks to tourism, which helps to promote cultural understanding.

The people interact with tourists from all over the world, and tourists, in turn, engage with the local traditions, customs, and languages of the destination they are visiting. This interchange fosters more mutual understanding as well as appreciation of one another's cultural backgrounds, which contributes to the development of a more inclusive and global worldview.

Participation in the Community:

Communities on a local level frequently take an active role in tourism-related endeavors, such as the provision of guided tours, the sale of local goods, and the dissemination of information regarding their cultural history. This kind of participation can give communities more agency, which in turn can increase their feelings of ownership and pride in their culture and surroundings.

Possibilities for Furthering One's Education:

Historically significant and culturally significant towns frequently become major centers for educational tourism. The cultural and historical research that is conducted in the town's schools, universities, and other research organizations contributes to the intellectual growth of the community as a whole and of its individual residents.

3. **Obstacles of a Cultural and Environmental Nature:**

Excessive tourism:

The phenomenon known as "overtourism" can occur when there are so many visitors to a certain location that it becomes unsustainable. It puts a pressure on the available regional resources, overloads the existing infrastructure, and is detrimental to the natural environment. The most important problem is to find a happy medium between economic gains and environmentally responsible methods.

The Degradation of Culture:
An overabundance of tourism can result in the commercialization of local culture and customs, which may hasten their decline. The strain that comes from having to pander to the expectations of tourists may end up changing or watering down the authenticity of a town's tradition.

Disparities in Socioeconomic Status:
Because local residents do not always benefit proportionally from the cash generated by the tourism industry, tourism has the potential to unintentionally worsen existing socioeconomic disparities. Finding a happy medium between economic growth and equal distribution is still one of the most difficult challenges.

4. **Tourism That Is Sustainable:**

It is vital that sustainable tourism practices be implemented in order to make the most of tourism's potential benefits to cities while also addressing the issues that tourism presents. The goal of sustainable tourism is to travel in a manner that has the fewest possible adverse effects on the surrounding natural environment as well as the cultural traditions of the people visited. The importance of responsible planning, conservation, and involvement in the community is emphasized.

Conservation of the Natural Environment:
To reduce the negative effects of tourism on the local ecosystem, municipalities might institute more sustainable policies and procedures. Among these are the encouragement of waste reduction, the use of sustainable energy, and the protection of natural areas.

Protecting Our Cultural Heritage:
Town planning should put an emphasis on making efforts to both maintain and develop the local culture. This could entail creating job possibilities for local artists, giving educational opportunities related to local culture, and protecting historical landmarks.

Participation in Community Activities:
It is essential to involve the local populations in the planning of tourism. It guarantees that locals will receive direct advantages from the industry and that their opinions will be taken into consideration during the decision-making process.

Education for Visitors:
It is possible to encourage responsible behavior in tourists by educating them about the local culture, environment, and sustainable practices. Some examples of

responsible behavior include reducing trash, honoring local customs, and safeguarding natural resources.

It is impossible to exaggerate the importance of tourism for cities and towns. It contributes to cultural preservation, intercultural dialogue, and community engagement in addition to offering economic diversity, job creation, and the development of infrastructure. However, in order for communities to maximize the benefits of tourism and reduce the issues it presents, sustainable tourism practices need to be implemented.

Because of the complicated link between tourism and communities, there is a pressing need for development that is both balanced and appropriate. The most important problem is to find a happy medium that allows for economic expansion while also protecting cultural traditions and the natural environment.

Nevertheless, municipalities who are adept at navigating these complications have the opportunity to capitalize on the transformative potential of tourism, which will ensure a profitable and sustainable future for their communities. To ensure that tourism continues to be a driving force for the growth of communities and keeps pace with shifting preferences and trends in the tourist industry, cities must learn to adapt to the ever-changing state of the world.

C. Purpose and Scope of the Book

The readers are given a clear knowledge of the author's goals as well as the parameters within which the book operates thanks to the book's purpose as well as its scope, which act as the core structure of the book. It is an essential component that plays an important role in shaping not just the content but also the style and the path that the work will take. In this essay, we will delve into the relevance of defining the purpose and scope of a book, studying how these factors influence the writing process and form the expectations of the reader. Specifically, we will look at how identifying the purpose and scope of a book may help a writer focus their efforts.

1. **The Reason for Writing This Book:**
   Getting to the Heart of the Matter:
   To articulate and communicate a book's essential meaning or overarching concept is the book's primary goal. Every book, whether it be a work of fiction, non-fiction, self-help, or academic research, aims to convey certain concepts, experiences, or information to the people who read it. The objective of the book is to convey the author's intention to share the information contained inside the book with the general public.
   Whether to enlighten, amuse, or inform:
   There are several reasons why a book might be written and published. Some books are written with the intention of informing and educating readers by providing helpful perspectives and information on a specific topic. Others aim to provide amusement by transporting readers to exotic lands, engrossing them

in compelling stories, or giving them opportunities to laugh and escape reality through their writing.

Motivate, sway, or test someone's resolve:

It's possible that a book's goal is to invigorate, convince, or test its audience's resolve. The purpose of inspirational novels is often to encourage readers to accomplish their objectives and to live lives that are more satisfying. It's possible that persuasive works will make an effort to change people's minds about a controversial topic. Books that are difficult to read inspire readers to rethink their worldviews and provoke reflection in the reader.

Fill a Void or Satisfy a Need:

In many instances, authors put pen to paper in order to fill a void in previously published works of literature or to satisfy a particular demand. For instance, academic books frequently investigate particular fields of knowledge, thereby contributing to the existing body of research and understanding. Books on self-help can provide direction and potential solutions for everyday problems that people face.

2. **The Subject Matter Covered in This Book:**

The Establishment of Boundaries:

The boundaries that the content of a book will be created within are determined by the scope of the book. It specifies what will be included as well as what won't be included. Determining the scope of the work is necessary in order to keep one's attention on the task at hand and to prevent the activity from becoming overly extensive, unfocused, or overpowering.

Both in depth and in scope:

The breadth as well as the depth of the book are both defined by the scope. Some books only scratch the surface of a vast variety of subjects but nonetheless manage to provide an overall summary. Others focus their attention intently on a specific aspect of research and present an analysis that is exhaustive. The decision about the scope has an effect on the amount of research and analysis contained within the book.

The Intended Viewers Are:

The people who are intended to read a book are intimately connected to its breadth. It determines if the book is meant for a wide audience or for a specialized readership in a certain field. The level of knowledge, vocabulary, and tone will be modified in order to cater to the specific audience that has been selected.

The period of time and the location in question:

When it comes to novels that cover historical topics, geographical topics, or cultural topics, the scope will frequently include a certain period of time or geographic place. Because of this, the author is able to present a narrative that is both specific and all-encompassing on a certain time period, location, or culture.

3. **Factors That Affect the Aim and the Scope:**
   Knowledge and enthusiasm of the Author:
   The author's familiarity with a topic and enthusiasm for the topic both have a big impact on the goals of the book and its scope. An author's familiarity with and excitement for a subject can result in an in-depth investigation of that subject, whereas an author's unfamiliarity with a subject may lead to a more general review of that subject.
   Expectations of the Reader:
   When attempting to define the aim and the scope of the project, it is essential to have a solid understanding of the expectations of the target readership. When writing a book, authors need to examine what their readers hope to gain from the text and then tailor the material accordingly.
   The Market and the Competition:
   The current level of competition and the requirements of the target audience both have an impact on the goals and objectives of a book. Authors may have the goal of distinguishing their work from other publications already in existence or of catering to a specialized audience that has not been adequately addressed.
   Investigation and Available Resources:
   One such factor that can influence the scope of a book is the accessibility of research materials and resources. If one conducts extensive study on a subject, one might be able to investigate it in greater depth; however, if one lacks access to certain data or materials, one might be forced to concentrate their efforts more narrowly.
4. **Striking a Balance Between the Purpose and the Scope:**

   The need for both Clarity and Consistency:
   In the early phases of the book-writing process, you should clearly define the goal and scope of the book, and you should keep those definitions consistent throughout the entire process. This guarantees that the book maintains its coherence throughout and conveys a consistent message to all who read it.
   Both in terms of relevance and engagement:
   Within the parameters of the goal and scope that have been specified, authors should continually evaluate how relevant and engaging their content is.
   It is possible that particular portions or themes will need to be amended or eliminated if they do not correspond with the primary message or the expectations of the audience.
   Ability to adapt:
   Although having a distinct aim and scope can help offer structure, authors should nevertheless be willing to acknowledge the need for some degree of adaptability.

Changes might need to be made in order to better serve the goals of the book if new research or insights become available, or if readers provide input.

The intention behind writing a book as well as the breadth of its subject matter are the directing factors that determine what goes into writing it. They create the parameters within which the content will be produced, in addition to defining the message that the author desires to express to the reader. Authors are able to construct books that effectively accomplish their intended purpose while also offering a pleasurable and educational experience for readers by giving careful consideration to the audience for whom the book is written, the author's area of expertise, and the subject matter of the book. In the end, having a purpose and scope that are clearly defined lead to a book having a greater impact and being more successful.

D. Methodology and Research Approach

Methodology and strategy for conducting research are essential components of any academic investigation. They offer a structured framework for carrying out research, accumulating data, and coming to conclusions. In this essay, we will investigate the significance of research technique and research approach in the research process. Specifically, we will investigate their definitions, components, and the ways in which they influence the quality and validity of research.

1. **A Definitive Analysis of Research Methodology and Procedure:**
   The methodology consists of:
   The term "methodology" refers to the organized structure and collection of guiding principles that direct the process of doing research. It includes the exact methods, techniques, and processes that were utilized to gather and analyze data, as well as the rationale for the selection of those particular methods, techniques, and procedures. The methodology acts as a road map, ensuring that the research is carried out in a manner that is both rigorous and ethical.
   Methodology of the Research:
   On the other hand, the research approach refers to the overarching strategy or perspective that is utilized in the process of framing and responding to research questions. It offers a more comprehensive theoretical framework within which the research can be carried out.
   The research strategy provides the foundation for the study design and contributes to the process of selecting the procedures that are the most appropriate.

2. **The following are the components of the methodology:**
   Methodology of the Research:
   The research design provides an overview of the entire procedure that will be followed to carry out the investigation. It involves making choices on the methodology of the research, such as whether it will be qualitative, quantitative, mixed-methods, experimental, observational, or focused on case studies.

The study design lays the groundwork for the gathering of data and the subsequent analysis.

Methods for the Collection of Data:
The methods of data collection are going to detail how the researchers are going to get the information or data that they need. Methods such as surveys, interviews, observations, experiments, content analysis, and literature reviews are examples of common research approaches. Researchers need to determine which approaches will be most useful for answering their research questions and accomplishing their goals.

Taking a Sample:
The selection of a subset of the population from which data will be collected is what is meant by the term "sampling." The objectives and parameters of the study will direct the choice of sampling method to be made by the researchers. Possible options include convenience sampling, stratified sampling, and random sampling.

Analysis of the Data:
The techniques for processing the data, coming to interpretations of the data, and drawing conclusions from those interpretations are outlined in the data analysis. The methodologies of quantitative and qualitative analysis, such as regression analysis, thematic coding, and content analysis, are outlined by the researchers who conduct the study.

Considerations of an Ethical Nature:
It is crucial that ethical considerations be taken into account while developing a methodology, as this will ensure that the research is carried out in an ethical and responsible manner. Researchers have a responsibility to address concerns regarding participants' rights to privacy and confidentiality as well as any risks to their health.

3. **Different Methods of Conducting Research:**

   Research that is Quantitative:
   Quantitative research seeks answers to study issues through the utilization of numerical data. It frequently involves the use of statistical methods and seeks to generalize findings to a more extensive population. Quantitative research often include things like questionnaires, experiments, and statistical breakdowns of the results.

   Research that is qualitative:
   The goal of qualitative research is to investigate and get a knowledge of complicated phenomena. In-depth interviews, focus groups, and content analysis are common components of this process. When analyzing qualitative data, researchers attempt to identify recurring themes, patterns, and subtleties.

   Research Using a Mixture of Methods:
   Research employing mixed methods brings together aspects of both quantita-

tive and qualitative approaches to the study of a topic. When researchers want to get a full grasp of a study subject or triangulate information from numerous sources, it is especially advantageous to employ this method.

Research Through Experiment:

The controlled and manipulated approach that experimental research takes is one of its defining characteristics. Researchers will often make changes to an independent variable in order to study how those changes affect a dependent variable. In the realm of experimental research, randomized controlled trials are quite common.

Research Using Case Studies:

In the field of research known as case studies, investigators do in-depth research on individual cases, which may focus on people, organizations, or events. The examples are investigated in great detail by the researchers so that they can make both specific and general conclusions.

Research through Action:

Researchers interact closely with practitioners or communities to find solutions to real-world problems through a process known as action research. This approach is frequently utilized in the field of education as well as the social sciences. Research is used as a tool in the effort to bring about positive change.

Investigations Into the Past:

Research in history investigates previous occurrences and their settings. For the purposes of constructing narratives, comprehending historical events, and evaluating the significance of those events, researchers rely on both primary and secondary sources.

4. **The Influence of Research Approach and Methodology:**

The Goals of the Research:

Both the methodology and the research approach need to be in line with the aims of the study. The researchers have to determine whether the quantitative, qualitative, or mixed techniques approaches are going to be the most effective in achieving their aims.

The Quality and Validity of the Data:

The rigor of the approach that was chosen has a direct impact on the quality and authenticity of the data. The dependability and credibility of the findings can be improved by carefully designing the research method.

Both in Breadth and Depth:

The scope and level of detail of the investigation are both influenced by the research methodology. The investigation of many facets of a research subject may call for the application of a variety of methodologies. For instance, qualitative research is useful for conducting in-depth studies, but quantitative research is helpful for conducting large-scale surveys and statistical analysis. Both types of research have their place in the world of academic inquiry.

Implications for Ethical Behavior:
Both the methodology and the strategy that researchers take to the research should take ethical considerations into account. The researchers have a responsibility to select procedures and strategies that are compliant with ethical standards and put the safety and confidentiality of the participants in their studies first.

Time Restraints and Resource Limitations:
Both the study approach and the methodology that is used are subject to the limits of practical issues such as limited time and resources. Because the research project is constrained in some ways, it may not be possible to implement certain methodologies because they call for additional time, resources, or specialized knowledge.

5. **Frameworks and paradigms for methodological research:**

When conducting research, it is common practice to adopt a strategy that is consistent with a certain methodological framework or paradigm. These conceptual frameworks serve as a guide for the research's underlying philosophical and epistemological assumptions.

Positivism entails:
The positivist philosophy places an emphasis on actual, observable phenomena and looks to quantitative data in an effort to demonstrate causal linkages. Quantitative research and an unbiased, value-neutral perspective are frequently mentioned in conjunction with it.

Interpretativism entails:
On the other hand, interpretivism places an emphasis on comprehending the individual's unique and personal experiences as well as points of view. It is consistent with qualitative research and aims to discover meaning and context through investigation.

Theory of Critical Thinking:
The critical theory approach places an emphasis on social criticism as well as the investigation of power structures and inequalities. It is frequently related with qualitative research that aims to challenge and modify the conventions and structures that exist within society.

Pragmatism entails:
Pragmatism is an inclusive approach that appreciates both quantitative and qualitative methodologies, putting an emphasis on the usefulness of research for the purpose of finding solutions to real-world problems.

The research process is not complete without a proper methodology and research approach, which will direct the method selection process, data gathering, and data analysis. It is impossible to conduct high-quality research that is in line with study objectives, upholds ethical standards, and generates findings that are meaningful and dependable without first making an informed decision regarding the technique and research approach to use. When it comes to making these kinds of important choices, researchers need to give serious consideration to their aims, limitations, and philosophical orientations. The path of the research and its impact on the area of study are eventually shaped by the methodical integration of research approach and technique.

E. Overview of Chapters

An overview of the chapters acts as the reader's road map and provides insight into the organization and subject matter of the work in the realm of books and academic writing. It gives a brief overview of what each chapter involves, the topics it covers, and the sequence in which those themes appear in the text. The purpose of this essay is to investigate the significance of an overview of chapters in terms of efficiently directing the reader through a book or research paper and explaining the author's intentions.

1. **The Aim of a Concise Introduction to the Chapters:**
   Providing Direction to the Reader:
   The purpose of an overview of chapters is to serve as a navigational aid for the reader, leading them through the various sections of the book or research paper. It gives the reader a sneak peek at what they may anticipate to find in each chapter, which makes it much simpler for them to comprehend how the work is structured.
   Indicating What Should Be Expected:
   The summary prepares the reader on what to anticipate regarding the range of coverage and the primary subject of each chapter. It provides insight into the important themes, ideas, and questions that will be addressed in the future parts, allowing readers to anticipate and engage with the material in a more effective manner, as it allows readers to predict what will be covered.
   Improving One's Capacity to Understand:
   When authors begin each chapter with a summary of its contents, they make it much simpler for readers to understand the material as they move forward through the work. This guarantees that readers will have a distinct mental framework within which they will be able to contextualize and process the material that is delivered in each chapter.
   Concerning the Content of the Chapter:
   In the overview, the connections and linkages between the various chapters are laid out and established. It creates a sense of consistency and continuity for the reader by assisting them in understanding how each chapter contributes to the overall narrative or argument of the book.

2. **Elements That Make Up an Outline of the Chapters:**
   Titles of the Chapters:
   The names of each chapter are presented in the overview in the same order as

they occur in the body of the text. The names of each chapter ought to be succinct while also providing pertinent information and a sneak peek into the chapter's subject matter.

A Few Descriptions in Brief:

A concise overview or description is presented for each chapter in this book. These descriptions ought to be condensed while still delivering a complete account of the primary ideas, subjects, and research issues that are discussed in each chapter.

Concepts and Aims Important to Understand:

The overview could highlight the most important themes, goals, or research purposes for each individual chapter. This ensures that the reader's expectations are in line with the author's aims by providing clarity regarding the precise objectives and primary focus of each chapter.

Structure of the Chapters:

An overview may also provide a description of the internal structure of each chapter, drawing attention to the subtopics, divisions, or approaches that were utilized. This gives readers an understanding of how each chapter is organized as well as the logical development of concepts included within it.

3. **The Importance of Having a Concise Summary of Each Chapter in a Variety of Works:**

The Book:

A full grasp of the organization and subject matter of a book can be gained by the reader by reading the overview of the book's chapters. It provides the reader with the option to read the entire text or to zero in on particular chapters that are pertinent to the reader's particular areas of interest. It is of utmost significance in works of non-fiction and academic writing, since readers of these types of literature are typically looking for precise information or an in-depth investigation of particular subjects.

Papers devoted to research:

An overview of the chapters of a research paper serves as a quick guide to the structure of the article as well as the most important findings. It makes it easier for readers to locate, at a glance, the parts of the text that are most pertinent to the research interests they have.

When viewed in this light, the overview of the chapters is typically located in the introduction or the abstract of the work.

Either Your Thesis or Your Dissertation:

It is essential for the examination committee and any other readers of a thesis or dissertation to grasp the research framework and the contributions made in each chapter. This can be accomplished by reading the overview of the chapters. Reviewers will find it much simpler to evaluate the methodology, findings, and conclusions when they can navigate the extensive study more easily thanks to this aid.

Works That Are Not Fiction:
An summary of the chapters is especially helpful in non-fiction works, such as books on self-help or educational topics. It enables readers to identify the chapters that contain the information or guidance they desire, providing them with a more efficient means of gaining access to content that is relevant to them.

4. **Developing an Effective Synopsis of the Chapters:**

Try to be Brief:
It is important to keep the descriptions and summaries brief while yet ensuring that they include the most important aspects of each chapter. Without becoming overburdened by long descriptions, readers should be able to get a feel for each chapter's major ideas quickly and easily.

Make Sure to Use Plain Language:
It is important that the language used in the overview be understandable to a wide variety of people. Avoid using jargon or terminology that are extremely technical as these can turn off readers who aren't already familiar with the topic.

Please Provide the Following Logical Sequence:
Check to see that the sequence of the chapters in the book or the research paper is followed logically in the summary. This makes it easier for readers to explore the content and understand the narrative as a whole.

Emphasize the Most Important Contributions:
Place an emphasis on the distinctive contributions that each chapter has made or the relevance that it holds. In what ways does each chapter advance our understanding, our knowledge, or our arguments? This gives readers an idea of the value that they can obtain from each subsection of the article.

Make Any Necessary Changes:
Make sure that the summary of the chapters reflects any changes that you make to the work, whether those changes involve revisions or updates. It needs to be an accurate representation of the finished book or research paper in terms of both its organization and its content.

When it comes to directing readers through a book or research paper, an overview of the chapters is an extremely important component. It helps readers engage more effectively with the material, clarifies what is expected of them, and improves their comprehension. In order for these overviews to effectively act as important roadmaps for the readers of the work, the authors need to properly build them. This will enable the readers to navigate the work with clarity and purpose. Whether it be in books, research papers, theses, or other works of non-fiction, the overview of chapters is an essential tool for communication that ensures readers can derive the greatest possible benefit from the material that is provided.

Chapter 1

The Foundations of Tourism Economics

The tourism industry has grown into a substantial economic force on a global scale, which has a positive impact on the expansion and growth of economies, communities, and regions. The study of tourism economics dives into the complex relationship that exists between tourism and economics. It investigates the ways in which tourism-related activities have an effect on the economy and the ways in which economic issues, in turn, have an effect on the tourism industry. This all-encompassing examination of the fundamentals of tourism economics attempts to present the reader with a profound comprehension of the fundamental principles, theories, and ideas that underpin this ever-evolving area.

1. **Theorizing the Economic Implications of Tourism**
   The Following Is an Explanation of Tourism Economics:
   The study of economics with an application to the tourism business is known as tourism economics. This subfield of applied economics focuses on the financial facets of the tourism sector. It encompasses the study of the interaction between tourism and a variety of economic issues, including the impact of tourism on local and national economies, employment, income production, and the general economic wellbeing of communities and regions.
   Components of the Economic Impact of Tourism:
   The study of tourism economics incorporates a variety of aspects, such as an analysis of demand and supply, evaluations of economic impact, cost-benefit analyses of tourism projects, analyses of tourism investment, and assessments of tourism policies and strategies. To fully grasp the multidimensional character of the tourism business from an economic vantage point, it is essential to have a solid understanding of the aforementioned components.
2. **An Overview of the Tourism Sector from a Macro Perspective**
   The Ever-Changing Nature of the Tourism Sector:

The tourism business is made up of a complex network of interconnected subindustries, such as transportation, lodging, food and beverage services, tour operations, and a wide variety of leisure pursuits. To fully grasp the economic significance and influence of this business, it is essential to have a solid understanding of the dynamics and interactions that occur within it.

The Tourism Industry Around the World:

The worldwide tourism industry is distinguished by the wide variety of locations, points of interest, and activities that can be experienced during trips. The distribution of tourist flows, the introduction of new tourism sites, and the shifting preferences and behaviors of tourists globally can be better understood by conducting an analysis of the structure and trends of the global tourism market.

3. **The Roles of Economics and Consumer Behaviour in Tourism**

   The following are the fundamentals of tourism's demand and supply markets:

   When applied to the tourist business, the concepts of demand and supply help explain the factors that influence both the demand for tourism services and the supply of tourism products. The equilibrium of the tourism market is heavily impacted by a variety of factors, including but not limited to price elasticity, income levels, consumer preferences, and external shocks.

   The Behaviour of Tourists as Customers:

   It is essential to have a solid understanding of consumer behavior in the context of tourism in order to develop successful marketing strategies and to successfully adjust tourism services to the ever-changing requirements and preferences of visitors. Tourist behavior and consumption patterns are shaped by a number of factors, including the reasons that people travel, the decision-making processes that they go through, and the impact that information and communication technology play.

4. **The Contributions of Tourism to the Economy**

   Effects that Have a Multiplier on the Economy:

   Tourism creates multiplier effects within local and national economies, which results in the creation of direct and indirect employment possibilities, the generation of income, and the stimulation of businesses such as retail, transportation, and entertainment that are connected to tourism. When these multiplier effects are analyzed, it is possible to gain insight into the wider economic benefits that the tourism industry brings.

   The Creation of Both Income and Employment:

   Tourism is a key source of income and employment for many communities and regions, particularly in regions with minimal economic diversity. This is especially true in places where economic opportunities are very restricted. When analyzing the direct and indirect contributions that tourism makes to income and employment, we can better understand the role that it plays in reducing poverty and improving people's standard of living.

Gains from Trading in Foreign Exchange and the Balance of Payments:
Many nations' improvements in their balance of payments can be attributed to the tourism industry, which typically represents a large source of foreign exchange revenues for those nations. Understanding the role that tourism plays in international trade and economic development requires conducting research into the trends of tourist spending, the amounts of foreign currency that are brought into national economies, and the effects that these have on those trends.

5. **The Role of Economic Policy in the Growth of Tourism**

Policy and Planning Concerning Tourism:
In order to encourage environmentally responsible growth in tourism and make the most of the economic opportunities presented by the sector, it is vital to design tourism policies and strategies that are effective. Policymakers are better able to design frameworks that support the expansion and competitiveness of the tourism sector when they have a solid understanding of the principles behind the formulation, implementation, and evaluation of tourism policies.

Development of Tourism That Is Sustainable:
The idea of sustainable tourism development places an emphasis on the necessity of striking a balance between economic growth, the preservation of the natural environment, and social inclusion.

An examination of the guiding principles of sustainable tourism development throws light on techniques for mitigating the unfavorable effects of tourism on the environment, on society, and on culture, while simultaneously maximizing the economic benefits of tourism over the long term.

6. **Tourism Economics: Obstacles to Overcome and Opportunities to Seize**

Excessive tourism and the deterioration of the natural environment:
The phenomenon of overtourism presents substantial challenges to popular tourist locations, which can result in the damage of the natural environment, the loss of cultural traditions, and the straining of the local infrastructure. It is essential, in order to reduce the negative consequences of overtourism, to conduct research into the underlying factors that contribute to the problem and investigate alternative methods of tourism management.

Developments in technology and the impact of the digital revolution:
The tourist sector has been radically altered as a result of the disruptive effects of digital technology, which have caused a revolution in the way tourism services are provided and utilized. It is vital to have an understanding of the ramifications of technological innovation in order to be able to react to the changing landscape of the tourism business. Some examples of technological innovation include online booking platforms, big data analytics, and virtual reality experiences.

The fundamentals of tourism economics are a complex web of ideas, hypotheses, and procedures that shed light on the complicated connection that exists between tourism and the economy. It is essential to have an understanding of the economic principles, implications, and regulatory frameworks that support the tourism industry in order to foster the growth of sustainable tourism and maximize the socioeconomic benefits that tourism provides to communities and regions all over the world. By delving deeper into the fundamentals of tourism economics, we are better able to handle the obstacles and opportunities presented by the always shifting tourism landscape. This allows us to ensure that tourism will continue to play an essential part in the growth of the global economy and the dissemination of cultural traditions.

1.1 Historical Evolution of Tourism

The idea of tourism, which can be defined as both a kind of leisure and an avenue for discovery, can be traced back quite far in human history. Alongside the development of society, technology, and the economy over the course of several centuries, the activity of traveling for leisure, religious, or educational reasons has also undergone significant development. The historical development of tourism can provide useful insights into the development of human societies, cultural exchanges, and the emergence of the current tourism sector if one has a good understanding of this history.

The purpose of this in-depth study is to follow the historical trajectory of tourism, beginning with its earliest origins and ending with the modern tourism environment around the globe.

1. **Early Methods of Transportation and Religious Journeys**
   The Ancient World and the Great Tours:
   During ancient times, travel was frequently related with commercial activities, religious journeys, and cultural interactions. The "Grand Tours," which were undertaken by the aristocracy of ancient civilizations such as the Greeks and Romans, are recognized as the earliest forms of leisure travel and cultural discovery. These journeys laid the groundwork for the growth of tourism as a cultural activity.
   Sacred Journeys & Religious Pilgrimages :
   Throughout the course of human history, religious tourism, including pilgrimages to holy sites and sacred locations, has been an important driver of travel. Travelers on their way to Mecca, Jerusalem, and other holy places have left their mark on the cultural and economic landscapes of the areas they passed through. As a result, pilgrimage routes and transport infrastructure have developed as a direct result of these travelers' activities.

2. **Travel and Recreation in the Early Modern Period and the Renaissance**
   Travel and Exploration in Early Medieval Europe:
   Travelers in Europe embarked on educational excursions, trading routes, and trips to cultural sites during the Middle Ages, which led to the development of

the earliest forms of tourism in Europe at that time. The development of trade routes, the introduction of the printing press, and the formation of colleges all played a part in the spread of knowledge and the cultural exchange that occurred between different places.

The Renaissance and the Exploration of Other Cultures:
The Grand Tour became more popular among the nobility and intellectuals of Europe during the Renaissance period, which coincided with a resurgence of interest in the dissemination of cultural knowledge and the creation of artistic works. During the Renaissance period, people were interested in learning more about classical antiquities, art, and history, which helped lay the groundwork for the current idea of cultural tourism as well as the appreciation of cultural heritage.

3. **The Emergence of the Spa Industry and the Age of Enlightenment**
The Benefits of Wellness Seeking and Spa Tourism:
The beginning of health and wellness tourism may be traced back to the 18th century, when a number of new spa towns and resorts opened their doors. Spa towns have sprouted out all over Europe as a result of the widespread appeal of the region's mineral springs, thermal baths, and other naturally curative elements. These spa towns are a popular destination for tourists in search of rest, rejuvenation, and curative therapies.

The Age of Enlightenment and the Exploration of Scientific Frontiers:
As a result of the Age of Enlightenment's encouragement of a spirit of scientific exploration and intellectual curiosity, a number of scientific expeditions and discovery trips were organized during this time period. The study of the natural world by explorers and naturalists led to the development of scientific tourism and the progress of knowledge in a variety of disciplines, including botany, zoology, and geography.

4. **The Beginning of the Industrial Revolution and the Development of Mass Tourism**
The Construction of New Transportation Facilities:
The transportation sector experienced a sea change as a result of the Industrial Revolution, which paved the way for the invention of steamships, railways, and eventually vehicles. The growth of transportation infrastructure made it easier for individuals to move between regions and continents. This paved the way for the development of mass tourism and the democratization of travel opportunities.

The Development of Seaside Resorts and the Leisure Tourism Industry:
As factory workers in metropolitan areas sought relief from their surroundings in coastal locations, the 19th century saw the emergence of seaside resorts and leisure tourism. The increased need for leisure and entertainment among the working class was catered to by the establishment of beach resorts, amusement

parks, and recreational facilities, which in turn transformed the dynamics of the tourism business.

5. **Tourism in the 20th Century and the Process of Globalization**
   Development of Tourism and the Economy After World War II:
   Tourism was an essential component in the economic reconstruction of war-torn countries in the decades after the end of World War II.

   The advent of international tourism as a crucial driver of global economic growth may be attributed, in large part, to the investments made by governments and other international organizations in the construction of tourism infrastructure. These organizations also promoted travel as a means of economic development and cultural exchange.

   The rise of the digital age along with other technological developments:
   Significant technological improvements were made in the latter part of the 20th century and the early part of the 21st century, ushering in a digital revolution that completely disrupted the travel and tourist sector. The introduction of commercial aviation, online booking platforms, and digital marketing have all had a significant impact on the way people travel. These developments have made it possible for the global tourism market to expand and have made it easier for travelers all over the world to have seamless travel experiences.

6. **Emerging Patterns in Tourism and Environmentally Responsible Development**

   Responsible vacationing and environmentally conscious tourism practices
   Sustainable tourism practices have emerged as a prominent force in the modern landscape of tourism as a direct response to worries about the environment as well as the requirement for responsible vacationing. The goal of initiatives that focus on ecotourism, community-based tourism, and cultural preservation is to reduce the amount of damage that tourism causes to the environment and the communities that it visits while simultaneously supporting sustainable development and the preservation of cultural heritage.

   The Expanding Scope of Specialized Tourism Markets:
   The modern tourist business has seen the emergence of niche tourism markets that cater to specific interests and preferences of travelers. The fields of adventure tourism, culinary tourism, heritage tourism, and medical tourism are becoming increasingly popular since they provide travelers with one-of-a-kind travel experiences while also fostering cultural diversity and welcoming attitudes in the context of the international tourism industry.

   The historical development of tourism is illustrative of the dynamic interplay that exists between human curiosity, the investigation of different cultures, and the growth of economies. The development of tourism is a reflection of the development of human societies and the ongoing search for knowledge, leisure, and cultural interchange. The first forms of tourism included educational endeavors and religious pilgrimages, while contemporary trends include environmentally responsible tourism and travel marketplaces catering to certain niches. By gaining an awareness of the historical underpinnings of tourism, we are able to develop a deeper appreciation for the role that travel plays in creating our cultural identities, fostering global connectedness, and promoting mutual understanding and respect among varied groups and areas all over the world.

1.2 Key Concepts in Tourism Economics

A multidisciplinary area, tourist economics investigates the interaction of economics and tourism, as well as the different factors that drive and influence the worldwide tourism industry. It comprises a wide range of important ideas that provide insights into the economic elements of tourism, such as the demand and supply of tourism services, economic impact evaluations, and the role of government policies and international organizations in the industry. It is essential to have a solid grasp of these fundamental ideas in order to realize the complex link that exists between economics and tourism, as well as the manner in which these two factors combine to form the landscape of global tourism. We will go into the underlying core principles in tourism economics as part of this in-depth research.

1. **The Role That Tourism Plays in the Economy**
   The Demand for Tourism:
   The term "tourism demand" refers to the desire, willingness, and ability of individuals or groups of people to go to particular locations for leisure, business, or any other purpose. Analyzing the elements that encourage persons to travel, such as personal preferences, income levels, cultural attractions, and the influence of external factors like economic conditions and currency rates, is necessary for gaining an understanding of the demand for tourism.

   Supply for Tourism:
   The term "tourism supply" refers to the variety of goods and services that are made available to fulfill the requirements of tourists. Accommodation amenities, transportation services, food and beverage choices, recreational activities, and tour package deals are all included in this category. When evaluating the infrastructure and capabilities of a place to meet the demands of tourists, the idea of tourism supply is one of the most important considerations.

   Expenditures Relating to Tourism:
   The term "tourism expenditure" refers to the amount of money spent by tourists while they are away on vacation. It includes money spent on lodging, meals, modes of transportation, tourist destinations, retail therapy, and any number of other products and services. The economic contribution that tourism has made to both local and national economies can be better understood through an analysis of tourism expenditures.

2. **The Effects of Tourism on the Economy**
   The effect of economic multipliers:
   In tourism economics, one of the most important concepts to understand is the economic multiplier effect. It explains how the preliminary expenditures made by visitors result in a chain of secondary and tertiary economic transactions, which in turn results in a higher total influence on the economy. For instance, when tourists spend money on accommodations, this expenditure results in additional income for the hotel personnel, as well as for local suppliers and other businesses located in the destination.
   The Creation of Both Income and Employment:
   In many areas, tourism constitutes a considerable portion of both the economic and
   employment base. It offers employment opportunities in a wide range of industries, including tourism, transportation, retail, and consumer goods manufacturing, among others. The development of income and employment is a fundamental economic benefit that can be derived from tourism, particularly in places where there is a lack of economic diversity.
   Losses and Losses in Economic Activity:
   When discussing the economics of tourism, the term "leakage" refers to the portion of tourist spending that does not contribute to the economy of the destination but rather is transferred to organizations that are located elsewhere. The term "leakage" refers to the practice of using money made from tourism to pay for imports, enterprises controlled by foreign nationals, or international tour operators. In order to maximize the economic benefits that tourism provides for the surrounding communities, one of the primary challenges that must be overcome is the reduction of leakage.
3. **Planning and Administration of Tourist Attractions**
   The Development of Destinations:
   The process of developing a destination includes the design, construction, and improvement of infrastructure and facilities that are intended to accommodate tourists. This includes the creation of networks for transit, options for accommodation, and attractions. It is essential to have efficient destination development in order to successfully attract and accommodate tourists while also assuring the destination's continued viability.
   Transportation Capacity:
   The carrying capacity of a location refers to the maximum number of guests that it can accommodate on a yearly basis without suffering adverse effects on its environment, society, or culture. Because exceeding the carrying capacity can lead to problems such as overtourism, environmental deterioration, and cultural erosion, it is a crucial topic in the management of destinations.

4. **Tourism Policy and Other Interventions by the Government**
   Policy Regarding Tourism :
   Policy in the tourist industry refers to the standards, regulations, and promotional techniques that are developed by governments and organizations in order to manage and advance the industry. The goal of effective tourism policy is to strike a balance between fostering economic growth and preserving the local environment, cultural traditions, and community development.
   The Role of Taxes and Fees:
   It is common practice for governments to levy taxes and fees on activities connected to tourism in order to generate money and finance local infrastructure and services. Because they have such a significant impact on the entire cost of tourism, visitors and local companies alike must make it a priority to become familiar with the destination's taxes and fee structures.
5. **The Function of Multinational Organizations**
   UNWTO stands for the World Tourism Organization:
   The World Tourism Organization, sometimes known as UNWTO, is the agency of the United Nations that is in charge of promoting responsible and environmentally friendly tourism on a global basis. In order to provide assistance for the expansion of tourism, UNWTO engages in research, offers advice on public policy, and helps governments collaborate with one another.
   The Tourism Industry's Contribution to International Economic Activity:
   Because it requires the transportation of goods and services across international boundaries, tourism is an important contributor to the growth of international trade. In order to properly evaluate the balance of payments, exchange rates, and trade agreements that pertain to the tourism industry, it is vital to have a solid understanding of the economic influence that tourism has on international trade.
6. **Ecotourism and Responsible Travel**
   Tourism with a Low Impact:
   To practice tourism in a manner that is environmentally, socially, and culturally responsible is to reduce the adverse effects of tourism while enhancing the positive effects of tourism. It incorporates ideas like participating actively in one's community, making responsible use of available resources, and protecting the natural environment. The implementation of sustainable tourism practices is essential to ensuring the economic health of tourist destinations over the long term as well as the prosperity of their surrounding communities.
   The Practice of Ecotourism:
   Ecotourism is a subset of sustainable tourism that places a premium on having outdoor, nature-based experiences as well as preserving the natural environment. It includes excursions to natural regions, the observation of various forms of animals, and the participation in various conservation projects. Education of

the environment and the preservation of natural ecosystems are both bolstered by the growth of ecotourism.

7. **Specialized Tourist Destinations**

   The Adventure Tourism Industry:

   Individuals who are looking for high-risk activities in the great outdoors, such as mountain climbing, trekking, and extreme sports are the target market for adventure tourism. It is essential for locations that provide adventure tourism experiences to have a solid grasp of the market for this type of tourism as well as the economic factors related with it.

   Tourism in the Medical Field:

   People who seek medical operations, treatments, or healthcare services often travel to other nations to acquire those services. This practice is known as "medical tourism." The cost reductions, improved quality of care, and expansion of medical infrastructure in destination nations are all components that contribute to the economic benefits of medical tourism.

8. **Developments in Technology and the Impact of the Digital Revolution**

   Platforms for Online Reservations:

   The proliferation of internet booking platforms like Expedia and Booking.com has brought about a revolution in the travel and tourism sector.

   These platforms have made it easier and more accessible for travelers to plan their journeys, book accommodations, and obtain information on destinations across the world. The interaction between tourists and businesses, as well as the way transactions are completed, has been revolutionized by online booking systems.

   Analytics for Big Data :

   The analysis of large amounts of data is of critical importance for comprehending tourism trends, consumer behavior, and the dynamics of the market. Businesses and tourist destinations are able to better cater their products and services as well as their marketing tactics to the ever-evolving tastes and requirements of customers by conducting in-depth analyses of massive databases.

   Understanding the economic elements of the tourism business on a global scale requires a solid grasp of the fundamental ideas underlying tourism economics. These concepts provide insights into the complex relationships that exist between tourism, economics, and sustainability. These interactions include analyzing tourism demand and supply, as well as determining the economic impact that tourism has on local and national economies. It is essential for decision-makers, firms, and individuals who want to navigate the changing terrain of tourism to have a solid understanding of these important ideas as the tourism sector continues to grow in response to technological breakthroughs, altering consumer tastes, and global issues.

   1.3 The Tourism Value Chain

The tourist business is a complex and multidimensional economic sector that encompasses a wide variety of activities, service providers, and stakeholders in its operations. We can examine the operation of this sector through the prism of the tourism value chain in order to have a better understanding of how it operates. The tourism value chain is a methodical framework that defines the many components and phases that are involved in the production and delivery of tourism services, beginning with the conception of travel and progressing all the way through the experience of traveling itself. With the help of this idea, we are able to break down the industry into its component elements and analyze the roles that various companies and individuals have played as well as the contributions they have made along the way. During this in-depth investigation, we will investigate the tourist value chain by investigating each stage as well as the relationships that are responsible for the expansion and development of the business.

1. **A General Introduction to the Tourism Value Chain**
   The tourism value chain is a comprehensive model that maps out the sequence of activities and services that together generate and deliver a complete travel experience. The model was developed by the World Travel and Tourism Council (WTTC). It all starts with the motivation and desire to go on an adventure and continues through a variety of stages, including the stages of planning, transportation, accommodation, entertainment, and services offered at the destination. By analyzing each stage, we are able to acquire a more profound comprehension of the complexities that are inherent to the industry as well as the roles that are played by the various actors.
2. **The Stage of Inspiring Thought**
   Marketing a Location as a Destination:
   The stage known as "inspiration" comes at the beginning of the tourism value chain. This is the point at which tourists are encouraged to visit unfamiliar places. When it comes to advertising their particular regions, destination marketing organizations, such as national tourism boards, regional tourism authorities, and municipal marketing agencies, play a crucial role. Their operations include things like advertising, branding, and public relations, as well as the transmission of information about the attractions, culture, and experiences that are accessible in their respective destinations.
   Travel Journalism:
   The travel media, such as magazines, websites, travel shows, and social media influencers, all play a part in setting the stage for inspiration by displaying beautiful locations and travel experiences that are meaningful to readers. These sites are frequently consulted by travelers in search of ideas and suggestions, which results in an increased demand for particular activities or locations.

3. **The Preparatory Work Stage**
   The Role of Travel Agencies:
   When it comes to vacation planning, tourists can rely on the assistance of travel companies and tour operators. They provide a variety of services, including as itinerary planning, booking flights, lodgings, and tours, as well as expert advise on locations and needs for travel.
   Platforms for Online Reservations:
   The planning stage has been revolutionized thanks to the rise of online booking platforms in this digital age. Travelers are able to conduct research, make comparisons, and make reservations for flights, rooms, and other services by using websites and apps such as Expedia, Booking.com, and Airbnb. These platforms make it easier to have flexibility and convenience when organizing trips.
4. **The Stage of Transportation**
   Airline companies :
   When it comes to the transportation stage of the tourism value chain, airlines play a vital role. They make it possible for travelers to arrive at their desired destinations by providing the means to do so. Travelers have a wide range of requirements and preferences, thus airlines provide a variety of service classes, itineraries, and amenities to meet those requirements and interests.
   Airports, which:
   Airports not only act as entry points to their respective destinations but also play an important part in the transportation stage. Terminals, runways, customs and immigration facilities, lounges, and transportation to and from the airport are some of the infrastructure, services, and amenities that are made available to passengers by these companies.
   Transportation on the Ground:
   In-destination travel is referred to as "ground transportation," and it encompasses a wide variety of conveyances, including buses, taxis, rental automobiles, and public transportation. The availability of ground transportation services during a tourist's stay ensures that they will have the mobility necessary to explore the attractions of their destination and to move between their accommodations and the activities they have planned.
5. **The Stage of Adjustment and Accommodation**
   In the case of Hotels and Resorts:
   There are many different styles of rooms, pricing ranges, and amenity packages available in hotels and resorts. During the course of their stay, they offer lodging in the form of guest rooms, as well as dining and dining facilities, leisure activities, and event services. Hotels range from those that are affordable to those that are luxurious, catering to a diverse variety of travelers' needs.
   Rentals for vacations:
   The accommodation market has been revolutionized by the proliferation of

online marketplaces for short-term rentals, such as Airbnb. Private homes, apartments, and other one-of-a-kind lodgings are available for rent to vacationers as an alternative to the conventional hotel setting. These accommodations also provide guests with opportunities to have experiences that are both distinctive and authentically local.

6. **The stage of experience**

   Amusements and other forms of entertainment:

   The activities, attractions, and entertainment possibilities that are offered at locations are the primary focus of the experiential stage. Cultural sites, amusement parks, museums, zoos, zoos, theaters, sporting events, and even more can fall under this category. These activities are sought after by vacationers so that they can become fully immersed in the history and entertainment of their place of choice.

   Experiences in Gastronomy, Including Restaurants:

   In the tourism industry, dining experiences are an essential component of the value chain. Local cuisine and one-of-a-kind dining experiences, ranging from food carts on the street to restaurants with Michelin stars, are frequently sought after by tourists. The restaurant and food service industry makes a major contribution to the vacation experience as a whole.

   Operators of Tours and Companies That Provide Activities:

   Travelers can enhance the quality of their experiences by participating in guided tours, outdoor activities, and other trip types offered by activity providers and tour operators. These kinds of enterprises give travelers experiences that they won't forget, whether it's a walking tour of the city, a wildlife safari, or a cookery lesson.

7. **The Destination Services**

   Centers for the Information of Visitors:

   It is necessary to have visitor information centers in order to assist travelers in navigating places. They offer advise and information on local attractions, services, and safety precautions in addition to providing maps and brochures about the area.

   Services Relating to Transportation:

   Taxis, ride-sharing platforms, and public transit are examples of the kinds of transportation options that help ensure visitors have an easy time getting about their destination of choice. They make it easier for visitors to move around the destination as well as connect them to various aspects of the area.

   Hospitality and Providing Service to Customers:

   The hospitality industry, which consists of establishments such as hotels, restaurants, and tourist destinations, is extremely important to the delivery of high-caliber customer service. Enhancing the overall travel experience, as well as

encouraging return visits and great evaluations, can be accomplished by cultivating an upbeat and friendly ambiance.
8. **The evaluation and comment stage**

Platforms for Reviews and User Feedback:
TripAdvisor and Yelp are two examples of popular internet sites that allow travelers to post reviews following their excursions and discuss their experiences. These reviews have an impact on the decisions of other travelers and offer constructive criticism to establishments and locations, allowing for ongoing enhancement.

DMOs are abbreviations for "destination management organizations"
In order to guarantee that visitors have a positive experience at the destination, organizations that administer destinations monitor visitor input, carry out surveys, and work in collaboration with local companies. They may decide to make adjustments, introduce new marketing techniques, or undertake new initiatives based on the input that they get.

The tourism value chain is an all-encompassing model that depicts the order of the various activities and services that go into the production and distribution of a tourist experience. It is crucial to appreciate this value chain in order to gain an understanding of the complexity of the tourist sector. This value chain involves a wide set of players and stakeholders, each of whom plays a distinct role and contributes in a different way. The tourism value chain provides insights into the complex dynamics of the sector at every point, from the first stages of inspiration and planning to the phases of transportation, housing, experiences, and destination services. By breaking down the value chain, locations, businesses, and individual travelers can all become more adept at navigating the tourism landscape, which will result in trips that are more memorable, more sustainable, and more rewarding.

1.4 Economic Drivers of Tourism
The tourism business is one that significantly contributes to the expansion and development of economies all over the world. It is both dynamic and significant economically. It acts as a critical driver for a variety of different economic sectors, creating income, employment, and earnings in foreign currencies. The tourist industry has a wide-ranging economic influence, one that can be felt across a variety of sectors and geographic areas. In this in-depth study, we will investigate the primary economic forces at work in the tourist industry, with a particular focus on the ways in which tourism contributes to economic expansion, promotes progress, and molds a variety of economic subfields around the world.

1. **The Creation of Employment Opportunities**
The function that tourism plays in the creation of employment opportunities is one of the key economic drivers that the industry plays. The tourism business is one that requires a large amount of work and employs a diverse spectrum of

professionals and support staff. These employees include hotels, tour operators, restaurant staff, tour guides, and transportation suppliers. This industry offers employment opportunities to persons with a wide range of skill levels, ranging from unskilled labor to highly specialized professions. The influx of tourists that visit popular tourist spots generates a need for various services, which in turn leads to the development of new employment opportunities in ancillary sectors like the building and retail sectors, as well as infrastructure development.

The employment opportunities that are created by tourism are especially beneficial in areas that have a limited variety of other economic options. It is common for coastal towns, cultural hubs, and natural attractions to place a significant amount of reliance on the tourism industry as a means of sustaining local livelihoods and lowering unemployment rates. Tourism generates both direct and indirect job opportunities, both of which contribute to an increase in the overall distribution of income and an improvement in the communities' standard of living.

2. **Sources of Financial Support**

Tourism is a significant source of money for individuals, corporations, and governments alike, making it one of the most effective means of generating income. The phases of inspiration and planning, in which travelers look for information and book services, are the first to produce a stream of income for the tourism industry. This stream of income is generated at numerous levels throughout the value chain. During their trips, tourists also spend money on things like lodging, meals, transportation, tourist attractions, and mementos, which contributes to the local economy.

Tourism is an essential source of revenue for businesses of all sizes, but particularly for small and medium-sized businesses (SMEs).

Many businesses in the area, including restaurants, souvenir stores, workshops for local artisans, and tour operators, are dependent on revenue from tourists. This additional revenue has the potential to assist the growth and expansion of these enterprises, which will stimulate entrepreneurship and innovation.

Taxes, levies, and licensing fees are all forms of revenue that can be generated for the government thanks to tourism. In many locations, taxes are levied on services such as lodging, dining, and transportation, which results in the generation of funds that can be invested in the improvement of infrastructure, the conduct of marketing campaigns, and the preservation of environmental resources. The revenue that is earned by tourism frequently helps to upgrades at destinations, which in turn improve the entire experience for tourists and attract additional tourists.

3. **Revenues Generated from Foreign Exchange**

Many nations' primary source of revenue in terms of foreign currency is derived from the tourism industry. When tourists from other countries visit a location, it is common practice for them to exchange the money of their home country for the currency of the host nation so that they may pay for their expenses while they are there. These profits in foreign currency serve to strengthen the destination's balance of payments and contribute to the economy's overall stability.

Earnings in foreign currency through tourism can have a substantial influence, in particular for nations that are strongly dependent on the export of tourism services. The country's currency reserves are typically bolstered when popular tourist locations experience an increase in the influx of foreign exchange. A nation's capacity to participate in international trade, service its external debt, and improve its overall financial situation is bolstered when there is consistency and availability in its revenues from foreign exchange.

Earnings in foreign currency from tourism are an important factor in balancing trade deficits for nations still in the process of building their economies. These revenues assist cover the cost of importing goods and services, ensuring the availability of vital products such as gasoline, technology, and machinery that may not be produced domestically and thereby helping cover the cost of importing those goods and services.

4. **The Diversification of the Economy**

Because it encourages the expansion of a variety of businesses and services within a location, tourism is one of the primary contributors to economic diversification. As more tourists arrive, other goods and services, in addition to housing and transportation, are required to meet their needs.

Because of the varied nature of consumer demand, a wide variety of enterprises, such as restaurants, retail stores, entertainment venues, and transportation services, are buoyed by economic activity.

The establishment of new enterprises and services that cater to the requirements and preferences of tourists is one aspect of the economic diversification that can be attributed to tourism's influence. Startups and entrepreneurs frequently uncover chances to supply customers with one-of-a-kind experiences or products, which, in turn, drives further economic expansion.

In addition, tourism has the potential to encourage the growth of regional agricultural and handicraft industries. These industries might be able to supply foodstuffs, beverages, and handmade goods in order to appeal to the varied preferences of vacationers. As a consequence of this, there is a greater demand for goods that are manufactured locally, which in turn stimulates economic activities that foster cultural authenticity and community identity.

5. **The Construction of New Facilities**

Destinations invest in transportation networks, hotel facilities, and cultural attractions so that they may better serve tourists, which supports the development of the infrastructure needed to support tourism. In order to improve accessibility, infrastructure including highways, ports, and airports are being upgraded and extended. A diverse selection of new places to stay has become available as a result of recent developments in the hotel, resort, and vacation rental industries. Construction, engineering, and other industries that are closely tied to infrastructure development frequently benefit from employment opportunities brought about by infrastructure development initiatives. The improvement of transportation and lodging facilities not only benefits tourists but also raises the standard of living for the people who live in the area. It's possible that communities may benefit from improved connectivity, modernized utilities, and renovated public places.

Investing in infrastructure not only helps the destination's hospitality industry, but it also provides long-term advantages to the local population, which in turn helps the destination's overall economy expand and flourish over the long run.

6. **Encouragement of Capital Formation**

   The lodging, food & beverage, and entertainment businesses all benefit from increased investment thanks to tourism's multiplicative effect. Investors from both locally and internationally understand the potential for profit that can be made in tourist sites, which has led to the building of new hotels, restaurants, and attractions as well as the development of existing ones.

   Investment in tourism-related enterprises may benefit from additional encouragement from government programs offering incentives and initiatives. The expansion of the tourism sector is helped along by the provision of financial incentives, such as reduced tax rates and government grants, to investors. These investments frequently result in improvements to the infrastructure and services of the destination, which contribute to an increase in the destination's overall attractiveness.

7. **The Financial Influence on the Surrounding Communities**

   Communities that are located in close proximity to popular tourist spots benefit significantly from tourism's positive effects on their economies. When tourists come to an area, they buy a wide variety of goods and services from local companies, which in turn helps the local economy. This expenditure helps small enterprises, provides cash for local entrepreneurs, and makes job possibilities available to local inhabitants.

   In many cases, local communities reap the benefits of increasing economic activity, which is made possible by the tourist industry, which encourages the expansion of a wide variety of industries, including agriculture, handicrafts, and cultural services. It is possible for smaller businesses to offer one-of-a-kind products or experiences specifically catered to tourists, which can provide substantial revenue streams.

   In addition, the money that is made from tourism can be used to improve a community's infrastructure and the quality of its public services. It is possible that this investment will lead to improvements in education, healthcare, and efforts to conserve the environment. In addition to this, it improves the occupants' quality of life in general.

8. Tourism's Future and the Obstacles That Stand in the Way

While there are many economic benefits to be gained from tourism, there are also challenges that it presents to the communities that are visited. The problems of overtourism, environmental deterioration, and cultural erosion are all aspects of the tourism industry that need to be managed carefully to preserve its long-term viability. The methods of sustainable tourism have as their overarching goal the reduction of tourism's deleterious effects while simultaneously increasing the industry's financial returns.

Reducing the overall number of tourists, protecting the area's natural resources, and retaining its historical significance are some of the potential solutions to these problems. tourist practices that are sustainable promote responsible travel and stimulate the development of tourist initiatives that are beneficial to the environment and based in local communities.

The tourist industry's economic drivers are very important to the expansion and development of economies all over the world. The tourism industry helps contribute to the creation of jobs, the distribution of income, and the earning of foreign currency. It encourages economic diversification, which in turn stimulates investment and pushes the development of infrastructure. In addition, tourism has a significant impact on the surrounding towns, helping to improve their economic well-being and providing support for businesses on a smaller scale.

Responsible and sustainable business practices need to be prioritized by destination management organizations, governments, corporations, and individual travelers if the tourism industry is to remain viable in the long term. The tourism sector has the potential to continue to be a major economic driver that is of benefit to both the local economies of destinations as well as the economy as a whole if measures are taken to strike a balance between economic growth and environmental and social responsibility.

Chapter 2

Tourism as an Economic Engine

The tourism industry has developed into a powerful economic force that is driving expansion, development, and wealth in a variety of locations across the globe. It is an industry that encompasses a wide variety of activities, ranging from leisure and recreation to cultural exploration and adventure. This industry is both diversified and active. Over the course of many years, tourism has evolved into a substantial engine of economic activity, making a contribution to the GDP, creating employment opportunities, and promoting the growth of many other industries. In this all-encompassing research, we are going to look into the complex function that tourism plays as an economic engine. Specifically, we are going to investigate its impact on national and local economies, the global tourist value chain, as well as the difficulties and opportunities that it brings.

1. **Tourism: A Driving Force Behind the World Economy**
   Significance to the Economy:
   The travel and tourism industry has grown to become one of the most important economic sectors in the world, making a sizeable contribution to overall GDP. According to the World Travel & Tourism Council (WTTC), the travel and tourism industry contributed 10.4% to the global GDP in 2019, and it was responsible for the maintenance of more than 330 million employment. Prior to the outbreak of the COVID-19 pandemic, the expansion of the tourism industry was outpacing that of the overall economy, and millions of tourists were visiting locations all over the world.
   Profits from Trading in Foreign Currency:
   The receipt of considerable amounts of foreign currency by nations is a direct result of the tourism industry. Countries are able to build up their foreign exchange reserves when they receive tourists from other countries who exchange their cash for the local currency. The management of trade deficits, the

maintenance of currency stability, and the facilitation of international transactions are all significantly aided by these reserves.

Employment Opportunities and Ways to Make Money:

The tourism industry is one that requires a significant amount of labor and provides employment for a diverse range of people.

Tourism is responsible for the employment of millions of people worldwide, particularly in the service industry (which includes hotels, restaurants, and tour operators), the transportation sector, the retail sector, and cultural attractions. Individuals' and communities' standard of living can be improved thanks to the money brought in by successful business endeavors and employment opportunities.

2. **The International Chain of Tourism Value**

   Stage of Inspiring Moments:

   The stage known as "inspiration" marks the beginning of the tourism value chain by providing the impetus for tourists to go out and discover new places. Inspiration for vacationers is significantly influenced by destination marketing agencies as well as the travel media. They spread knowledge on sights, cultures, and experiences, which in turn fuels the urge to travel and experience new things.

   The Stage of Planning:

   Travelers typically seek the services of travel companies and online booking platforms throughout the planning stage of their trips. The process of trip planning is simplified and made more accessible and convenient by the presence of these organizations, which offer itinerancy planning, flight and hotel bookings, and professional advise on destinations and travel requirements.

   The Transportation Phase Is:

   The transportation stage is comprised of services provided by airlines, airports, and ground transportation companies. Airports act as entry points to the places that travelers choose to visit, while airlines are responsible for providing the means by which passengers can get to their destinations of choice. Movement within destinations can be made much simpler by utilizing ground transportation options such as taxis, rental automobiles, and buses.

   The Stage of Accommodations:

   Hotels, resorts, and rental homes for short-term stays all play a part in the accommodation stage. These accommodations are tailored to accommodate a wide range of traveler interests, from economical to opulent. The accommodation industry is responsible for providing services in the form of lodging, dining establishments, leisure activities, and event planning.

   Phase of the Experience:

   The experiential stage places a significant emphasis on the attractions and entertainment that are available.

To fully immerse themselves in the history and nightlife of their location of choice, tourists look for cultural attractions, amusement parks, museums, zoos, theaters, and sporting events to attend while they are there. The experience of a tourist can be improved by tour operators and activity providers, as well as by restaurants and other forms of gastronomic entertainment.

Services at the Destination Stage:
The destination services stage necessitates the presence of crucial components such as visitor information centers, transportation services, hospitality, and customer service. These organizations provide maps, information, and support to visitors, making it easier for them to traverse the destination.

Evaluating and Receiving Feedback:
Reviews and feedback platforms, in addition to destination management organizations, each have a part to play in this step of the review and feedback process. Through evaluations, tourists communicate their impressions to fellow tourists and offer constructive criticism to establishments and places of interest in the hope that they can be improved.

3. **The Tourism Industry's Contributions to the Economy**

   Creation of Employment Opportunities:
   The function that tourism plays in the creation of jobs is one of the most important and major economic drivers that it plays. The industry is highly dependent on human labor and provides employment opportunities in a wide variety of fields, such as retail, transportation, hospitality, and operation of tour businesses. Particularly in regions where there is not a great deal of economic diversity, tourism is an essential source of both income and a means of subsistence.

   Production of Cash Flow:
   Tourism is a significant source of money for individuals, corporations, and governments alike, making it one of the most effective means of generating income. At various points in the process, money can be made. This includes the phases of getting ideas and preparing, as well as the stages of actually traveling and spending money on things like lodging, food, transportation, attractions, and souvenirs.

   Profits from Trading in Foreign Currency:
   Many nations' primary source of revenue in terms of foreign currency is derived from the tourism industry. To pay for their vacations in a foreign country, tourists typically exchange the money of their home country for the currency of the country they are visiting.
   The nation's balance of payments and economic stability both benefit from the nation's earnings in foreign currencies, which support those earnings.

   Diversification of the Economic System:
   The emergence of a variety of different sectors and service providers within a location is facilitated by tourism, which in turn supports economic diversity.

A wide variety of companies, such as restaurants, retail stores, entertainment venues, and transportation services, are fueled by the demand for products and services.

The Development of Infrastructure:
The expansion and improvement of airports, roads, railroads, ports, and hotels are all direct results of tourism's role as a driver of infrastructure construction and improvement. Construction of new infrastructure not only improves transportation and living conditions, but also generates employment prospects.

Motivating Financial Investment:
Investment is encouraged in a variety of tourism-related industries, such as the hospitality, food & beverage, and entertainment sectors. Investors from both locally and internationally understand the potential for profit that can be made in tourist sites, which has led to the building of new hotels, restaurants, and attractions as well as the development of existing ones.

Economic Influence on the Surrounding Communities:
Local communities see an improvement in their economic well-being as a result of tourism since it helps to maintain and grow small enterprises and provides cash for local entrepreneurs. Tourists are served by microbusinesses that sell a variety of goods and services, which helps to further stimulate economic activity.

4. **Obstacles and the Future of Sustainable Tourism**

   Excessive tourism:
   Popular tourist places often face the big difficulty of having too many visitors. It happens when an excessive number of tourists overrun a location, which can lead to the destruction of the environment, the erosion of cultural traditions, and the straining of the infrastructure. To prevent overtourism and ensure the industry's long-term viability, thorough management and oversight are required.

   Deterioration of the Environment:
   The environmental impact of tourism can be significant, with factors such as pollution, deforestation, the destruction of habitat, and the generation of trash all adding to the overall degradation of the ecosystem. The practices of sustainable tourism have as their primary objective the reduction of these impacts through various eco-friendly initiatives and various conservation activities.

   The Degradation of Culture:
   Over-commercialization and excessive numbers of tourists can lead to a loss of cultural significance. The arrival of tourists has the potential to have an impact on local customs, dialects, and ways of life. It is necessary to encourage cultural preservation as well as tourism that is responsible in order to stop the degradation of cultures.

   Reaching Your Goal of Resilience:
   Destinations for tourism are susceptible to a variety of risks, including those posed by natural disasters, political unrest, and economic downturns. For a

location to become more resilient, it must first build its infrastructure, then improve its emergency preparedness, and finally diversify its tourism offers in order to reduce potential hazards.

5. **Methods of Environmentally Responsible Tourism**

Traveling in a Responsible Manner:
Responsible travel encourages travelers to behave in a way that is ethical and respectful toward the destinations, cultures, and landscapes they visit. It is recommended that tourists lessen their impact on the environment, show respect for local traditions, and contribute to the economic and social prosperity of the communities they visit.

Ecotourism refers to:
Experiences that are both environmentally responsible and centered in natural settings are at the heart of ecotourism. It encourages the preservation of natural habitats and animal populations by putting an emphasis on environmental education and the adoption of responsible tourism practices.

Tourism that is based on local communities:
Tourism that relies on the participation of local communities in its organization and management is known as community-based tourism. It helps to preserve the town's culture while also ensuring that the community benefits economically from the activity.

The Protection and Preservation of Cultural Heritage:
The cultural assets of locations are the focus of initiatives to conserve cultural heritage. These efforts strive to protect and preserve those assets. The revitalization of historical sites, the promotion of traditional arts, and the protection of languages and cultural practices are some of the initiatives that are being undertaken.

The tourism industry is a robust economic engine that plays a significant role in the expansion, employment, and development of destinations all over the world. Because it is such a dynamic and varied industry, it has an effect on a wide range of other industries as well, including transportation, lodging, attractions, and local businesses. The stages of inspiration, planning, transportation, lodging, experiential, destination services, assessment, and feedback are all a part of the global tourism value chain, which demonstrates the complex interaction between these stages.

Opportunities and benefits for nations and regions are created by the economic drivers of tourism, which include the generation of employment and income, earnings in foreign exchange, economic diversification, infrastructure development, investment, and economic influence on local communities. However, the sector is also confronted with obstacles, such as excessive tourism, the damage of the natural environment, and the erosion of cultural traditions. In order to combat these issues, sustainable tourism practices and responsible travel behaviors are required.

In a world that is undergoing rapid transformation, it is of the utmost importance to encourage environmentally responsible tourism practices such as ecotourism, community-based tourism, and the preservation of cultural heritage. Not only does sustainable tourism guarantee the long-term financial stability of destinations, but it also helps to protect the local ecosystem, culture, and heritage for the benefit of future generations. Destinations are able to continue to reap the benefits of this ever-evolving business while simultaneously preserving their distinct characteristics and cultural identities if they acknowledge the varied role that tourism plays as an economic engine and strive toward sustainable practices.

2.1 The Role of Tourism in Local Economies

Tourism is a powerful economic force that has the capacity to reshape local economies, stimulate growth, and generate a variety of opportunities for communities all over the world. These positive effects can be seen in many different countries. The tourism industry can have a number of different effects on local economies, including the creation of income and jobs, the promotion of new business formation, and the expansion of existing physical infrastructure. This examination looks deeply into the complex link that exists between tourism and local economies. It investigates the relevance of the tourist industry from an economic standpoint, as well as the various spheres of society that it has an effect on, as well as the difficulties and possibilities that it poses.

1. **The Contribution of Tourism to the Economic Well-Being of the Area**
   Production of Cash Flow:
   The local economies of these areas benefit enormously from the revenue generated by tourism. When people go to a certain location, they spend their money on a range of different goods and services. These can include things like lodging, food, transportation, entertainment, and mementos. Spending money in this way generates a direct influx of revenue into the local economy, which benefits both local businesses and inhabitants.
   Creating New Jobs:
   Local economies typically rely heavily on tourism as an important employment generator. This results in the creation of a diverse range of work opportunities, including positions in the hospitality industry (e.g., hotels and restaurants), as well as roles in the transportation industry, retail, and cultural attractions. The tourism industry offers a variety of job opportunities, which are beneficial for both skilled and unskilled labor, and they contribute to a decrease in the local unemployment rate.
   Expanding of Small Businesses:
   The expansion of small enterprises brought on by tourism is beneficial to the economies of the surrounding areas. When tourists come to an area, local businesses like restaurants, souvenir shops, tour operators, and others that are on a smaller scale experience a surge in revenue. These companies frequently offer experiences that are one of a kind and exclusive to the area, which further

promotes the culture and personality of the place.

The Distribution of Income:

The revenue generated by tourism is dispersed over a wide variety of fields and industries within the local economy. Because of this distribution, a wide variety of economic sectors, ranging from agriculture to handicrafts, are able to profit from expenditures brought on by tourism. The equitable distribution of income is critical to the elimination of economic inequalities and the improvement of the health of the communities in which people live.

Tax Collections:

Tax money is brought in by tourism for the benefit of local governments. Taxes levied on lodging establishments, dining establishments, and other tourism-related businesses provide revenue that can be re-invested in the expansion of tourism-related infrastructure, marketing initiatives, and environmental protection. The financial status of local authorities is improved when more money is collected in taxes.

2. **The Impact of Tourism on Diversifying the Economy**

   Multiple Fields of Economic Activity:

   Through its stimulation of a wide range of industries, tourism contributes to the promotion of economic diversification. Demand is created for a wide variety of goods and services, including but not limited to restaurants, retail stores, entertainment venues, and transportation services, as a result of this phenomenon. The emergence and expansion of numerous enterprises is directly attributable to the variety of needs that exist.

   Enterprise on your own:

   Entrepreneurship and the growth of small businesses are frequently fostered in areas that are popular for tourism. The discovery by entrepreneurs of chances to supply tourists with one-of-a-kind goods and experiences, which spurs innovation and investment, is a primary driver of this industry. This enterprising spirit contributes to the growth of the local economy by establishing new avenues for income collection.

   Industries Related to Agriculture and Crafts:

   The growth of local agriculture as well as the handicraft industry is encouraged by tourism. These industries might be able to supply foods, beverages, and handcrafted goods in order to satisfy the varied preferences of vacationers. The expansion of economic activities and the promotion of cultural authenticity are both facilitated by the demand for locally made goods.

3. **The Construction of New Facilities**

   The Means of Transport:

   The expansion of existing infrastructure, notably in the transportation sector, is propelled by the tourism industry. The nation's ports, roadways, airports, and railways are all undergoing expansion and modernization projects so that they can better accommodate the growing number of tourists. Enhanced connectivity and convenience are two benefits that accrue to both tourists and local inhabitants when the transportation infrastructure is improved.

The Accommodation Facilities Are As Follows:

The expansion of the tourism industry frequently calls for the development of brand-new lodging options, which may take the form of hotels, resorts, or private vacation homes. As a result of this growth, there will be a wider variety of housing alternatives available to tourists, which will in turn benefit local firms in the construction and hospitality industries.

Places Open to the Public

It is possible that improvements in public areas and utility systems will arise from investments in infrastructure that are brought about by an increase in tourism. There may be improvements made to parks, public transportation, and other public facilities in communities. These sorts of improvements raise the standard of living for the people who live in the area.

4. **Financial Activity and the Expansion of Businesses**

   Investing in the Neighborhood:

   Locations with a strong tourism industry tend to be attractive to local investors because of the sector's strong potential for profit. Entrepreneurs within the community might consider making investments in businesses that provide lodging, food and drink, entertainment, and other services aimed at tourists. These investments will ultimately result in the production of new jobs and will drive economic growth.

   Investiture a l'échelle internationale:

   The creation of foreign direct investment is frequently the result of international investors looking for opportunities in tourist spots. The influx of foreign capital can promote the construction of hotels, resorts, and infrastructure projects, further contributing to the expansion of the economy.

   Initiatives of the Government:

   When governments want to stimulate investment in tourism-related industries, they usually provide financial incentives. These incentives could take the form of tax cuts, government subsidies, or grant money. The establishment of businesses and the expansion of economic activity within communities can both be stimulated by government efforts.

5. **The Financial Influence on the Surrounding Communities**

   Help for the Neighborhood Businesses:

   Local economies benefit from tourism in a variety of ways, from the creation of small restaurants and shops to the operation of large hotels and service providers. This support establishes an economic environment that allows for the growth of local enterprises, which in turn helps to contribute to the economic well-being of the community and the employment of local residents.

Possibilities for Employment:
The tourism industry provides local citizens with work possibilities, which helps to lower the area's overall unemployment rate and raises the overall quality of life. Employment opportunities are available in a variety of different industries in addition to the hotel business. These other industries include transportation, retail, and cultural attractions.

Investing in the Community:
The money brought in by tourists frequently goes toward investing in the local community. The quality of life in a community can be further improved by local governments by allocating funding to improve public services such as education and healthcare, which would ultimately benefit the town's citizens.

Protecting Our Cultural Heritage:
Tourism is beneficial to the communities that surround a cultural site because it helps to preserve the site's history and culture. Because tourists are interested in genuine experiences, local communities have an incentive to preserve their traditions, languages, and other cultural practices. It is imperative that cultural traditions be preserved in order to protect the identities and histories of local communities.

6. **Obstacles and the Future of Sustainable Tourism**

Excessive tourism:
Popular tourist locations are frequently confronted with the huge obstacle of overtourism. It happens when an excessive number of tourists overrun a location, which can lead to the destruction of the environment, the erosion of cultural traditions, and the straining of the infrastructure. The methods of sustainable tourism strive to lessen the impact that excessive tourism has on its surroundings.

Deterioration of the Environment:
The effects of tourism on the local ecosystem aren't always positive. The degradation of the environment is caused in part by factors such as pollution, deforestation, the destruction of habitat, and the production of garbage. The goal of sustainable tourism is to reduce these impacts as much as possible through eco-friendly practices and various conservation measures.

The Degradation of Culture:
Over-commercialization and excessive numbers of tourists can lead to a loss of cultural significance.
The arrival of tourists has the potential to have an impact on local customs, dialects, and ways of life. For the sake of preventing the deterioration of cultural traditions, it is imperative that tourism practices be culturally sensitive.

Reaching Your Goal of Resilience:
Destinations for tourism are susceptible to a variety of risks, such as those posed by natural disasters, political unrest, and economic downturns. For a location

to become more resilient, it must first build its infrastructure, then improve its emergency preparedness, and finally diversify its tourism offers in order to reduce potential hazards.

7. Methods for a Sustainable Tourism Industry

Traveling in a Responsible Manner:

Travel that promotes ethical and respectful behavior toward places, cultures, and surroundings is considered to be responsible travel. It is recommended that tourists lessen their impact on the environment, show respect for local traditions, and contribute to the economic and social prosperity of the communities they visit.

Ecotourism refers to:

Experiences that are both environmentally responsible and centered in natural settings are at the heart of ecotourism. It encourages the preservation of natural habitats and animal populations by putting an emphasis on environmental education and the adoption of responsible tourism practices.

Tourism that is based on local communities:

Tourism that relies on the participation of local communities in its organization and management is known as community-based tourism. It helps to preserve the town's culture while also ensuring that the community benefits economically from the activity.

The Protection and Preservation of Cultural Heritage:

The cultural assets of locations are the focus of initiatives to conserve cultural heritage. These efforts strive to protect and preserve those assets. The revitalization of historical sites, the promotion of traditional arts, and the protection of languages and cultural practices are some of the initiatives that are being undertaken.

The tourism industry is extremely important to local economies since it helps generate cash, builds employment opportunities, encourages the growth of local businesses, and supports the expansion of physical infrastructure.

Tourism is a major economic force that supports economic diversification by fostering entrepreneurialism and stimulating the growth of different industries, ranging from agriculture to handicrafts.

Transportation, lodging, and public space can all be improved as a direct result of tourism-driven infrastructure development, which is to the advantage of both locals and visitors. Economic expansion and job creation are both stimulated by investments made in enterprises domestically and abroad that are tied to tourism. In addition, local communities feel the economic impact of tourism in the form of job opportunities, support for local businesses, investments in community projects, and the maintenance of existing cultural traditions and historic sites.

However, in order to ensure the continued profitability of destinations over the long term, it is necessary to pay attention to issues such as overtourism, environmental deterioration, and cultural erosion. Sustainable tourism practices can help. To achieve a healthy equilibrium between economic expansion and the preservation of native ecosystems, cultural practices, and historical sites, responsible tourism practices such as ecotourism, community-based tourism, and cultural heritage conservation are absolutely necessary.

Communities are able to reap the benefits of tourism while still maintaining their distinct characteristics and cultural identities if they acknowledge the critical function that tourism plays in their economy and adopt methods that are friendly to the environment.

2.2 Economic Impact Assessment Models

Models of economic impact assessment are crucial instruments that are utilized in the process of evaluating the consequences of a wide range of economic activities on local, regional, and national economies. These models are useful for helping policymakers, businesses, and researchers understand the effects of particular actions, policies, or events on key economic variables like employment levels, income levels, production levels, and tax revenues. They give stakeholders the ability to make educated decisions, plan strategically, and evaluate the potential benefits and drawbacks of specific activities. This in-depth investigation goes into the most important economic impact assessment models, their respective methodology, and the significance of these models in terms of understanding and influencing economic policy.

1. The Analysis of Inputs and Outputs

The input-output analysis, also known as I-O analysis, is a model of economic impact assessment that is commonly used to investigate the interrelationships between the various parts of an economy.

This model allows analysts to analyze the ripple effects of changes in one sector on other industries by quantifying the movement of goods and services from industry to industry. The I-O model offers extremely helpful insights into the total influence of a particular economic activity, such as a new investment or a change in policy, on the economy as a whole.

The methodology consists of:

I-O analysis makes use of a table that describes the transactions that take place between the various parts of the economy. This table is called an input-output table. This table provides an overview of the buying and selling of products and services that occurs in various sectors, including households, businesses, and the government. These data are utilized by analysts in order to compute direct, indirect, and induced impacts. Direct impacts are the initial changes that occur in the sector that is the focus of attention, whereas indirect effects are the changes that occur in other sectors as a result of interdependencies. The variations in household expenditure that occur as a direct result of changes in income are reflected by induced effects.

The Importance of:

I-O analysis provides policymakers and businesses with the tools necessary to better comprehend the linked nature of the economy. It highlights the necessity of studying multiplier effects by shedding light on how changes in one sector can have a cascading effect on other sectors and providing insights into how these changes can occur. This model is helpful in evaluating the overall impact of changes in policy, investments, or shocks. As a result, stakeholders are able to make informed decisions that are beneficial to the growth and stability of the economy.

Models that Can Be Computed Using the General Equilibrium (CGE)

Computable General Equilibrium (CGE) models are comprehensive economic instruments that examine the effects of numerous economic shocks or policy changes on many sectors of an economy at the same time. CGE models were developed in the 1970s. These models provide a comprehensive explanation of the ways in which shifts in one industry might have repercussions on other industries, pricing, and factor markets. CGE models are especially helpful when examining the larger ramifications of policy decisions, such as those regarding trade policies, changes in taxation, and regulatory reforms.

The methodology consists of:

CGE models make use of a set of equations to depict the interactions between the various participants in the economy, such as the government, the customers, and the producers. In order to model the results of shifts in policy or external shocks, these equations contain data on supply and demand as well as production functions and factor markets.

CGE models provide a full view of the dynamics of the economy because they take into account both the market-clearing mechanisms as well as the behavioral responses of economic actors to changes in policy.

The Importance of:

CGE models are extremely helpful when studying the many relationships that exist within an economy and attempting to forecast how various policy shifts will play out over the long run. They make it possible for policymakers to evaluate the trade-offs associated with different policy options, comprehend the distributional consequences on diverse economic players, and foresee probable market distortions. The formulation of efficient and well-balanced policies that foster sustainable economic growth and development is made significantly easier with the use of CGE models.

The Cost-Benefit Analysis (CBA) is the third section

The Cost-Benefit Analysis, also known as CBA, is a fundamental economic tool that is used to analyze the economic sustainability of a project, policy, or investment by comparing the costs of those aspects to the benefits that such aspects provide. CBA makes it possible for decision-makers to evaluate whether or not the potential benefits of a proposed action outweigh the associated costs and to determine whether or not the project can be carried out economically. This model is utilized frequently in the process of evaluating public works projects, investments in infrastructure, and policy interventions.

The methodology consists of:

The steps of identifying, quantifying, and putting a monetary value on the costs and benefits of a project or policy are included in a cost-benefit analysis (CBA). The benefits include both direct and indirect economic gains, such as increased output and employment, while the expenses include investment costs, operational costs, and maintenance costs. Indirect benefits include environmental and social implications. CBA takes into account the changing value of money over time and makes a comparison between the total present value of costs and the total present value of benefits.

The Importance of:

CBA provides a methodical framework for examining the possible returns of a project or policy,

which enables politicians and corporations to make more educated investment decisions. It makes sure that resources are distributed effectively and that the projects that will have the greatest overall positive impact on society are given priority. CBA plays a significant role in the promotion of transparency and accountability in decision-making, making it possible for stakeholders to think about the wider social and economic ramifications of their actions.

IV. Models With Multipliers

The indirect and induced impacts that changes in an economy have on major economic variables like output, income, and employment are analyzed by multiplier models. These models assess the magnifying effect that a change in one area has on other sectors, which reflects the overall influence that the change has on the economy. The purpose of multiplier models is to gain an understanding of the economic relevance of particular actions or occurrences and to quantify the effects that specific activities or events have on other areas of the economy.

The methodology consists of:

The employment multiplier, the income multiplier, and the output multiplier are three examples of multipliers that are utilized by multiplier models in order to estimate the entire impact that a change in a particular sector will have on the economy as a whole. Taking into account the interdependencies and links that exist between different industries, these multipliers calculate the additional economic activity that is generated as a result of an initial change. The potential benefits of investments or policy shifts can be evaluated in terms of their total contribution to the expansion of the economy with the assistance of multiplier models.

The Importance of:

When it comes to gaining an understanding of the interrelated nature of the economy, multiplier models are a vital tool for policymakers, corporations, and scholars alike. These models provide insights into the broader implications for employment, income distribution, and overall economic growth. They do this by measuring the spillover effects of changes in certain sectors, which allows them to provide these insights. The use of multiplier models to strategic decision-making and resource allocation enables stakeholders to determine which industries have the most potential to stimulate economic activity and generate positive multiplier effects, hence guiding strategic decision-making and resource allocation.

V. Social Accounting Matrices (often referred to as SAMs)

The Social Accounting Matrices (SAMs) are comprehensive economic models that represent the interactions between various economic agents, such as households, enterprises, and the government. SAMs are also known as social accounting matrices. It is possible for analysts to evaluate the distributional consequences of policy changes, shocks, or interventions on diverse subsets of the population by using SAMs because they provide a thorough picture of the entire economy. These models are extremely helpful in determining the social and economic effects that various policies and programs have had on various subsets of the population of the society.

The methodology consists of:

SAMs take into account information regarding an economy's production, consumption, and distribution of income in addition to the activities of the government.

These data have been arranged in the form of a matrix, which depicts the transactions that take place between the various economic agents and sectors. With the help of SAMs, analysts are able to examine the distributional consequences of policy changes on income, employment, and welfare, taking into consideration the many different socio-economic groups as well as the relationships between them within the economy.

The Importance of:

When it comes to evaluating the fairness and social effects of policy measures, SAMs are an indispensable tool for scholars and politicians alike. These models assist in identifying the prospective beneficiaries and victims of particular policies, which enables policymakers to devise measures that encourage inclusive growth and alleviate socioeconomic inequalities. The SAMs provide insights into the linked nature of the economy and society, stressing the significance of considering the broader social and economic welfare in the policy formation and implementation processes.

Statistical and Econometric Models

Statistical methods known as econometric models are employed in the process of analyzing and forecasting economic relationships on the basis of previous data. In order to estimate the parameters of these models and the correlations that exist between economic variables, economic theory and statistical methods are used. Using econometric models to forecast future economic trends, evaluate the consequences of policy shifts, and get a better knowledge of the elements that influence economic outcomes are all extremely beneficial endeavors.

The methodology consists of:

In order to evaluate the connections between the economic variables, econometric models make use of both time series data and cross-sectional data. In order to discover causal linkages and forecast economic outcomes, these models make use of regression analysis, time-series analysis, and statistical approaches. Forecasting, policy effect assessment, and scenario analysis are all important applications where econometric models come in handy.

The Importance of:

Econometric models give governments, entrepreneurs, and researchers a powerful framework for studying economic linkages and making decisions based on that information. These models give stakeholders the ability to foresee the possible effects of policy shifts and evaluate the elements that influence economic results. The formulation of evidence-based policies and initiatives that foster economic growth and stability can be significantly aided by the utilization of econometric models.

Models of economic impact assessment are vital tools for evaluating the implications of various economic actions, policies, and events on local, regional, and national economies. These models can be used by policymakers, enterprises, and researchers to examine these consequences. These models provide vital insights into the interrelated nature of the economy, which enables stakeholders to make educated decisions, plan strategically, and evaluate the possible benefits or drawbacks of various activities.

The analysis of inputs and outputs looks at the interdependencies between different sectors as well as the consequences that changes in one sector have on other areas. To be computed Models of general equilibrium give a complete study of the effects that changes in policy have on numerous sectors at the same time. These analyses take into account market-clearing mechanisms as well as the behavioral responses of economic agents. The Cost-Benefit Analysis, also known simply as a "Benefit-Cost Analysis," is one of the most important tools for determining whether or not a proposed project, policy, or investment will be profitable. The objective of multiplier models is to quantify the indirect and induced effects of changes on important economic indicators in order to gain an understanding of the more far-reaching consequences for employment, income, and overall economic growth. Analysts are able to evaluate the distributional implications of policy changes on a variety of socio-economic groups by utilizing social accounting matrices, which represent the interactions that occur between the many economic agents in a system. In order to examine and anticipate economic interactions, econometric models make use of statistical approaches. This provides stakeholders with the ability to predict economic trends, evaluate the implications of policy, and gain an understanding of the elements that influence economic results.

The formulation of economic policy, the promotion of economic growth, and the advancement of social and economic welfare are all significantly influenced by the models presented here. Stakeholders are able to make well-informed decisions that are to the economic advantage of all levels—local, regional, and national—when they successfully apply models of economic impact assessment.

2.3 Challenges and Opportunities

Models of economic impact assessment offer insightful information regarding the effects of a wide range of economic actions, policies, and occurrences on the economies of local, regional, and national communities. In spite of the fact that these models have a number of major benefits in terms of the ability to make well-informed decisions and to plan strategically, they also present their own unique set of problems and opportunities. In this analysis, we will investigate the primary difficulties as well as the potential benefits that are connected to economic impact assessment methods.

The Obstacles:

The Availability and Quality of the Data:

The availability and quality of the data are one of the most significant obstacles in the process of evaluating the economic impact. In order to arrive at reliable conclusions, economic models need to be fed copious amounts of extensive and current data on a wide range of economic factors, such as production, consumption, employment, and the activities of the government. Particularly in places or industries that have a deficient data infrastructure, ensuring that data is of a high quality and is easily accessible can be a considerable difficulty.

A Sensitivity to Assumptions:

Models used for assessing the economic impact typically rely on a set of assumptions, which can include things like consumption patterns, production functions, and the behavior of economic agents. The degree to which the results are sensitive to these assumptions might be a challenge, given that even slight modifications to the assumptions can result in substantial deviations from the expected outcomes. When analyzing the results of a study, policymakers and analysts need to be mindful of the sensitivity of the topic and proceed with caution.

Making Predictions Amid Uncertainty:

In the practice of economic forecasting, economic models are routinely applied, despite the inherent unpredictability of the subject matter. The accuracy of projections can be thrown off by a variety of external factors, including swings in global markets, alterations in legislation, or unforeseen events (like natural catastrophes). Those in charge of making decisions, who need to develop plans based on these estimates, have difficulties as a result of the ambiguity.

The concept of causality as well as counterfactuals:

When determining the economic impact of a particular policy or initiative, it might be difficult to establish a chain of causality between the two. It is not always easy to determine what would have transpired in the absence of the intervention. This is referred to as the counterfactual. This difficulty can give rise to discussions about whether the impacts that have been observed are, in fact, the outcome of the intervention that is being evaluated.

Results Based on Distribution:
It's possible that economic impact evaluations don't represent the distributional consequences of policies or projects as well as they should. A policy may have beneficial effects on an economy as a whole, but it may have disproportionately favorable or negative effects on some groups or regions of the economy. The difficulty that must be addressed by policymakers is making certain that the benefits are dispersed in a fair manner.

Occasions to seize:

The Art of Making Informed Decisions:
Models of economic effect assessment offer an important possibility for informed decision-making. They provide a structured framework that researchers, businesses, and politicians can use to examine the potential repercussions of a number of different solutions. By making efficient use of these models, stakeholders are able to make decisions that are not based on intuition or political concerns, but rather on the data and analysis that supports them.

Evaluation of Public Policy:
Models of economic impact assessment make it possible to evaluate both the impact of existing policies and the impact of changes to policies that are being proposed. These models can be used by policymakers to gain an understanding of how various policy alternatives may affect their economies and to assist them in making decisions based on an exhaustive analysis of the potential benefits and drawbacks of such options.

The Process of Strategic Planning
Strategic planning can make use of economic impact assessment models, which can be utilized by businesses and organizations. Because of these models, they are able to evaluate the prospective results that could come from a variety of strategies, investments, and expansions. Organizations are able to design well-informed strategies that optimize economic benefits when they make use of the resources available to them.

Distribution of Resources:
The use of economic impact models offers a methodical approach to the distribution of resources. When governments and organizations have a better grasp of the economic repercussions of various initiatives or interventions, they are better able to allocate resources in an effective manner, directing those resources to areas where they will have the greatest impact on the growth and development of the economy.

Identifying Potential Commercial Openings:
The results of economic impact assessments can be used to assist in locating economic prospects in a variety of industries or geographical areas. When stakeholders are aware of the opportunities for expansion and development, they are better able to direct their efforts toward those domains in which investments are most likely to result in a profit.

Advocacy & Raising Awareness Among the Public:

It is possible for economic impact studies to be utilized as effective advocacy tools. Advocates can make a compelling argument for the implementation of particular projects or policies if they quantify the economic benefits that those initiatives or policies will bring about. These evaluations have the additional potential to raise public knowledge and support for programs that promise to stimulate economic growth.

Chapter 3

Planning and Development of Tourism Infrastructure

Tourism is a sector that is both active and continuously expanding, and it makes a considerable contribution to the economy of many countries all over the world. To foster and sustain the expansion of the tourism industry, the construction of new tourist amenities and facilities is of critical importance. It is necessary for destinations to engage in careful planning and make investments in infrastructure if they wish to meet the requirements and expectations of visitors, deliver unforgettable experiences, and protect the natural world. This in-depth study investigates the planning and development of tourism infrastructure, delving into its significance, important components, obstacles, sustainable practices, and case studies that illustrate effective solutions.

1. **The Importance of Tourist Facilities and Attractions**
   Growth of the Economy:
   The infrastructure of tourist destinations is a driver of economic expansion. It offers the physical underpinning that is required for activities related to tourism, such as transportation, accommodation, and attractions. The creation of new jobs, the generation of new money, and the attraction of new investments are all direct results of economic development being stimulated by investments in infrastructure.
   Destination: competitiveness in the marketplace
   In order to be more competitive in the international tourism market, a location should have tourism infrastructure that has been carefully planned out and built. Tourists are more likely to visit a location if it features airports, hotels, transit networks, and attractions that are on par with the best in the world. The standard of a location's infrastructure has the potential to differentiate it from other similar destinations.
   Enhancements Made to Accessibility:
   The expansion of infrastructure improves visitors' abilities to reach tourism

destinations.

It is much simpler for tourists to reach their desired destinations when there are well-developed transportation networks in place, such as airports, roads, and public transportation. This increased accessibility has the potential to attract a greater variety of guests.

Sustainability in Relation to the Environment:

The design and implementation of sustainable infrastructure are both important contributors to the conservation and protection of natural and cultural resources. Sustainable methods lessen the damage that tourism causes to the natural world and contribute to the economic vitality of destinations over the long term.

2. **Essential Elementa de la Infraestructura Turistica**

Infrastructure for Transportation and Travel:

1. **Airports and Airline Companies:** The use of aircraft as a mode of transportation is the most common way to access overseas destinations. The ability to effectively manage an influx of tourists requires both up-to-date airports and reliable airline services.
2. **Roads and Highways:** For ground transit within destinations, well-maintained road networks are needed. Connectivity and accessibility are both enhanced when the road infrastructure is of a high standard.
3. **Public Transportation:** Buses, subways, and trams are all examples of public transportation systems that play an important part in transporting tourists around inside locations and minimizing the amount of traffic congestion.

Infrastructure for Lodging and Dining:

1. **Hotels and Resorts:** The hospitality industry includes lodging establishments such as hotels, resorts, motels, and lodges. These establishments provide a variety of room types to accommodate a wide variety of traveler tastes.
2. **Vacation Rentals:** As an alternative to conventional hotels, vacation rental platforms provide vacationers the opportunity to stay in private houses or apartments rather than in a hotel.
3. **Camping facilities and eco-lodges:** Camping facilities and eco-lodges provide travelers who are looking for more nature-oriented experiences the opportunity to stay in more rustic settings inside or close to natural attractions.

Facilities & Tourist Attractions:

1. **Museums, Historical Sites, and Other Cultural Attractions:** Attractions of a cultural nature, such as museums, historical sites, and art galleries, highlight the legacy and culture of a destination.
2. **Theme Parks and Other amusement Venues:** Tourists have a variety of options for amusement and leisure while visiting a destination that features theme parks, water parks, theaters, and sports stadiums.
3. **Natural Attractions:** Natural wonders, such as national parks, beaches, and wildlife reserves, are essential components of many of the locations that are popular with tourists.

Infrastructural Support for Communication:

1. **Connectivity to the Internet:** It is essential for travelers to have access to high-speed internet in order to share their experiences, organize their vacations, and stay connected during their travels.
2. **Mobile Networks:** Stable mobile networks guarantee that vacationers will be able to make phone calls and utilize data services while they are away from home.
3. **Tourist Information Centers:** Tourist information centers give visitors with assistance on sites, activities, and services in addition to providing them with maps and brochures.

Infrastructural Support for Services:

1. **Restaurants and Eating Out:** The food and beverage industry provides a wide array of options for eating out, ranging from food carts on the street to fine dining establishments.
2. **Retail and Shopping:** Tourists' shopping requirements are met by shops selling trinkets and souvenirs, local markets, and retail outlets.
3. **Access to Medical Facilities and Emergency Services:** The availability of medical facilities and emergency services is absolutely necessary for the protection and well-being of tourists.

III. Obstacles Facing the Development of Tourism Infrastructure
Finance and business investment:

It might be difficult to secure finance for infrastructure improvements related to tourism. Because of the high original expenditures as well as the requirement for continuous maintenance and modifications, significant financial commitments are necessary. In order to appropriately fund these initiatives, it is frequently required to obtain backing from the government, investments from the private sector, and money from overseas sources.

Influence on the Environment:

The expansion of tourism infrastructure can have negative effects on the surrounding environment, including the destruction of habitat, the depletion of resources, and an increase in carbon emissions. In sustainable development, one of the most important challenges is striking a balance between the economic benefits of infrastructure and efforts to save the environment.

Limitations on Available Capacity:

The rapid expansion of tourism can cause overcrowding and put a strain on the infrastructure that already exists. When it comes to capacity, popular places frequently struggle with issues such as overloaded airports, congested highways, and lodgings that are filled to full. Finding a happy medium between rising tourist numbers and finite resources is a significant problem.

Maintenance of the Infrastructure:

The infrastructure needed to support and maintain tourism is a challenge that never goes away. When maintenance is neglected, it can lead to a degradation in the quality of the infrastructure, which can have an influence on both the experience that visitors have and the competitiveness of the destination. It is crucial to have adequate planning and resources in place for maintenance.

Impact on the Local Community:

The establishment of new tourist infrastructure may have an effect on the surrounding community. Gentrification, an increase in the expense of living, and shifts in local cultures and ways of life are all potential side effects of increased tourism. Finding a happy medium between the needs of those who live in the area and those who work in the tourism business can be a difficult task.

IV. The Creation of an Ecologically Sound Tourism Infrastructure

Considerations Regarding the Environment

The construction of environmentally responsible tourism infrastructure places a priority on the protection and conservation of the environment. It include carrying out environmental impact studies, putting in place environmentally friendly construction practices, and making use of renewable energy sources.

Participation in Community Activities:

Participation from the surrounding community in the planning and development of infrastructure is absolutely necessary for achieving sustainable results. Participation from the community helps ensuring that local residents benefit from infrastructure improvements, that cultural traditions are preserved, and that community well-being is improved.

Protecting Our Cultural Heritage:

The building of tourism infrastructure should show respect for cultural heritage and customs and encourage their continued preservation. Increasing a location's authenticity and cultivating a greater awareness for its culture can both be accomplished by designing public spaces to incorporate local architecture, art, and cultural elements.

Capacity for the Transport of Tourists:

The conservation of natural and cultural resources is aided by the management of tourism's impact through practices such as limiting the total number of tourists and restricting their access to sensitive regions. The implementation of measures to increase carrying capacity can help reduce capacity restrictions.

Collaborations between the public sector and the private sector:

A successful partnership between the public and private sectors is essential to the process of funding and creating tourism infrastructure. Public-private partnerships (PPPs) are beneficial to the development of sustainable infrastructure projects because they capitalize on the respective strengths of both the public and private sectors.

Fostering economic growth, encouraging competitiveness among destinations, and improving the quality of experiences offered to tourists all require careful planning and development of the tourism infrastructure that supports these endeavors. Destinations with better infrastructure in terms of accessibility, hotels, attractions, and services for tourists are more likely to see an increase in visitor numbers.

Nevertheless, it also comes with complications regarding funding, affects on the environment and capacity, restrictions on capacity, impacts on the community, and upkeep of infrastructure.

It is vital to consider environmental protection, community involvement, cultural preservation, tourism carrying capacity, and public-private partnerships while developing tourism infrastructure in order to achieve sustainable tourism infrastructure development. Destinations are able to reap the economic benefits of tourism while also preserving their natural and cultural resources if they put into practice environmentally responsible business strategies and encourage collaboration among various stakeholders.

Case studies that were successful highlight the possibility of tourism infrastructure development that is both well-planned and sustainable. These examples demonstrate the positive outcomes that can be achieved through careful planning and development of infrastructure, whether it be a luxurious resort in Singapore, conservation efforts around Machu Picchu, innovative accommodations in the Maldives, a scenic highway in Iceland, or a thriving international airport in Dubai. All of these examples can be found around the world.

3.1 Infrastructure Requirements for Tourism

The tourism business is one that is ever-changing and complex, and its success is strongly dependent on the presence of many types of physical infrastructure. The infrastructure plays a critical part in shaping the tourism experience, easing travel, and enabling the expansion of this industry. It is vital to have well-planned and developed infrastructure in order to accommodate the varied requirements and expectations of tourists. This includes transportation networks, hotel facilities, attraction systems, and communication systems. In this in-depth study, we will investigate the requirements for tourism infrastructure, with a particular focus on the relevance of these requirements, as well as the main components and sustainable practices involved.

1. **The Importance of Tourist Facilities and Attractions**
   The Engine of the Economy:
   The development of adequate tourism infrastructure is a primary factor in many nations' and regions' rates of economic expansion. It creates cash, encourages investments, and helps to facilitate the creation of new jobs. When both domestic and foreign tourists are drawn to a location, the economy of that location might see a large boost as a result of the destination's well-developed tourism infrastructure.
   Destination: competitiveness in the marketplace
   The ability of a location to compete successfully in international markets is improved by the quality of its tourism infrastructure. Today's vacationers are looking for convenience, comfort, and an experience that will stick with them forever. It is essential to have well-functioning infrastructure in order to entice tourists and to keep them happy once they have arrived at your destination. This includes things like highways, airports, and hotels.
   Obtainability and Availability of Connectivity:
   Accessibility and connection are both improved by the infrastructure supporting tourism, particularly the various transit networks. Airports, highways, railroads, and other modes of public transportation that run smoothly and efficiently make it simpler for tourists to travel to and experience their locations. Increasing a location's accessibility creates opportunities for that location to tap into markets that are both broader and more diversified.
   Sustainability in Relation to the Environment:
   The practices of sustainable tourism infrastructure strive to strike a balance between the expansion of the economy and the preservation of the environment. Long-term sustainability is achieved by the building of infrastructure that minimizes its environmental imprint, reduces waste, and promotes energy efficiency. This helps to ensure that natural resources are preserved for future generations.
2. **Essential Elementa de la Infraestructura Turistica**

Infrastructure for Transportation and Travel:

1. **Airports and Airline Networks:** In order to successfully attract tourists from other countries, it is necessary to have up-to-date airports and an extensive airline network. As the initial point of contact, these gateways are responsible for making the very first impression, which ought to be a good one.
2. **Roads and Highways:** For ground mobility within destinations, having a road network that is well-maintained is absolutely necessary. It improves accessibility

and connection, which in turn makes it easier for tourists to travel to a variety of locations.
3. **Public Transportation:** Tourists have a much easier time getting around inside locations when they take advantage of public transportation options like buses, subways, and trams.

Infrastructure for Lodging and Dining:

1. **Hotels and Resorts:** The hospitality industry is comprised of a wide variety of establishments, including hotels, resorts, motels, lodges, and inns. These offer a variety of lodgings, ranging from those that are affordable to those that are luxurious, appealing to the various preferences of travelers.
2. **Vacation Rentals:** As an alternative to conventional hotels, vacation rental platforms provide vacationers the opportunity to stay in private houses or apartments rather than in a hotel.
3. **Camping and Eco-lodges:** Camping facilities and eco-lodges provide travelers who are interested in having experiences related to nature the opportunity to stay in more rural settings inside or close to natural attractions.

Facilities & Tourist Attractions:

1. **Museums, Historical Sites, and Other Cultural Attractions:** Attractions of a cultural nature, such as museums, historical sites, and art galleries, highlight the legacy and culture of a destination.
2. **Theme Parks and Other amusement Venues:** Tourists have a variety of options for amusement and leisure while visiting a destination that features theme parks, water parks, theaters, and sports stadiums.
3. **Natural Attractions:** Natural wonders, such as national parks, beaches, and wildlife reserves, are essential components of many of the locations that are popular with tourists.

Infrastructural Support for Communication:

1. **Connectivity to the Internet:** It is essential for travelers to have access to high-speed internet in order to share their experiences, organize their vacations, and stay connected during their travels.
2. **Mobile Networks:** Stable mobile networks guarantee that vacationers will be able to make phone calls and utilize data services while they are away from home.

3. **Tourist Information Centers:** Tourist information centers give visitors with assistance on sites, activities, and services in addition to providing them with maps and brochures.

Infrastructural Support for Services:

1. **Restaurants and Eating Out:** The food and beverage industry provides a wide array of options for eating out, ranging from food carts on the street to fine dining establishments.
2. **Retail and Shopping:** Tourists' shopping requirements are met by shops selling trinkets and souvenirs, local markets, and retail outlets.
3. **Access to Medical Facilities and Emergency Services:** The availability of medical facilities and emergency services is absolutely necessary for the protection and well-being of tourists.

III. Obstacles Facing the Development of Tourism Infrastructure
Finance and business investment:

It might be difficult to secure finance for infrastructure improvements related to tourism. Because of the high original expenditures as well as the requirement for continuous maintenance and modifications, significant financial commitments are necessary. In order to appropriately fund these initiatives, it is frequently required to obtain backing from the government, investments from the private sector, and money from overseas sources.

Influence on the Environment:

The expansion of tourism infrastructure can have negative effects on the surrounding environment, including the destruction of habitat, the depletion of resources, and an increase in carbon emissions. In sustainable development, one of the most important challenges is striking a balance between the economic benefits of infrastructure and efforts to save the environment.

Limitations on Available Capacity:

The rapid expansion of tourism can cause overcrowding and put a strain on the infrastructure that already exists. When it comes to capacity, popular places frequently struggle with issues such as overloaded airports, congested highways, and lodgings that are filled to full. Finding a happy medium between rising tourist numbers and finite resources is a significant problem.

Maintenance of the Infrastructure:

The infrastructure needed to support and maintain tourism is a challenge that never goes away. When maintenance is neglected, it can lead to a degradation in the quality of the infrastructure, which can have an influence on both the experience that visitors have and the competitiveness of the destination. It is crucial to have adequate planning and resources in place for maintenance.

Impact on the Local Community:

The establishment of new tourist infrastructure may have an effect on the surrounding community. Gentrification, an increase in the expense of living, and shifts in local cultures and ways of life are all potential side effects of increased tourism. Finding a happy medium between the needs of those who live in the area and those who work in the tourism business can be a difficult task.

IV. The Creation of an Ecologically Sound Tourism Infrastructure

Considerations Regarding the Environment

The construction of environmentally responsible tourism infrastructure places a priority on the protection and conservation of the environment. It include carrying out environmental impact studies, putting in place environmentally friendly construction practices, and making use of renewable energy sources.

Participation in Community Activities:

Participation from the surrounding community in the planning and development of infrastructure is absolutely necessary for achieving sustainable results. Participation from the community helps ensuring that local residents benefit from infrastructure improvements, that cultural traditions are preserved, and that community well-being is improved.

Protecting Our Cultural Heritage:

The building of tourism infrastructure should show respect for cultural heritage and customs and encourage their continued preservation. Increasing a location's authenticity and cultivating a greater awareness for its culture can both be accomplished by designing public spaces to incorporate local architecture, art, and cultural elements.

Capacity for the Transport of Tourists:

The conservation of natural and cultural resources is aided by the management of tourism's impact through practices such as limiting the total number of tourists and restricting their access to sensitive regions. The implementation of measures to increase carrying capacity can help reduce capacity restrictions.

Collaborations between the public sector and the private sector:

A successful partnership between the public and private sectors is essential to the process of funding and creating tourism infrastructure.

Public-private partnerships (PPPs) are beneficial to the development of sustainable infrastructure projects because they capitalize on the respective strengths of both the public and private sectors.

3.2 Public and Private Sector Involvement

The development of tourism infrastructure is a complex enterprise that frequently calls for the participation of both the public sector and the commercial sector in collaborative efforts. This relationship is essential to enable the smooth planning, financing, and execution of infrastructure projects that are necessary to support the expansion of the tourism industry. Within the scope of this investigation, we will investigate the responsibilities, problems, benefits, and instances of public and private sector involvement in the development of tourism infrastructure.

1. **Parts to Play and Duties to Assume**
1. **Participation of the Public Sector**
   Planning and Regulatory Procedures:
   A substantial part of the responsibility for the design and management of tourism infrastructure falls on the public sector, which is comprised of government agencies operating at all three levels of government (local, regional, and national). To ensure that broader economic and environmental objectives are met, it is the responsibility of public authorities to formulate the guidelines, regulations, and standards that will regulate the expansion of existing infrastructure.
   Finance and business investment:
   Through budget allocations, grants, and subsidies, governments frequently contribute essential money to the expansion of existing physical infrastructure. Common examples of public investments include airports, highways, and public transportation networks. These funds are helpful in getting initiatives off the ground, particularly in sectors where private investments may not be enough on their own.
   Responsibility for the Ownership and Management of Infrastructure:
   Airports, seaports, and public transit networks are examples of vital pieces of infrastructure that are frequently owned and managed by public agencies. This guarantees that vital infrastructure will continue to be available to the general public and will be subject to regulation in order to keep the required levels of safety, quality, and service.
   Conservation of Both Natural Resources and Cultural Objects:
   In order to guarantee that tourism infrastructure projects adhere to environmental and cultural preservation criteria, participation from the public sector is very necessary. It is the responsibility of the authorities to carry out environmental impact assessments (EIAs) and put in place sustainable practices in order to preserve natural resources and cultural assets.
2. **Participation of the Private Sector**

   Investing and Financial Support:
   The majority of the funding for tourism infrastructure projects comes from individuals and organizations within the private sector. This includes firms, investors, and developers. They frequently make substantial financial investments in order to fund the building, operation, and upkeep of facilities such as hotels, resorts, and amusement parks.
   The Building Process and Day-to-Day Operations:

Construction and operation of tourism-related infrastructure are both currently being actively worked on by private businesses. They are in charge of the development of various infrastructures, including those for transit, attractions, and lodging. In addition to this, they are responsible for managing the day-to-day operations, maintenance, and upgrades that are necessary to keep the infrastructure competitive and operational.

The Relationship Between Innovation and Competitiveness

The participation of the private sector encourages creativity as well as healthy competition. Businesses that want to maintain their competitive edge and draw in customers invest in cutting-edge technologies, designs, and services. This results in the creation of tourism infrastructure that is both distinctive and of a high quality.

Employment and Its Impact on the Economy:

The participation of the private sector in the development of tourism infrastructure results in the production of new job openings and makes a major contribution to both the regional and national economies. It does this by bringing in new money, new tax contributions, and new opportunities for business, all of which encourage economic growth.

II. Obstacles and Potential Rewards

1. the Obstacles

   Vacancies in Funding:

   When it comes to funding, the development of tourism infrastructure frequently runs into financial shortages, as the resources available from the public sector may not be enough to cover the total cost of a project. Filling these gaps might be difficult and might call for creative new finance alternatives.

   Influence on the Environment:

   The development of tourism infrastructure presents a difficulty in striking a balance between economic growth and environmental sustainability. Participation from the private sector may place an emphasis on profit, which may result in damage to the environment. It can be difficult to find a middle ground that takes into account the needs of both of these groups.

   Limitations on Available Capacity:

   It is possible for capacity restrictions to arise as a result of rapid infrastructure development in popular tourist areas. The experience that visitors have and the community as a whole can be badly impacted when there are not enough available hotels, overcrowded airports, and congested highways.

   Maintenance of the Infrastructure:

   The difficulty of ensuring the continued upkeep and viability of tourism-related infrastructure over the long term is a typical one. When maintenance is neglected, the quality of the infrastructure can deteriorate, which has a negative influence on both the experience that visitors have and the competitiveness of the location.

2. **The Advantages**

Growth of the Economy:
The involvement of both the public and private sectors in the development of tourism infrastructure is beneficial to the expansion of the economy. The private sector is responsible for generating money through its investments and operations, while the public sector is responsible for contributing to and regulating a climate that is conducive to economic growth.

Both originality and quality:
Participation from the private sector is essential for fostering innovation and ensuring the quality of infrastructure. Tourists are able to profit from the competition that exists among private businesses because it motivates those businesses to provide the greatest services, accommodations, and attractions possible.

Creating New Jobs:
The generation of jobs is helped forward by both of these areas. The private sector provides employment opportunities in a wide variety of fields, such as hospitality and construction. The participation of the public sector also results in employment prospects, including positions in regulatory oversight, administrative management, and spatial planning.

Destination: competitiveness in the marketplace
The level of a destination's competitiveness can be improved via the combined efforts of the public and private sectors. A place that stands out from its rivals and has well-developed infrastructure, such as an international airport or a five-star resort, is likely to see an increase in the number of tourists that visit.

III. Methods That Are Ecologically Sound
The creation of environmentally friendly, socially just, and economically viable tourism infrastructure requires the adoption of strategies that take into account all three of these consequences. Participation from both the public and business sectors is necessary to advance these practices.

1. **Initiatives for Environmental Stewardship in the Public Sector**
   Policies and Regulations That Are Friendly to the Environment:
   The establishment of enduring policies and regulations that direct the growth of tourism infrastructure can be accomplished by public bodies. This includes the establishment of environmental standards, the planning of land use, and the implementation of conservation techniques.
   Grants and other financial incentives:
   To stimulate investments in environmentally friendly infrastructure from the private sector, governments may provide financial incentives and subsidies.

Companies can be motivated to prioritize the protection of natural and cultural resources by receiving financial incentives in the form of tax breaks, subsidies, or low-interest loans.

The Process of Monitoring and Enforcing:
Monitoring and enforcing environmental and sustainability norms falls under the purview of public authorities, who are charged with this responsibility. Infrastructure developers must be subjected to routine audits and inspections to verify that they comply with rules and engage in environmentally responsible activities.

2. **Initiatives Towards Sustainability in the Private Sector**

Greener Methods of Production and Construction:
Infrastructure projects undertaken by private firms can benefit the environment by incorporating environmentally responsible elements of design and methods of operation. This includes technologies that are more efficient in energy use, methods that reduce waste, and renewable sources of energy.

Participation in the Community:
Entities from the private sector can actively interact with local communities to guarantee that the construction of new infrastructure will be to the people' benefit. This may involve the creation of new job opportunities, the expansion of existing capacities, and investments in the community.

Certification and Honors Received:
In the process of developing tourism infrastructure, a large number of private enterprises actively seek certifications and awards for environmentally responsible practices. Not only does this designation justify their efforts, but it also draws tourists who are environmentally sensitive.

The process of developing tourism infrastructure is complex and varied, and it requires the involvement of both the public sector and the business sector. Each industry plays an essential part, with the public sector being in charge of planning, regulation, funding, and the protection of the environment, and the private sector concentrating on investments, innovation, quality, and operation. This cooperation may bring difficulties, such as inadequate finance, adverse effects on the environment, insufficient capability, and inadequate maintenance of the underlying infrastructure.

The participation of the public and private sectors, on the other hand, results in considerable benefits, such as increased economic growth, innovation, job creation, and the competitiveness of the destination. When it comes to ensuring that the development of infrastructure is in line with environmental, economic, and social goals, sustainable practices are absolutely necessary.

Both industries may work together to produce tourism infrastructure that is beneficial not only to tourists but also to the destinations themselves if they adhere to high standards, implement policies that are sustainable, engage local communities, and follow through on their commitments. Case studies of tourism infrastructure's successful implementation of effective collaboration and sustainable development come from all around the world and highlight its potential.

3.3 Sustainable Tourism Development

Tourism is a global sector that, when managed in a sustainable manner, has the potential to deliver significant economic advantages to destinations while also maintaining the natural and cultural history of those locations. The development of sustainable tourism strives to achieve a balance between economic growth, environmental responsibility, and the welfare of the communities that are directly affected by tourists. In the course of this in-depth investigation, we are going to discuss the idea of sustainable tourism development, as well as its significance, important concepts, problems, and potential solutions for making the tourism industry more responsible and environmentally friendly.

1. **The Importance of Promoting Eco-Friendly Tourism Development**
   Influence on the Economy:
   In a large number of nations and geographic areas, tourism is one of the most important economic drivers. The development of tourism in a sustainable manner guarantees that the economic benefits of tourism are maximized and distributed fairly, thereby promoting the creation of jobs as well as small companies and communities on the ground.
   Conservation of the Natural World:
   The preservation of natural resources and ecosystems should be given top priority in the development of sustainable tourism. Its goal is to lessen the negative effects that tourism has on the surrounding environment by cutting down on pollution, the destruction of habitats, and excessive exploitation of natural areas.
   Protecting Our Cultural Heritage:
   An essential component of environmentally responsible tourism is the protection and celebration of the local cultural heritage. It encourages respect for local customs, traditions, and historical locations, so halting the loss of cultural practices and promoting an understanding for diverse cultures.
   Responsibility to One's Community:
   The development of sustainable tourism is dedicated to improving the overall health of the communities that are visited. It ensures that citizens of the surrounding area benefit from tourism activities and are actively engaged in the decision-making processes of such activities.
2. **Principles of Responsible and Lasting Growth in the Tourism Industry**
   Concern for the Environment and Safety:
   Practices that safeguard the environment and maintain the integrity of natural and cultural resources are essential components of sustainable tourism development. The protection of fragile ecosystems and heritage places can be assisted by

taking actions such as restricting the number of visitors, encouraging responsible behavior, and putting conservation schemes into action.

Possibility of Financial Success:

The tourism industry must be able to maintain its economic vitality in order to achieve long-term success. To ensure that tourism is beneficial to all parties involved, sustainable tourism development must encompass the production of economic possibilities, the distribution of income, and the investment in local communities.

Participation in the Community:

The empowerment of local communities is a crucial component of the development of sustainable tourism. Residents are more likely to have a feeling of ownership over their environment and cultural heritage when they are given opportunities to participate in tourism planning and development, as well as income sharing.

Authenticity and quality are guaranteed.

The development of sustainable tourism fosters the production of tourism experiences that are both of a high quality and of a genuine nature. Visitors are more interested in having authentic experiences with the local culture and marvels of nature than in seeing artificially made sites.

3. **Obstacles Facing the Growth of Tourism in a Sustainable Manner**

Striking a Balance Between Economic and Environmental Concerns:

Finding a happy medium between expanding the economy and protecting the natural world is one of the most difficult challenges we face.

The development of sustainable tourism must take into account the repercussions that tourism activities will have in the long run and find a middle ground between making a profit and protecting the environment.

Excessive tourism:

The problem of overtourism arises when vacation spots have an excessive number of guests, which can result in overcrowding, damage to the natural environment, and disagreements with the residents of the area. In many popular sites, successfully managing the influx of visitors is a considerable task.

The Development of Infrastructure:

It might be difficult to build environmentally friendly infrastructure that caters to the tourism industry without having a detrimental effect on the surrounding area. Transportation, lodging, and other types of facilities need to be created in a way that minimizes their impact on the environment and cuts down on the amount of resources they use.

Implications for Culture and Society:

Because tourism can bring about changes and outside influences, it can be difficult to maintain the authenticity of local cultures and ways of life over time.

This presents a continuing problem. It is a difficult task to manage these repercussions while simultaneously fostering the preservation of cultural traditions.

4. **Methods for the Accomplishment of Ecologically Sound Tourism Development**

Management of the Destination:
Destination management organizations, often known as DMOs, are extremely important to the process of fostering the growth of sustainable tourism. They devise plans and put them into action in order to control the influx of tourists, preserve natural resources, and provide assistance to the community at large.

Education and a Consciousness of the Facts:
It is crucial to educate tourists about the need of responsible travel. This includes educating people about environmental conservation, cultural standards, and the significance of minimizing one's own environmental impact when traveling.

Regulations and Administrative Procedures:
Regulations imposed by the government are absolutely necessary to guarantee the growth of tourism in a way that is environmentally responsible. These rules could include things like zoning, land use, protections for the environment, and the creation of codes of conduct for tourists.

Investing in the Future of Sustainability:
It is possible for businesses in the private sector, such as hotels and travel agencies, to make investments in environmentally friendly procedures. This may involve the implementation of waste-reduction measures, the promotion of community engagement, and the use of environmentally friendly technologies.

It is vital to grow tourism in a sustainable manner if one want to strike a balance between the economic benefits of tourism and the preservation of both the environment and cultural traditions. Conservation, economic viability, community engagement, and the promotion of high-quality, authentic experiences are core tenets of the concept of sustainability. Managing overtourism and lessening tourism's effects on culture and society are among the challenges that need to be overcome. Striking a balance between economic and environmental interests is another obstacle.

Destination management, education, and laws, as well as investment in sustainability from the corporate sector, are some of the strategies that can be used to achieve sustainable tourism development. Case studies of successful tourist development in Bhutan, Costa Rica, Palau, New Zealand, and the Galápagos Islands illustrate the possibilities for responsible tourism development and exhibit the benefits of an approach that is sustainable. The tourist industry has the potential to flourish while also preserving the natural and cultural assets of the world for the benefit of future generations if it adopts a sustainable approach.

3.4 Funding and Investment Sources

The provision of financial resources and the making of financial investments are both vital components of the development of tourism infrastructure. These elements are what drive the building and upkeep of essential facilities that are necessary for the tourism industry. It is possible to acquire funding from a variety of sources, including the governmental sector, the corporate sector, and international organizations. In this concise review, we will investigate the key sources of finance and investment for tourism infrastructure. These include both public and private funding.

1. **Funding from the Public Sector**
   Budgets for Governments:
   The budgets of governments at all levels, including local, regional, and national, are typically the source of the public financing that is used to develop tourism infrastructure. The preservation of cultural heritage, the construction and upkeep of public transit networks, the provision of public utilities, and the protection of environmental resources all receive funding from the government.
   Donations and Financial Aid:
   It is possible for governments to provide financial assistance in the form of grants and subsidies in order to promote infrastructure projects related to tourism, particularly in areas where tourism is an important economic driver. These grants can assist in getting projects off the ground and promote involvement from the private sector.
   Funding from Donors and International Assistance:
   It is possible that international help and donor funds could be beneficial to the development of
   tourism infrastructure in less developed regions in certain circumstances. Both multilateral organizations like the World Bank and bilateral donors have the ability to provide financial support for initiatives that are in line with their respective organizations' respective development aims.
2. **Investment from the Private Sector**
   Investment from Businesses:
   Investments in tourism infrastructure are typically made by private businesses, such as hotel chains, airlines, and other tourism operators. They provide funding for the development and operation of various infrastructures, including those for lodging, attractions, and transportation.
   Putting Money Into Real Estate:
   Property developers frequently make investments in tourist infrastructure, particularly in regions that have a significant tourism potential. They construct hotels, resorts, and other holiday properties, all of which have the potential to considerably contribute to an area's allure as a tourist destination.
   PPPs, often known as public-private partnerships:
   A public-private partnership (PPP) is a type of joint venture in which both the

public sector and the private sector collaborate in the physical infrastructure of a tourist destination. When it comes to funding and managing projects, these partnerships draw on the advantages offered by both industries. Some examples include joint ventures for the building of hotels and resorts as well as concessions at airports.

3. **Organizations at the International and Multilateral**

    Both the IMF and the World Bank:

    Funding and investment are provided by multilateral institutions such as the World Bank and the International Monetary Fund (IMF) for tourism infrastructure projects in underdeveloped nations. These organizations concentrate their efforts on projects that have the potential to increase economic growth, decrease poverty, and advance sustainable development.

    The Role of Regional Development Banks in

    There are a number of regional development banks around the world, such as the Asian Development Bank and the Inter-American Development Bank, that provide financial assistance for the development of tourism infrastructure in particular geographic regions. They put in effort to address the one-of-a-kind problems and possibilities that are specific to their areas of expertise.

4. **Initiatives at the Local and Regional Level**

    Taxes and Levys Applied to Tourism:

    Bed taxes and airport departure fees are two examples of the types of tourist-related taxes and levies that many locations impose in order to earn cash for the expansion of their tourism infrastructure. The majority of the time, these fees are paid by tourists and then invested back into the local infrastructure.

    Destination Marketing Organizations, abbreviated as "DMOs," are as follows:

    Destination management organizations (DMOs) in popular tourist areas typically set aside a portion of their budgets to subsidize tourism infrastructure. They make investments in marketing and promotion with the goal of luring a larger number of tourists to the region, which, in turn, creates cash that can be used for the expansion of the existing infrastructure.

5. **Organizations Concerned with the Environment and Conservation**

    The acronym "NGOs" stands for "non-governmental organizations"

    Many nongovernmental organizations (NGOs) with an emphasis on environmental protection and conservation make investments in the creation of environmentally responsible tourism infrastructure. These organizations might be able to give financing and support for projects that save natural regions and animals while still catering to the needs of responsible tourism.

    Funding from Foundations and Grants:

Another potential source of funding for environmentally responsible tourism infrastructure projects comes from charitable organizations and private foundations that award grants. They may make funding available to organizations that support efforts to preserve the environment, engage the local community, and conserve resources.

Chapter 4

Marketing and Promotion of Towns as Tourist Destinations

The tourism business is one that is dynamic and is expanding at a quick rate, and municipalities all over the world are beginning to recognize the potential economic benefits of attracting tourists. When it comes to exhibiting the one-of-a-kind experiences, cultural offerings, and attractions that a town has to offer, having an effective marketing and promotion strategy is absolutely essential. Within the scope of this comprehensive guide, we will investigate the many facets of marketing and promoting towns as tourist destinations, including the significance of destination branding, digital marketing, stakeholder engagement, and environmentally responsible tourism practices.

1. **A Comprehension of the Function That Towns Serve as Tourist Attractions**
   Why Cities and Towns Are So Important:
   Travelers who are looking for a more laid-back and genuine experience will find that towns, which are often smaller than major cities, each have their own distinct allure and personality, making them appealing locations. They provide a view into local culture, traditions, and a slower-paced way of life, which can be a welcome contrast to the hustle and bustle of urban centers and can be a source of inspiration.
   Advantages to the Economy:
   The creation of jobs, the generation of cash, and the stimulation of the growth of small enterprises are all ways in which tourism can considerably augment an area's economy. Visitors put money into the local economy by spending it on things like souvenirs, meals, and souvenirs, as well as hotels and attractions.
   Protecting Our Cultural Heritage:
   Additionally, tourism can assist communities in maintaining their cultural traditions. As a result of the interaction that tourists have with local customs, works

of art, and historical places, there is an incentive to preserve and promote these components of the town's character.

2. **Establishing a Powerful Identity for Your Community**
   Marketing Your Destination:
   Developing a distinct and alluring image for your city is a necessary step in the process of effective destination branding. It ought to convey the town's identity as well as its culture and the experiences that are available to tourists in the area. In a tourism market that is already very competitive, successful branding can help your town stand out.

   The process of determining one's Unique Selling Points (USPs):
   What makes your town unique in comparison to others? When it comes to branding, it is crucial to identify the particular selling characteristics of your community, whether those selling factors be pristine natural landscapes, historical landmarks, cultural festivals, or a special culinary scene.

   Maintaining Coherence in Branding:
   It is essential to have a consistent branding strategy across all marketing platforms. This includes employing a logo, color scheme, and messaging that are all consistent with one another in order to create a cohesive picture of your municipality.

   Narrative expression:
   When it comes to branding a destination, storytelling is a powerful tool. If you want to develop an emotional connection with possible visitors to your area, tell them engaging stories about the history of your community, local heroes, or unusual events.

3. **The Use of Online Marketing to Promote the Town**
   The Development of Websites:
   The foundation of your town's online presence should be a website that is not just attractive but also rich in content and easy to navigate. It should include necessary information on places to stay, things to see and do, restaurants, and other events.

   The presence of social media:
   Make use of various social media sites in order to interact with prospective visitors. Make it a habit to share interesting content on a regular basis, such as photographs, movies, and tales that highlight the one-of-a-kind characteristics of the town.

   Optimizing a website for search engines (SEO):
   Make an investment in search engine optimization (SEO) to make sure that the website for your town appears prominently in the results returned by search engines when potential tourists are looking for places to visit.

   Marketing with content:
   Develop meaningful material for your audience that both enlightens and

entertains them. It is possible to attract and engage potential tourists to the town by writing blog posts, articles, and guides on the area's attractions, culture, and experiences.

Advertising on the Internet:
It may be beneficial to target certain audiences interested in visiting your town by using online advertising channels such as Google Ads and the advertising options provided by social media platforms.

4. **Working Together with Various Stakeholders**

Local Organizations and Their Services:
Work together with local companies, such as hotels, restaurants, tour operators, and transportation services, to develop vacation packages and specials that will make the most of the time that tourists spend in the area.

Participation in Community Activities:
Engage with the community at large in order to encourage them to take an active role in the marketing activities being undertaken by the town. This can be accomplished through the organization of local events, festivals, and other activities that highlight the culture of the area.

Collaborations with Neighboring Municipalities:
Creating regional tourist packages and promoting cross-visitation can be accomplished by collaboration with surrounding towns, which is beneficial to all of the towns involved.

Governing at the Local Level:
For the purpose of ensuring that tourism is conducted in a responsible manner, it is important to
have tight working relationships with the authorities of the local government in order to align marketing efforts with town development goals, infrastructure upgrades, and regulations.

5. **Methods of Environmentally Responsible Tourism**

Tourism that takes responsibility:
It is important to encourage responsible tourist activities that take into account the environment, the culture of the area, and the health of the people. Visitors should be encouraged to treat the environment with respect, patronize locally owned companies, and participate in the community in a meaningful way.

Conservation of the Natural Environment:
Bring attention to the fact that your municipality is actively working to preserve the environment. This may involve the promotion of sustainable transportation options, recycling programs, and conservation projects. Other examples include programs that collect recyclable materials.

Protecting Our Cultural Heritage:
Participate in activities that help to preserve cultural heritage, such as providing

assistance to regional artisans and craftsmen, organizing cultural events, and safeguarding historical sites.

6. **Advertising Efforts and Publicity-Seeking Activities**
Local Celebrations & Happenings:
To encourage people to visit your community, you should host or promote local festivals, events, and cultural festivities. These events have the potential to deliver one-of-a-kind experiences and contribute to the town's image of vivacity.

Unique Deals and Promotional Bundles:
Come up with unique vacation packages, bargains, and marketing campaigns to lure tourists to check out the various activities and sights that the city has to offer.

Destination Marketing Organizations, abbreviated as "DMOs," are as follows:
Think about becoming a member of an existing destination marketing group or starting one of your own so that you can better organize and support promotional efforts and campaigns.

7. **Evaluating Performance and Making Adjustments to Tactics**

KPIs, or Key Performance Indicators, are as follows:
Establish key performance indicators in order to evaluate how well your marketing strategies are working. These may include the amount of visitors, the traffic on the website, the participation on social media, and the influence on the economy.

Comments Left By Visitors:
The feedback of tourists should be gathered and analyzed in order to have an understanding of their experiences and preferences. The use of this information may help shape future marketing efforts.

Making Adjustments to Tactics:
Be willing to alter your marketing and promotional methods based on the data and feedback that you have acquired in order to better match the requirements and desires of the audience that you are trying to reach.

The process of marketing and promoting cities and towns as tourism attractions is a multi-faceted activity that demands careful planning, ingenuity, and a dedication to sustainable practices. The development of a powerful brand, the implementation of digital marketing, the formation of partnerships with various stakeholders, and the execution of promotional campaigns and events are all necessary elements of an effective marketing plan. The implementation of these methods allows towns to protect their cultural and natural legacy while also attracting visitors and stimulating economic growth; this ensures the towns' continued success as tourist attractions over the long run.

4.1 Destination Marketing Strategies

The field of destination marketing is one that is always changing and developing, and it is essential to the process of luring tourists and highlighting the qualities that make a location special. As a result of the advent of the digital age, destination marketing techniques have evolved to take advantage of the power offered by the internet, social media, and data analytics. This in-depth guide examines the essential components of destination marketing strategies, the use of technology, sustainable tourism practices, and the significance of stakeholder participation in the process of successfully promoting a location.

1. **Comprehending the Concept of Destination Marketing**
   The Importance of Marketing a Destination to Visitors:
   The purpose of destination marketing is to attract tourists and travelers by promoting a particular location or place, such as a city, region, or even a country, as a vacation or business destination. The objective is to highlight the one-of-a-kind encounters, cultures, activities, and attractions that may be found at the location.
   The Importance of Travel and Tourism:
   The tourism industry is an important economic driver for many different locations, as it helps to create jobs, brings in cash, and encourages the expansion of local small companies. To fully capitalize on the potential financial benefits of tourism, it is imperative to implement successful destination marketing tactics.
2. **Elements That Make Up Successful Destination Marketing Strategies**
   Creating a Brand and an Identity:
   The establishment of a robust brand for a destination serves as the cornerstone of marketing operations. Defining the identity, values, and distinctive selling points of the location are involved in this process. Branding that is effective in communicating the essence of a destination and distinguishing it in the eyes of passengers is considered to be successful.
   The Intended Viewers Are:
   It is crucial to determine who the intended audience is and have a knowledge of them. This contains information about the visitor's demographics, interests, preferences in travel, and reasons for wanting to visit the destination.
   Distribution Methods in Marketing:
   It is essential to utilize a variety of marketing platforms if one wishes to attract a sizable audience. This comprises both traditional channels like as print media, television, and billboards, and digital channels such as websites, social media, email marketing, and search engines. Traditional and digital channels are both included in this category.
   Production of Content:
   One of the most important aspects of marketing a destination is producing content that is both interesting and instructive, and that does it in a way that

showcases the attractions and activities available there. This content can be presented in a variety of formats, such as blogs, videos, photographs, and articles.

Working Together and Forming Partnerships:

It is possible to improve the experience of tourists by working together with local establishments such as hotels, restaurants, and other tourist destinations. The establishment of package deals, special discounts, and events that are geared toward attracting tourists can be the consequence of partnerships.

Insights and Analysis of the Data:

Utilizing data analytics and gaining insights from visitors are both helpful in improving marketing efforts. Destinations may make their marketing efforts more effective by better tailoring them to the behaviors of tourists if they have a solid grasp of those behaviors.

3. **The Impact of Digital Technology on Tourism Destination Marketing**

   Presence on the Internet:

   When it comes to modern destination marketing, having a robust online presence is an indispensable component. Among these responsibilities is the upkeep of a website that is both comprehensive and easy to navigate, with the goal of providing travelers with the information they require.

   Optimizing a website for search engines (SEO):

   Making an investment in SEO strategies guarantees that the destination's website will rank prominently in the results of search engines, which increases the likelihood that prospective tourists will find the destination online.

   The Marketing of Social Media:

   By utilizing social media platforms such as Facebook, Instagram, and Twitter, locations have the ability to connect with tourists, publish material that is interesting, and reply to questions in real time.

   Marketing with content:

   Travelers can be successfully attracted to a destination through the use of content marketing. Not only does the production of useful material, such as travel guides, articles, and blog entries, provide information to tourists, but it also establishes the location in question as an authority on the attractions available there.

   Marketing based on influencers:

   The effectiveness of attempts to market a destination can be increased by forming partnerships with individuals who have a sizable number of followers on the internet. It is possible for influencers to create material that is genuine, interesting, and compelling for their audience.

4. **Methods for a More Eco-Friendly Tourism Industry**

   Promotion of a Responsible Tourism Policy:

   Practices that contribute to sustainable tourism place an emphasis on responsible tourism, which takes into account the health of the local community, the natural environment, and cultural traditions. Marketing a destination should encourage visitors to behave responsibly while they are there.

Conservation of the Natural Environment:

To attract environmentally conscientious tourists, it's a good idea to highlight the location's commitment to environmental conservation and sustainable practices. This can include things like recycling programs, efforts to preserve nature, and alternative modes of transportation that are more environmentally friendly.

Protecting Our Cultural Heritage:

The protection of cultural heritage also ranks high on the list of essential components of sustainable tourism. In order to preserve and highlight the destination's one-of-a-kind heritage, it is important to support local craftspeople, cultural events, and historical landmarks.

5. **Collaborative Efforts with Stakeholders**

   Local Organizations and Their Services:

   It is crucial to work together with local businesses in order to improve the experience that tourists have while they are in the area. Some examples of such businesses include hotels, restaurants, and transportation services. The formation of partnerships can lead to the creation of attractive package packages and other offers for tourists.

   Participation in Community Activities:

   Community involvement is important for ensuring that people will be willing partners in any

   destination marketing efforts. Residents of a location may experience a greater feeling of ownership and pride if the community hosts events, festivals, and other efforts that highlight the culture of the location.

   Participation of the Government:

   In order to match marketing activities with destination development goals, infrastructure improvement plans, and regulations, it is vital to work closely with local government authorities. This will ensure that tourism is practiced in a responsible manner.

6. **Evaluating Performance and Making Adjustments to Methods**

   KPIs, or Key Performance Indicators, are as follows:

   Determine the key performance indicators that will be used to assess the effectiveness of destination marketing efforts. These may include the amount of visitors, the traffic on the website, the participation on social media, the economic impact, and the comments from travelers.

   Comments Left By Visitors:

   Collect and evaluate the comments and suggestions made by tourists in order to obtain a better understanding of their experiences, preferences, and requirements.

This information can be used to guide future marketing initiatives and assist contribute to the improvement of the experience for visitors.

Adjustments Made to Tactics:

Be willing to alter your marketing and promotional plans based on the data and feedback that you have acquired in order to better satisfy the requirements and requirements of the audience that you are trying to reach.

It is necessary to have efficient destination marketing strategies in place in order to successfully attract tourists and promote the distinct features of a location. In this day and age, destination marketing has progressed to include the utilization of technology, environmentally responsible tourist practices, and cooperative efforts with local stakeholders. The attention of tourists can be drawn to a location so that it can reap the economic benefits of tourism. This can be accomplished by developing a powerful brand, determining the audience for which the brand is intended, diversifying the marketing channels used, producing content that is compelling, and embracing sustainable tourism practices.

4.2 Digital and Social Media Marketing

The proliferation of digital and social media has had a significant impact on the way marketing is done today. Businesses, brands, and organizations in this day and age have access to a plethora of options to interact with their target audience, increase brand awareness, and drive conversions. This all-encompassing guide delves into digital and social media marketing, outlining the most important components, methods, and platforms, as well as the tremendous impact that these channels have on current marketing efforts.

1. **The Scenario of Marketing in the Age of Digital and Social Media**
   The rise of digital technology:
   The term "digital marketing" refers to all promotional activities that take place online, such as those conducted on websites, in emails, on search engines, and on social media platforms. Because of its effectiveness and its capacity to communicate with a large and varied customer base, it has developed into an essential component of modern marketing strategy.
   The ubiquitous nature of social media:
   The use of social media platforms is rapidly becoming one of the most influential parts of digital marketing. It encompasses websites and apps such as Facebook, Instagram, Twitter, and LinkedIn, as well as TikTok, which enable users to communicate with one another, build professional networks, and share information. The purpose of social media marketing is to interact with an audience in order to promote a product or service by utilizing various channels.

2. **The Most Important Aspects of Online Marketing**
   The Development of Websites:
   The foundation of successful digital marketing initiatives is a website that is not

just informational but also easy to navigate. It performs the function of a digital shop, where customers may learn about a brand's products and services and interact with the company.

Optimizing a website for search engines (SEO):
The process of enhancing a website's visibility in search engine results is referred to as search engine optimization (SEO). To boost a website's exposure to consumers, it is necessary to make use of pertinent keywords, provide high-quality content, and enhance the website's performance.

Marketing with content:
The goal of content marketing is to attract and keep the attention of a specific audience while also educating them about relevant topics. Blog posts, articles, movies, infographics, and webinars are all examples of the many different formats that content can take.

Marketing using E-mail:
Email marketing makes use of email campaigns in order to communicate with prospective and current customers. It is an effective method for sending promotional messages, updates, and news articles directly to the inboxes of subscribers.

3. **The Most Important Elements of Social Media Marketing**

Determine Your Platform:
It is vitally important to select the appropriate social media sites. When it comes to demographics and hobbies, several platforms appeal to specific groups. For instance, LinkedIn is an excellent platform for business-to-business marketing, whereas Instagram and TikTok are very well-liked by younger audiences.

Production of Content:
Creating content that is interesting and engaging for users is at the core of social media marketing. Posts, photos, videos, tales, and live streaming are all different types of content. The content ought to be congruent with the message conveyed by the brand and resonant with the audience in question.

Participation in the Community:
Responding to followers' comments and direct messages and engaging in other forms of conversation with them are all part of engaging with the community on social media. The cultivation of trust and loyalty through the development of a robust online community.

Marketing based on influencers:
Influencer marketing is a form of marketing that promotes goods or services by capitalizing on the notoriety and credibility of influential users of social media. As a result of their ability to provide genuine content that strikes a chord with their audience, influencers make for effective marketing partners.

4. **Strategies for Online and Digital Marketing**
   SEM stands for search engine marketing
   Paid advertising on search engines, such as Google, is a component of search engine marketing (SEM). Pay-per-click (PPC) campaigns, in which companies pay for ad spots in search results, are included in this.
   Strategie de marketing de contenu :
   Create a content marketing plan that takes into account both the brand's objectives and its target demographic. The regular publication of high-quality material contributes to the development of authority and increases traffic.
   Campaigns for Marketing Via Email:
   Develop engaged relationships with subscribers by launching tailored email marketing campaigns. Ensure that the appropriate content is delivered to the appropriate recipients by customizing messages, dividing the audience, and utilizing automation.
   Marketing via Affiliate Links:
   Affiliate marketing entails forming partnerships with other affiliates who, in exchange for a commission on sales, promote your goods or services to potential customers. This might make your brand more accessible to a wider audience and generate more leads.
5. **Strategies for Marketing Through Social Media**
   Calendar of the Content:
   By planning and scheduling social media posts with the help of a content calendar, businesses can ensure a steady flow of content that is in line with the messaging and promotions of their brands.
   Promotional Activities on Social Media:
   There are paid advertising choices available on a number of social media platforms, including Facebook Ads, Instagram Ads, and Twitter Ads, among others. These allow companies to increase their awareness while also targeting particular demographics.
   Prize Drawings and Competitions on Social Media:
   The engagement and participation of followers can be increased through the use of contests and giveaways. These programs have the potential to increase brand visibility while also generating content from end users.
   Collaborations with Influencers:
   Collaborate with social media influencers who already have a sizable audience and whose beliefs are congruent with those of the brand. Influencers are able to assist in expanding both your reach and your trustworthiness.
6. **Evaluating and Assessing One's Level of Success**
   KPIs, or Key Performance Indicators, are as follows:
   Determine the key performance indicators that will be used to evaluate how well digital and social media marketing is working. These may include the amount

of visitors to a website, the conversion rate, the click-through rate, the amount of engagement on social media, the growth in the number of followers, and the email open rate.

Insights and Analytical Work:
Use the analytics tools supplied by the platform to monitor performance. Examples of such tools are Google Analytics and social media insights. These technologies supply extremely helpful information regarding the demographics, tastes, and behaviors of audiences.

Testing with A and B:
The purpose of A/B testing is to discover which version of a webpage, email, or social media post is more successful in terms of traffic and engagement. It assists in the refinement of strategies and the optimization of content in order to achieve higher levels of engagement and conversion.

7. **The Influence That Technology And Automation Have On Society**
Automation of Marketing Strategies:
Marketing automation solutions simplify marketing activities by streamlining activities such as email campaigns, lead nurturing, and the scheduling of social media posts. They allow for more tailored marketing efforts to be made while also improving overall efficiency.

The acronym AI stands for "artificial intelligence"
Artificial intelligence systems can examine vast datasets to get insights into the behavior of consumers. Artificial intelligence-driven chatbots improve both customer service and engagement.

The terms augmented reality (AR) and virtual reality (VR) refer to the same thing
AR and VR technologies provide prospective clients with experiences that are fully immersive. They can be utilized to provide virtual tours as well as exhibit products.

8. **Obstacles Facing Marketing in the Digital and Social Media Age**
Saturation and rivalry in the market:
The online environment is cluttered with content and adverts from various companies. Making yourself noticeable in a sea of information is a difficult task.

Adjustments to the Algorithm:
The algorithms used by social media platforms are frequently updated, which might have an effect on the content's reach and visibility. It is essential to adjust oneself to these changes.

Concerns Regarding Privacy:
Privacy and the safety of one's data have recently emerged as major concerns. Marketers have a responsibility to follow privacy legislation as well as the desires of their customers.

Overabundance of Content:

Consumers are sometimes overcome by an excess of information. It is crucial to craft material that is succinct, interesting, and pertinent.

9. **Emerging Patterns in the Promotion of Businesses via Digital and Social Media**

Marketing with Videos:
The consumption of content presented in video form is gaining ground. It is anticipated that live streaming, 360-degree videos, and short-form media would dominate the landscape of the digital world.

Optimizing Results for Voice Search:
Voice search optimization will become increasingly important as the use of voice-activated technology, such as smart speakers, becomes more widespread.

Content that can be interacted with
Increased user engagement can be achieved through the usage of interactive content such as polls, quizzes, and shoppable posts.

Personalization Determined by AI:
Personalization will continue to be enhanced by AI, allowing users to access content that is more pertinent and targeted.

The method in which companies and brands communicate with their customers has been fundamentally altered by the advent of digital and social media marketing. These platforms provide effective avenues for increasing brand exposure, interacting with customers, and generating conversions. The power of digital and social media marketing may be harnessed by organizations to help them thrive in the digital era. This can be accomplished by putting strategies into action, monitoring success, and keeping up with the latest trends and technical breakthroughs.

4.3 Event and Festival Tourism

Attending or taking part in numerous events, festivals, and celebrations in different locations across the world is fueling a growing subset of the travel business known as event and festival tourism. These meetings provide tourists one-of-a-kind experiences while showcasing a variety of cultural traditions, creative expression, and artistic expression. In this review, we will discuss the relevance of event and festival tourism, its influence on local economies, and the aspects that contribute to the allure of these get-togethers among tourists.

1. **The Importance of Tourism in the Form of Events and Festivals**
   Participation in a Culture:
   Tourism at events and festivals offers visitors the chance to become fully immersed in the culture of the location they are visiting. Visitors are able to obtain a deeper understanding of the local way of life by attending festivals because these events frequently reflect the history, values, and customs of the community.
   Unforgettable Adventures:

The experiences that one can have at events and festivals are one of a kind and cannot be had anywhere else. The Rio Carnival is one example of a large-scale celebration, whereas the Albuquerque International Balloon Fiesta is an example of a gathering that focuses on a specific interest. People go to these events in the hopes of having an unforgettable experience and seeing something that is out of the norm.

Influence on the Economy:
Tourism related to events and festivals makes a substantial contribution to the economy of the area. These events bring in tourists who spend money on things like lodging, food, transportation, and souvenirs, which is beneficial to the local economy and helps to create jobs.

2. **Varieties of Gatherings and Celebrations**
Festivals de la Culture:
Heritage, traditions, and practices within a community are honored and celebrated during cultural festivals. Celebrations of the Chinese New Year are held all over the world. Some examples include Diwali in India, Oktoberfest in Germany, and other similar events.

Festivals de musique:
Music festivals celebrate a wide variety of musical styles and are attended by music fans from all around. Iconic examples include festivals such as Coachella in the United States and Tomorrowland in Belgium.

Competitions in Sports:
Attracting competitors and spectators from all over the world, sporting competitions such as the Olympic Games, the FIFA World Cup, and the Tour de France do just that. These events foster a sense of togetherness and offer cause for celebration.

Festivals of the Arts and Film:
Festivals of art and film feature a variety of creative works, ranging from the visual arts and cinema to the written word and the performing arts. In this field, some of the most prestigious events include the Cannes Film Festival, the Venice Biennale, and the Sundance Film Festival.

3. **The Attractiveness of Tourism for Events and Festivals**
Interactions with Other People:
The chance to engage in social conversation and network with individuals whose lives have been shaped by a variety of experiences can be found at events and festivals. It is possible for travelers to make ties and friends not just with locals but also with other tourists.

For your amusement:
These get-togethers are fun and typically feature performances of music, dancing, painting, and various other forms of expression. The entertainment component attracts people who are looking for an experience that is both enjoyable

and culturally stimulating.

When it comes to social media and photography:
Because event and festival tourism delivers moments that are both visually appealing and shareable, it is an ideal topic for photography and the sharing of images on social media. The tourists document and talk about their adventures, which brings more attention to the event and the location that is hosting it.

Delectables for Your Mouth:
The cuisine and peculiarities of a region are regularly highlighted at events and festivals. The fact that vacationers are able to partake in local culinary customs and delicacies contributes to the overall quality of the trip.

4. **Impact on the Economy and the Communities in the Area**

Growth of the Economy:
The tourism associated with events and festivals has a considerable effect on the economy. It results in increased revenue for local businesses, hospitality and tourism-related services, which frequently leads to the creation of new jobs and the expansion of existing infrastructure.

Participation at the Local Level:
Communities on a smaller scale are of critical importance when it comes to the planning and execution of events and festivals. This involvement helps to preserve cultural traditions, increases feelings of pride in the community, and creates opportunity for local merchants and artists to display and sell their wares.

Practices That Are Sustainable:
The importance of event and festival management that is more environmentally responsible continues to rise. The long-term profitability of event tourism is improved by making concerted efforts to reduce the industry's negative influence on the surrounding environment, effectively manage waste, and engage the community in event planning.

5. **Opportunities and Obstacles to Overcome**

Management of the Crowd and the Infrastructure:
The management of huge crowds can be difficult at times. It is imperative to have adequate infrastructure as well as crowd control in place in order to assure the visitors' and participants' satisfaction and safety.

Influence on the Environment:
The generation of waste and the disruption of habitat are two examples of the severe environmental impacts that can be caused by events and festivals. In order to lessen the severity of these consequences, sustainable behaviors are required.

Balance in the economy:
Finding a happy medium between the potential economic rewards and the need to protect the cultural identity of an area can be difficult. Achieving this equilibrium

is essential for ensuring that local communities continue to prosper while preserving their unique cultural identities.

Event and festival tourism provide tourists with one-of-a-kind experiences as well as opportunity to become fully immersed in the culture of the location they are visiting. These events not only offer amusement and unique experiences, but also contribute significantly to the economic well-being of the towns in which they are held. Nevertheless, they also bring up difficulties in terms of infrastructure, the influence on the environment, and the economic equilibrium. Event and festival tourism has the potential to continue to flourish and benefit the world's travel sector if it adheres to three key tenets: preserving cultural authenticity, promoting environmental responsibility, and providing efficient crowd management.

4.4 Branding and Identity

Branding and identity are essential concepts in the world of business and marketing that extend far beyond simple logos and slogans. They are about making an impression that is one of a kind and one that lasts, which differentiates a company, product, or service from those of its competitors. In this overview, we discuss the relevance of branding and identity, as well as its essential components and the effect that they have on the perception and loyalty of customers.

1. **The Importance of Branding and Identity in Today's World**
   The difference is in:
   A company or product can differentiate itself from its rivals through the development of its brand and identity. They come up with a one-of-a-kind positioning that communicates what it is about the brand that makes it stand out and why consumers should care about it.
   Recognizance :
   A brand that maintains its identity and branding in a consistent manner is easier to recognize. Consumers develop a recognition for a certain business or brand over the course of time by coming to link particular colors, logos, and slogans with that business or brand.
   The values of Trust and Loyalty:
   Consumers are more likely to put their faith in a brand that has been carefully crafted and possesses a distinct identity. Because customers have faith in what the brand stands for, it inspires loyalty among them and motivates them to make additional purchases.
2. **Essential Elements of a Brand's Identity and Presentation**
   Logo:
   A brand's logo serves as a graphical representation of the company, and it is frequently the first thing that consumers take note of. It need to be easily recollected, adaptable, and indicative of the personality of the brand.
   A Selection of Colors:

Colors have the ability to elicit certain feelings and have psychological connotations. Color schemes are selected for their ability to express particular emotions and messages by companies. As an illustration, the color blue may stand for dependability and trust, but the color red may denote excitement and zeal.

The art of typing:
The identity of a brand can be affected by typography, which refers to the selection of typefaces and the style of the text. The personality of a brand, whether it be classic, contemporary, or whimsical, may be conveyed by its choice of fonts.

A Phrase to Remember or Slogan:
A memorable slogan or tagline is a brief statement that conveys the essence of a company or the promise it makes to consumers. Consider the Nike slogan "Just Do It" as well as the Apple slogan "Think Different."

Voice and Messaging of the Brand:
The manner in which a company conveys its messages to its target audience has a direct impact on how the company is understood. The voice of a brand can be helped to be defined by the choice of language that is used, whether it be official, colloquial, or amusing.

3. **The Importance of Branding and Identity to the Way Customers See Themselves**

   Always consistent:
   It is crucial to maintain consistency in branding in order to establish an image that is distinct and unified. Customers are more likely to form a solid and reliable perception of a brand when its visual and message features are maintained over all of its touchpoints.

   Connecting on an Emotional Level:
   Customers are prompted to feel something when a brand successfully conveys its identity. The name of the brand begins to be connected with a range of emotions, including pleasure, excitement, melancholy, and trust. A meaningful relationship with a consumer might result in brand loyalty.

   Credibility and reliability:
   Trust and credibility may be built with the help of a clearly defined identity and consistent branding. When customers are aware of what to anticipate, they are more likely to put their faith in the claims and standards made by a brand.

   Relationship with Core Beliefs:
   The core principles and core beliefs of a brand are frequently communicated through its branding and identity. This association has the potential to attract customers who share those beliefs, which will develop stronger connections.

4. **Adapting to the Era of Digital Technology**

   Presence on the Internet:
   Because we live in a digital age, the presence of a brand online is an essential component of its identity and branding. A website that is easy to use, social

media profiles that are interesting to follow, and online advertising all add to the image of a company.

Content that can be interacted with

Interactive content, such as polls, quizzes, and user-generated material, is becoming
increasingly popular among brands as a strategy for increasing audience engagement and developing a more dynamic identity.

Transparency in Branding:

Transparency is something that consumers respect, and brands are now expected to be open and honest with their customers. The identity of a brand need to represent the company's commitment to ethical and environmentally responsible business operations.

Engagement of the Customer:

The use of social media and participation in online forums give venues for direct interaction with clients. These places are being utilized by brands in order to fortify their existing relationships and adapt their identities in response to the comments and suggestions of their target audiences.

5. **Opportunities and Obstacles to Overcome**

Changing Expectations of the Consumer Market:

The expectations of consumers shift throughout time, and companies have to evolve to continue to have an impact on consumers' lives. This gives opportunities for rebranding and updating the identity of a brand in order to satisfy the expectations of modern consumers.

Keeping the Same Thing Over and Over:

When there are so many different ways that people can communicate with one another, it can be difficult to keep a consistent branding and identity. However, maintaining this consistency is absolutely necessary in order to construct and protect the image of a brand.

Authenticity of the Brand:

Authentic brands are becoming an increasingly attractive option for consumers. The difficulty lies in striking a balance between authenticity and commercial success, making sure that the brand identity reflects both of these aspects.

The era of globalization:

The difficulty of keeping a consistent identity across a variety of cultures and markets is one that is frequently faced by global brands. Finding the right balance between adapting to local expectations and maintaining the essential essence of the brand can be challenging.

The potential of a company's brand and identity to impact the views, loyalty, and trust of its customers is significant. A powerful and unique identity helps a company stand out from the competition and establishes emotional connections with its target audience. Because the opportunities and challenges associated with branding and identity are constantly shifting in this digital age, it is absolutely necessary for organizations to change while continuing to uphold their fundamental principles and commitments.

Chapter 5

Community Engagement and Tourism

The relationship between community participation and tourism is one that is dynamic and advantageous for both parties. Local communities and tourists meet one another at the point where these two spheres overlap, forging linkages that not only enhance the tourism experience but also promote economic growth, cultural preservation, and social cohesion in the destination. In this in-depth book, we investigate the tremendous impact that community engagement has on tourism, the rewards and problems that come along with it, and the ways in which destinations may use this relationship to create travel experiences that are both sustainable and gratifying.

1. **The Importance of Involvement with Local Communities in the Tourism Industry**
   Tourism with a Focus on Local Communities
   Participation of local people in tourism activities is not a passing fad; rather, it is essential to the idea of tourism that is both sustainable and responsible. The participation of local communities in the tourism business helps to ensure that the advantages of tourism are distributed fairly and positively impacts the well-being of the local population.
   The protection of cultural and historical assets:
   Communities on a local level are responsible for maintaining cultural practices, historical locations, and legacy. Including them in tourism-related endeavors contributes to the protection and maintenance of these priceless assets for the benefit of future generations.
   Real and Genuine Experiences:
   When visiting a new location, tourists are looking for experiences that are more genuine and immersive than ever before. Tourists are able to go deeper into a location, experience the culture of the area, and create experiences that they will remember forever if they interact with the local people.

Advantages to the Economy:
Participation in community activities helps to strengthen local economies. Residents have the opportunity to produce income, acquire jobs, and start their own small companies if they take part in tourism-related activities. The community as a whole will benefit from this increase in economic activity.

2. **Components of Community Involvement in Tourist Attractions**
   Local Organizations and Their Services:
   A fundamental aspect of community involvement is providing assistance to and raising awareness about the existence of local companies, such as hotels, restaurants, tour operators, and retail establishments selling handmade goods. It is important to guarantee that the community benefits from tourism profits, and one way to do this is to encourage tourists to patronize local companies.
   Encounters with other cultures:
   By extending an invitation to tourists to take part in cultural activities such as traditional dance performances, craft workshops, or cooking classes, communities get the chance to engage with visitors and visitors get a better understanding of the culture of the community they are visiting.
   Practices That Are Sustainable:
   Community engagement frequently includes the implementation of environmentally responsible tourism activities. Local communities play a crucial part in the implementation and promotion of environmentally friendly programs, responsible wildlife encounters, and responsible conduct recommendations for tourists. These are all areas in which tourists can have an impact on the environment.
   Craftsmen & Artisans in the Neighborhood:
   Tourists provide opportunity for local artisans and craftsmen to demonstrate their abilities,
   wares, and customs, which in turn fosters opportunities for economic growth and the preservation of culture. Craft markets and workshops are wonderful places for this kind of involvement.

3. **The Advantages of Involving Local Communities in Tourism**
   Protecting Our Cultural Heritage:
   Participation of the local community in tourism-related endeavors contributes to the preservation of cultural traditions and history. Communities that are heavily invested in the tourism business have a vested interest in preserving their culture and making it more resistant to the effects of change because of this investment.
   Growth of the Economy:
   The health and happiness of a community are both improved by tourism's contribution to economic progress. The number of unemployed people and those living in poverty is brought down while at the same time the number of jobs

and the success of enterprises are brought up.

Experiences That Are Better:

Experiences that are more genuine, immersive, and satisfying can be had by tourists who interact with the communities in which they visit. These are the kinds of experiences that are likely to be remembered and talked about, leading to an increase in the number of tourists who visit the location.

a higher level of social cohesion:

Participation in community activities helps to strengthen the social bonds that exist among members of the local population. It is possible for locals to develop a sense of pride and a sense of shared responsibility for the destination's overall health and prosperity when they take part in tourism-related activities.

4. **The Difficulties Associated with Community Involvement in Tourism**

Finding a Happy Medium Between Tourism and Everyday Life:

The local communities may find it difficult to maintain a healthy balance between their regular lives and the activities associated with tourism. An over reliance on tourism can occasionally cause disruptions to the routines of local residents, which can be a source of inconvenience for these people.

Managing the Appropriation of Cultural Practices:

It is possible for tourism to result in cultural appropriation, which is the commercialization or distortion of traditional components of a community's culture.

The engagement of the community need to have the goal of preventing such problems and ensuring cultural respect and authenticity.

Influence on the Environment:

Participation in community activities may, unintentionally, lead to environmental problems such as increasing waste and pollution and the destruction of natural habitats. To lessen the impact of these problems, sustainable tourism measures need to be put into place.

Distribution of Benefits in an Equitable Manner:

It can be difficult to ensure that the economic and social benefits of tourism are spread fairly among the inhabitants of a community, but this is a goal that should be pursued. It is possible for there to be disparities in income and opportunity, both of which need to be addressed in order to promote community cohesion.

5. **Methods of Community Involvement That Are Efficient in the Tourism Industry**

Participation of Members of the Community in Decision-Making:

Local communities should be given the opportunity to weigh in on choices, regulations, and plans pertaining to tourism. Because of their active participation, tourism activities will always be in line with the interests and values of the community.

Education and Professional Development:
It is necessary to make educational and training options available to the population of the area. Because of this, they are equipped with the knowledge and abilities essential to participate in tourism activities in an efficient and environmentally responsible manner.

Instruction on Sensitivity to Culture:
Travelers and tourism industry workers alike should participate in cultural sensitivity training in order to better understand, respect, and value local rituals and traditions. This helps to prevent the appropriation of other cultures and ensures that interactions are genuine.

Advertising and public relations:
The cultural experiences and opportunities for community engagement that are included in a destination's tourism offers can be actively marketed and promoted by the destination. This appeals to vacationers who are looking for immersive experiences and are interested in giving back to the places they visit.

6. **Measurement of Success and Viability in the Long Term**

KPIs, or Key Performance Indicators, are as follows:
The success of programs to involve the community can be evaluated with the help of KPIs that are identified. KPIs might include things like improved income and employment generation, as well as metrics of tourist happiness and cultural preservation.

Continuous Observation and Course Adjustment:
Continuous monitoring of community involvement efforts provides destinations with the ability to change and advance their plans in response to shifting requirements and obstacles.

Practices That Are Sustainable:
Adhering to responsible tourist practices, limiting environmental impact, and resolving socio-economic imbalances within the community are all important steps to take if one wishes to ensure that community participation is sustainable.

Community engagement and tourism are inextricably interwoven; local communities are at the heart of a destination's cultural preservation and economic prosperity, making community engagement particularly important. When community engagement efforts are successful, they lead to travel experiences that are genuine, gratifying, and immersive for tourists, while also producing possibilities for locals. However, in order to overcome obstacles such as cultural appropriation and striking a balance between tourist and daily life, proactive initiatives and unceasing efforts are required. Destinations have the ability to harness the transformative potential of community participation in order to create a tourism sector that is both more fulfilling and more environmentally sustainable if they promote community involvement, education, cultural sensitivity, and sustainable practices.

5.1 Balancing Local Interests and Tourism

Finding a happy medium between the needs of the host community and the demands of tourists is an ongoing challenge for locations all over the world. As the tourism industry continues to expand, the requirements and goals of the communities that tourists visit frequently overlap with those of the towns themselves. To achieve sustainable and responsible tourism, striking a healthy balance between the two is essential. This ensures that the advantages of tourism are shared fairly, that local cultures and habitats are protected, and that inhabitants and tourists can coexist happily. In this extensive guide, we delve into the complicated dynamics of this connection, analyzing the relevance, problems, tactics, and case studies connected to maintaining a healthy equilibrium between local interests and tourism.

1. **The Importance of Striking a Balance Between Community Concerns and Tourism**
   Tourism with a Low Impact:
   Finding a happy medium between tourism and local interests is essential to the development of
   sustainable tourism. It guarantees that the social, economic, and environmental aspects of a location are taken into consideration, hence protecting the tourism industry's potential to thrive in the long run.
   Growth of the Economy:
   In many different locations, tourism is a vital contributor to economic growth, as it helps to generate money and jobs, as well as stimulates the growth of local small businesses. A distribution of economic advantages that is fair requires that competing local interests be taken into account.
   Protecting Our Cultural Heritage:
   Maintaining a healthy balance between local interests is another important step in protecting a destination's cultural identity and legacy. The preservation of local cultures is aided by tourism that shows consideration for the local norms, values, and customs.
   Integration of Society:
   Social cohesiveness can be encouraged by maintaining positive relationships between locals and visitors to the area. It fosters a sense of belonging within the community as well as a sense of shared responsibility, which contributes to the overall improvement of its health.
2. **The Difficulties Associated with Striking a Balance Between Tourism and Local Interests**
   Inadequate space:
   An excessive amount of tourism can result in overcrowding, which in turn interferes with the normal activities of the local community and places a pressure on the infrastructure, resources, and public services.
   Disparities in the Economy:

In many cases, tourism results in income inequities, with some industries benefitting more than
others from the industry. It's possible that the locals will feel left out of the economic benefits of tourists, which could lead to confrontations.

Appropriation de la culture:
It is possible for tourism to result in cultural appropriation, which is the commercialization or distortion of traditional components of a community's culture. This can lead to problems relating
to cultural sensitivity and can weaken the validity of a culture.

Influence on the Environment:
The presence of a substantial number of tourists can exacerbate environmental problems such as pollution, the loss of habitat, and the excessive consumption of natural resources. This poses a risk to the local ecosystems as well as the continued health of the environment.

3. **Methods for Striking a Balance Between Local Concerns and Tourist Activities**

   Participation in Community Activities:
   Tourism-related decision-making processes should include active participation from the communities that are directly impacted by those decisions. They ought to be given a voice in matters pertaining to the formulation of tourist policies and the planning of related activities.

   Best Practices for Responsible Tourism:
   It is essential, in order to lessen the damage that tourism does to the natural environment, to put into practice environmentally conscious tourism measures such as waste management, protection of wildlife, and sustainable transportation.

   Education and Professional Development:
   Residents of a community can acquire the information and skills necessary to participate in tourist operations in an efficient and environmentally responsible manner if educational and training opportunities are made available to them.

   Sensitivity to culture and awareness of culture:
   The local customs and traditions should be respected and appreciated by tourists as well as those who work in the tourism industry, hence cultural sensitivity training should be required of both groups. This helps to prevent the appropriation of other cultures and ensures that interactions are genuine.

4. **Measurement of Success and Continuity of Activity**

   KPIs, or Key Performance Indicators, are as follows:
   The identification of key performance indicators (KPIs) helps measure the efficacy of programs in striking a balance between local interests and tourists. KPIs can include things like the number of visitors, the advantages to the economy, the level of happiness felt by residents, environmental measures, and cultural preservation benchmarks.

Continuous Observation and Course Adjustment:
Continuous monitoring of tactics and the impact they have enables destinations to adjust and advance their strategy as necessary to meet the ever-evolving demands and obstacles.

Practices That Are Sustainable:
It is necessary to make sure that sustainable practices are incorporated into the strategies for striking a balance between local interests and tourists. This includes the implementation of environmentally sustainable legislation, cultural preservation projects, and responsible tourist programs.

It is necessary to strike a balance between local interests and tourism if the travel industry is to flourish in a way that is both sustainable and responsible. Destinations may foster a peaceful and mutually beneficial interaction between locals and tourists by actively including local populations in decision-making processes, implementing responsible tourism practices, providing education and training, and fostering cultural sensitivity and understanding. The obstacles are substantial, but the rewards of attaining this balance are profound. It will result in economic growth, the preservation of cultural traditions, social cohesion, and the wellbeing of communities as well as tourists. In a world where the number of people traveling is only expected to increase, striking this balance is more important than it has ever been.

5.2 Involving the Community in Tourism Development

Involving the local population in the process of developing tourism is a vital component of ethical and environmentally conscious vacationing. It acknowledges the significance of the local people as stakeholders in the tourism business and makes an effort to guarantee that the benefits of tourism are fairly divided among all of the local citizens. This in-depth guide investigates the relevance of community involvement in tourism development, as well as its associated problems, solutions, and case studies. Its purpose is to shed light on the tremendous impact that community involvement has on destinations and the wellbeing of the citizens of those destinations.

1. **The Importance of Community Involvement in the Creation of New Tourist Attractions**

   Tourism with a Low Impact:
   The participation of local people in the expansion of tourism is essential to ensuring its continued viability. It helps to ensure that the economic, social, and environmental aspects of a destination are taken into consideration, which in turn contributes to the sustainability of tourism over the long run.

   Economic Self-Determination:
   Residents in the surrounding area get actively involved in the tourism industry, which can lead to economic empowerment in the form of job creation, opportunities for business ownership, and the generation of money.

   Protecting Our Cultural Heritage:

The cultural character and heritage of a location can be better protected and preserved via the participation of the local population. It guarantees that local customs, traditions, and historical sites are respected and maintained in their original state.

Integration of Society:
Participation in community activities helps to strengthen the social bonds that exist among members of the local population. It fosters a sense of pride and collective responsibility for the health of the location, which contributes to an improvement in the general quality of life in the community.

2. **The Difficulties Associated with Community Participation in Tourism Development**

   The absence of adequate representation:
   When local communities are not adequately represented in the decision-making processes pertaining to tourism, this can result in the imposition of development plans that are not in line with the interests of the community.

   Disparities in the Economy:
   The expansion of tourism can occasionally result in economic inequalities, with some industries benefiting more than others from the development. This has the potential to exacerbate existing tensions within the community.

   Consideration for Other Cultures:
   Respect for the norms and practices of the community at large is of the utmost importance. It is possible for tourism development to unwittingly produce cultural insensitivity problems when there is a lack of appropriate awareness and respect for the local culture.

   Influence on the Environment:
   Large-scale tourist development may lead to environmental problems such as the destruction of habitat, an increase in waste production, and pollution, all of which pose a risk to the viability of local ecosystems and the environment.

3. **Methods of Community Involvement That Are Proven to Be Successful in Tourism Development**

   Planning for Tourism Based on the Community:
   Include input from the local community in the planning and development of tourism. Involve members of the community in the decision-making process to ensure that their needs and priorities are taken into account.

   Education and Professional Development:
   Make it possible for locals to participate in tourism activities in an efficient and environmentally responsible manner by providing them with educational and training opportunities that will equip them with the skills and information they need.

   Instruction on Sensitivity to Culture:
   The local customs and traditions should be respected and appreciated by

tourists as well as those who work in the tourism industry, hence cultural sensitivity training should be required of both groups. This helps to prevent the appropriation of other cultures and ensures that interactions are genuine.

Advertising and public relations:

Promote community-based tourist projects as well as businesses that are owned by local residents actively. Develop marketing efforts that put the spotlight on the genuine experiences that the community has to offer.

4. Measurement of Success and Continuity of Activity

KPIs, or Key Performance Indicators, are as follows:

When it comes to tourist development, identifying key performance indicators (KPIs) is helpful in assessing the success of community participation projects. KPIs might include things like improved income and employment generation, as well as metrics of tourist happiness and cultural preservation.

Continuous Observation and Course Adjustment:

The continuous monitoring of community involvement activities enables destinations to adjust and advance their approach as necessary to meet the ever-evolving demands and obstacles.

Practices That Are Sustainable:

It is crucial to make certain that community involvement activities contain environmentally responsible techniques. This includes the implementation of environmentally sustainable legislation, cultural preservation projects, and responsible tourist programs.

Participation from the local community in the growth of tourism is a vital component of ethical and environmentally conscious vacationing. Destinations have the potential to provide equitable economic growth, the preservation of cultural traditions, and social cohesion through active engagement with the local community. The obstacles are enormous, but the benefits of good community involvement are profound. These benefits result in the well-being of both inhabitants and tourists, which is essential to the sustainability of tourism over the long run. It is impossible to overestimate the significance of community participation in this day and age, when responsible and environmentally conscious travel is becoming increasingly emphasized.

5.3 Cultural Preservation and Heritage Tourism

Heritage tourism and cultural preservation are two interwoven concepts that aim to appreciate the richness of a location's history, customs, and cultural identity. Heritage tourism is a subset of cultural tourism. Heritage tourism gives visitors the opportunity to become completely submerged in the history, artwork, and customs of a particular location, whereas cultural preservation works to protect and pass on these priceless artifacts to subsequent generations. In this book, we discuss the relevance of cultural preservation and heritage tourism, as well as the challenges and opportunities presented by these two topics, as well as the strategies for protecting cultural heritage through the responsible use of tourism.

1. **The Importance of Maintaining Cultural Authenticity and Promoting Heritage Tourism**
   Identifying One's Culture
   The cultural character of a site can be maintained and celebrated in large part through the practice of heritage tourism and preservation of cultural artifacts. They contribute to a feeling of continuity by linking the current generation to the generations who came before them.
   Education and a Consciousness of the Facts:
   Visitors get a better understanding of the past and a greater appreciation for culture as a result of participating in heritage tourism. Tourists have the opportunity to get a more nuanced awareness of the world's myriad cultures when they visit historical sites, museums, and participate in local customs.
   Advantages to the Economy:
   There are enormous financial advantages to be gained from heritage tourism. Admission fees, guided tours, and the sale of locally made wares all contribute to the organization's financial success. at addition to this, it generates job possibilities at cultural institutions and enterprises that are connected to the cultural sector.
   Development that is Sustainable:
   The protection of cultural traditions and the promotion of tourism that values heritage are essential to sustainable development. They bring in tourists who place a high value on genuine and significant experiences, which in turn leads to the protection of cultural treasures and the promotion of tourism policies and procedures that are responsible.
2. **Obstacles to Overcome and Opportunities to Seize**
   The Degradation of Culture:
   Erosion of culture takes place whenever traditional ways of life and beliefs are put in jeopardy by industrialization and globalization. Through the promotion and protection of cultural assets, heritage tourism presents a potential opportunity to fight against this deterioration.
   Inadequate space:
   Overcrowding is a common problem at popular heritage sites, which can ultimately lead to erosion and destruction. It is necessary to have management techniques in place in order to protect both the sites and the experience of the visitors.
   Appropriation de la culture:
   When travelers participate in activities that distort or exploit the culture of their destination, this behavior can be considered cultural appropriation. In order to

avoid having to deal with this problem, education and awareness are absolutely necessary.

Striking a Balance Between Conservation and Development:
It might be difficult to strike a balance between the need to preserve cultural traditions and the need for economic growth brought by tourism. In order to guarantee that both goals will be accomplished, sustainable procedures have to be put into place.

3. **Methodologies for the Protection of Cultural Assets and the Promotion of Heritage Tourism**

In the Interest of Education and Interpretation:
Education and explanation ought to be a part of all aspects of cultural preservation and historic tourism. It is sometimes easier to explain the historical and cultural significance of a location and its traditions through the employment of interpretive programs, museums, and guided tours.

Participation in Community Activities:
It is crucial for local communities to be involved in tourism related to heritage. The upkeep of cultural practices and historical sites frequently falls on the shoulders of members of the community. Their engaged engagement contributes toward making the conservation of heritage a more likely possibility.

Practices That Are Sustainable:
It is essential to implement sustainable tourism practices in order to safeguard cultural assets and the environments in which they are located. Some examples of these measures are crowd management, waste minimization, and responsible visitor conduct.

Consideration for Other Cultures:
It is essential for travelers as well as those who work in the tourism industry to be culturally sensitive. They ought to respect the local customs, traditions, and sacred locations in order to cultivate an environment that values and respects cultural diversity.

4. **Measurement of Success and Continuity of Activity**

The Happiness of Our Guests:
The level of satisfaction experienced by tourists is an essential indicator of the success of heritage tourism. The provision of enriching experiences as well as instructional value is essential to the accomplishment of cultural preservation goals.

Influence on the Environment:
It is essential to keep an eye on how heritage tourism affects the surrounding ecosystem. The natural environment around cultural places ought to be preserved in order for preservation efforts to be successful.

Advantages to the Economy:

It is crucial for establishing the viability of historical tourism to conduct an analysis of the economic benefits it provides, such as the creation of jobs, the generating of cash, and the support it provides for local companies.

Celebrating the richness of a location's history and customs while simultaneously supporting sustainable development requires the preservation of cultural artifacts and the growth of heritage tourism. They teach visitors about the past, produce economic advantages, and encourage ethical tourism practices, as well as save cultural heritage for future generations and ensure that it is passed down to them. There are a number of challenges that need to be addressed, including cultural erosion, overcrowding, cultural appropriation, and striking a balance between preservation and development. Destinations are able to assure the continuous celebration and protection of their cultural heritage through the use of heritage tourism if they embrace strategies that place an emphasis on education and interpretation, community involvement, environmentally sustainable practices, and cultural sensitivity.

5.4 Managing Overtourism

Overtourism is a developing global phenomenon that arises when a location suffers an unsustainable inflow of tourists, resulting to negative social, cultural, economic, and environmental repercussions. This occurs when a place receives an influx of tourists that exceeds its capacity to accommodate those tourists. This topic has risen to the forefront as a result of increased accessibility to travel and the struggle that destinations face in coping with the effects of high visitor volumes. We examine the relevance of overtourism, its underlying causes, the impacts it brings, as well as ways for regulating overtourism to ensure sustainable travel in this all-encompassing book.

1. **The Importance of Over Tourism in the First Place**
   Influence on the Economy:
   The economy of a destination can suffer greatly if there is too much tourism. Although it has the potential to bring in a significant amount of money through tourism, it also has the potential to cause income gaps and an overreliance on a single business, which leaves the location economically vulnerable.
   Protecting Our Cultural Heritage:
   The arrival of a large number of visitors poses a potential risk to the cultural integrity of a site. At cultural and historical landmarks, an excessive number of visitors can result in property damage and the loss of long-held customs.
   Influence on the Environment:
   An excessive amount of tourism is one of the factors that contribute to environmental degradation, which includes pollution, the destruction of habitat, and an excessive use of resources. These characteristics can be detrimental to the ecosystems in the area, which in turn can impair the viability of tourism.
   The Standard of Living:
   Overcrowding, growing costs of living, and the loss of community spaces are

common factors that contribute to a decline in the quality of life for residents of areas that are overrun with tourists. This may result in increased social tensions and a weakened sense of belonging in the community.

2. **The Foundational Factors Behind Excessive Tourism**

   Travel by Air for a Low Price:
   People find it much simpler and more economical to go to faraway places as a result of the widespread availability of affordable air travel, which contributes to congestion.

   The Internet and Its Related Mediums:
   Travel has become more popular as a result of the proliferation of digital platforms and social media, which has led to an increase in the number of people traveling to scenic locations throughout the world.

   Tourism Aboard Cruise Ships
   The tourism industry associated with cruise ships can bring in enormous numbers of visitors to a region, which can overwhelm the area's infrastructure.

   Insufficient Government Oversight:
   The negative effects of over tourism are made worse when there is little control and oversight, which can allow tourism to expand unchecked and further exacerbate the problem.

3. **The Effects of Excessive Tourism**

   The Degradation of Culture:
   An increase in the number of tourists visiting an area can have a negative effect on its culture by prompting local customs to be adapted or changed to satisfy the needs of visitors.

   Deterioration of the Environment:
   Overtourism has a number of negative effects on the surrounding ecosystem, including the destruction of habitats, excessive use of resources, and pollution.

   Disparities in the Economy:
   There is a possibility that tourism would cause income disparities, in which some industries will gain more than others, ultimately leading to social and economic inequality.

   Infrastructure That Is Under Stress:
   Infrastructure in the area frequently becomes stressed, which can lead to problems such as traffic congestion, overcrowding in public spaces, and excessive usage of available utilities.

4. **Methods for Controlling Excessive Tourist Visitation**

   Methods of Environmentally Responsible Tourism:
   Responsible waste management, energy-efficient transportation, and water conservation are examples of sustainable tourist practices that can be implemented to help prevent negative impacts on the surrounding environment.

   Administration of Visitors:

Implement techniques for managing visitors, such as capping the number of people who can enter a place each day, charging admission, and setting up reservation systems at popular destinations.

Participation in Community Activities:
Ensure that local communities are involved in the decision-making process and that they receive benefits as a result of tourism.

Zoning and Regulatory Measures:
Establishing laws and zoning requirements is an effective means of controlling the expansion of tourist lodgings and avoiding unchecked development.

5. **Measurement of Success and Viability in the Long Term**

The Happiness of Our Guests:
Determine whether or not over tourism management techniques are successful by gauging the level of satisfaction expressed by visitors. Visitors who had a positive experience are more inclined to return to the location and to suggest it to others.

Advantages to the Economy:
After measures have been taken to manage overtourism, it is vital to conduct an analysis of the economic benefits that tourism provides. This involves the development of new jobs, the generating of new money, and support for existing neighborhood companies.

Influence on the Environment:
Maintain a close watch on the ecological footprint left by tourism management practices in order to guarantee the conservation of the natural setting. The issue of overtourism is a complicated one that poses a threat to the long-term viability and original character of many sites. Nevertheless, it is possible to effectively manage it through the implementation of responsible tourism practices, visitor management, community involvement, and regulation. The strategies that are used to manage overtourism need to be adapted to each destination's particular set of problems and advantages. By doing so, we can assure the preservation of cultural history, the conservation of the environment, and the overall well-being of both the locals and the tourists who visit here. It is possible to find a solution to the issue of overtourism; but, this will take thoughtful planning, active participation, and a commitment to travel that is both sustainable and responsible.

Chapter 6

Hospitality and Accommodation

The travel and tourism sector is incomplete without the presence of hospitality and lodging as essential components. It is essential to the travel experience to provide guests with a place to stay that is not just pleasant but also accommodating and fun to be in during their trip. In this all-encompassing book, we investigate the realm of hospitality and accommodation, diving into its significance, the development of the industry, important factors that contribute to visitor happiness, sustainable practices in lodging, and upcoming trends in the field.

1. **The Importance of Providing Hospitality and Accommodating Guests**
   The Heart and Soul of the Travel Experience:
   The provision of hospitable service and comfortable lodging is essential to the success of any trip. The standard of these services has a significant bearing on both the overarching travel experience and the desire to return to a particular location.
   Influence on the Economy:
   The hospitality business is a vital force that propels the economy of the entire world. As a result of its ability to foster the growth of local enterprises, bring in additional tax money, and provide employment opportunities, this industry is an essential component of the economy.
   The Exchange of Cultures:
   The provision of hospitality and lodging is of critical importance in the process of cultural exchange. The staff at the lodging establishments provide opportunities for guests to engage in conversation with locals, provide exposure to regional customs and cuisine, and educate visitors about the culture of the area.
   Security and ease of living:
   It is extremely important for tourists that the accommodations they choose provide both safety and comfort. The enjoyment of travel and one's sense of

calm are both improved by the presence of a location that is both safe and comfortable.

2. **The development of the tourism, hospitality, and lodging industries**
   Throughout the course of history:
   The practice of offering travelers a place to rest their heads and hospitality extends back to the earliest known civilizations. Throughout the course of history, inns, guesthouses, and taverns have been extremely important institutions for promoting both economic and cultural interaction.

   The process of modernizing and standardizing:
   The hospitality and hotel sector became more standardized and professionalized in the 19th century as a direct result of the emergence of mass tourism that occurred around the same time period as the industrial revolution. Hotels and other types of accommodation companies started offering standardized services and amenities to their guests.

   Innovation and technological advancement:
   The business world has been completely disrupted by developments in technology, most notably the proliferation of mobile apps and the internet. Travelers now find it much simpler to conduct research, book accommodations, and customize their trips thanks to the proliferation of online booking platforms, review websites, and smartphone check-in services.

   The Economy Based on Sharing:
   The traditional hospitality industry has been shaken up by the sharing economy, which is best demonstrated by websites like as Airbnb and HomeAway. These websites make it possible for individuals to rent out their houses and other properties for shorter periods of time.

3. **Crucial Components in the Production of Extraordinary Visitor Experiences**
   Assistance to Customers:
   An unforgettable experience for guests is built on a strong foundation of exceptional customer service. The experience of a guest is improved when the staff people they interact with are attentive, pleasant, and knowledgable.

   Keeping things clean and maintaining them:
   It is non-negotiable for there to be clean and well-maintained accommodations. The contentment and comfort of the guest can be ensured by maintaining a room that is clean and attractive.

   Personalized expression:
   It is possible to greatly boost customer happiness and loyalty by customizing the guest experience through the provision of bespoke facilities, services, and recommendations.

   Experiences in Dining and the Culinary Arts:
   The meals that guests consume are an essential component of their overall

experience.

Opportunities for life-changing gastronomic adventures can be found in a wide range of dining establishments, from upscale restaurants to laid-back cafes.

4. **Environmental Responsibility of Lodging**

    Practices That Are Sustainable:

    It is critical for the hospitality business to practice sustainability in order to lessen its impact on the environment. Contributing factors to sustainability include the use of lighting that is more efficient with energy usage, the conservation of water, the reduction of trash, and responsible sourcing of products.

    Programs for Professional Accreditation:

    Hotels and other types of lodgings can demonstrate their dedication to environmentally responsible operations by participating in certification programs such as LEED (Leadership in Energy and Environmental Design) and Green Key.

    Eco-friendly Architecture:

    Eco-friendly elements, such as energy-efficient construction, solar panels, and water recycling systems, are rapidly being incorporated, more and more, into the design of accommodation buildings.

    Participation in the Community:

    Sustainability and strong community relationships can be fostered by engagement with local communities, which can be accomplished by providing support to local artists and companies and contributing to community development.

5. **Predictions for the Hospitality and Accommodations Industry in the Near Future**

    The Integration of Technology:

    The incorporation of various forms of technology will be a prevalent movement in the future. There will be an increase in the prevalence of smart rooms that have voice-activated controls, smartphone check-in, and digital concierge services.

    The state of one's health and well-being:

    The visitor experience will be significantly enhanced by the inclusion of a variety of wellness amenities and services, including as fitness centers, spa facilities, healthy dining alternatives, and mindfulness programming.

    Longevity and kindness to the environment:

    In the future, sustainability will continue to be a top goal, and many lodging establishments will work toward achieving carbon neutrality, decreased waste, and responsible sourcing.

    Hyper-personalization, also known as:

    The future of the hospitality industry will include hyper-personalization, which will occur when data-driven insights enable accommodations to anticipate visitor preferences and create experiences that are suited to the individual.

6. **Assessing Success and the Level of Satisfaction of Guests**

Commentary from Guests:
It is possible to gain useful insights into the visitor experience and areas for improvement by soliciting feedback from guests, collecting that data, and then doing an analysis of that feedback.

Calculating Occupancy Rates:
The occupancy rates and revenue generated per available room, abbreviated as RevPAR, are critical performance measures for hotels and other types of accommodation establishments, demonstrating how successful they are financially.

The Satisfaction of Employees:
The contentment of a company's employees is frequently associated with that of its customers. It is more likely that employees who are happy and involved in their work will give outstanding customer service.

Hospitality and accommodation are essential components of the travel experience, playing a significant role in the formation of tourists' memories and impressions of the places they visit. The landscape has undergone significant change as a result of the expansion of the sector, which has been accompanied by advances in technology, the rise of the sharing economy, and an increasing emphasis on sustainability. The ability to provide excellent experiences for guests depends on a number of elements, including customer service, cleanliness, customisation, and the kind of food options available.

Many hotels and motels are beginning to recognize the importance of incorporating environmentally conscious policies and procedures into their operations. Continued innovation, such as the incorporation of technology, wellness and well-being initiatives, sustainability efforts, and hyper-personalization, are all expected to characterize the hospitality and accommodation business in the years to come.

In spite of the fact that the hospitality industry is always undergoing change, the fundamental tenets of the hospitality trade, which include guaranteeing the guests' comfort, safety, and overall pleasure, will continue to be at the center of providing excellent guest experiences, which in turn will encourage beneficial cultural interchange and economic expansion.

6.1 Types of Accommodation

The lodging that one chooses is one of the most important aspects of their trip because it has such a huge impact on the level of comfort, convenience, and overall enjoyment they have. The changing requirements and tastes of travelers are reflected in the wide variety of lodging options that are accessible in different parts of the world. The purpose of this in-depth guide is to examine a wide variety of lodging options, ranging from standard hotels to unusual and out-of-the-way places to stay, with the goal of casting light on the significance of these accommodations, the characteristics they offer, and the unique experiences they provide to tourists.

1. **The Importance of Making Arrangements for Accommodations**
   Affordability and practicality:

Accommodation provides passengers with a comfortable and secure location to rest, which in turn improves the overall quality of the trip experience for the tourist.

Travelers are able to maintain their well-being, recharge their batteries, and stay organized when they stay in accommodations that are comfortable.

Experiences Unique to the Area:

The type of lodging that one choose can have a considerable impact on the overall quality of the trip. Travelers can gain a deeper understanding of the culture, lifestyle, and architecture of a place by staying in a variety of various types of accommodations throughout their trip.

Different preferences and spending capacities:

The hospitality sector is able to accommodate customers with a diverse range of financial constraints and personal tastes. It is possible for vacationers to locate hotels that are appropriate for both their budgetary constraints and their unique preferences, making it possible for everybody to find suitable lodging.

Unforgettable Adventures:

Some lodgings provide their guests with one-of-a-kind and unforgettable experiences, enabling them to make memories that will last a lifetime. Some examples of these are stays in treehouses, underwater hotels, or old castles.

2. **Types of Accommodations That Have Been Around for Years**

    The Hotels:

    Hotels are one of the most typical kinds of places to stay, and there is a wide range of prices and levels of comfort available. They provide a selection of amenities including as restaurants, fitness centers, concierge services, and room service for their guests.

    Hotels: Motels :

    Motels are often located along highways and are well-known for the convenience of their location as well as their reasonable rates. They are suitable for people going on road trips or traveling who are looking for basic facilities.

    Hotels and Resorts:

    The purpose of resorts is to provide both a relaxing atmosphere and exciting activities. They frequently offer a variety of dining options, swimming pools, spas, and other forms of entertainment, so providing guests with a comprehensive vacation experience.

    B&B stands for "bed and breakfast"

    The innkeepers at bed and breakfasts typically serve breakfast and provide guests with information on the surrounding area. They are especially common in places of interest that are rich in history and character.

    The Hostel:

    Hostels are great places to stay for budget-conscious solitary travelers as well as those who want to be in an environment with other people. They frequently include rooms in a dormitory layout as well as common areas.

Rentals for vacations:

The term "vacation rentals" refers to a wide variety of lodging options, including apartments and houses, as well as cabins and villas. These are great options for smaller or bigger parties, especially families.

3. **Accommodations That Are Unlikely to Be Found Elsewhere**

   Cabins in the trees

   Treehouses provide visitors a one-of-a-kind and immersive experience in nature by putting them in the middle of the forest canopy during their stay. These are ideal for people who love the outdoors and are always looking for new experiences.

   Hotels Submerged in Water:

   The stunning sights of marine life and underwater sceneries may be seen from the rooms of underwater hotels, which are located below the surface of the water. They offer an experience that is in every way immersive.

   The Castle Remains:

   Travelers who choose to spend their nights in a castle are afforded the opportunity to relive the splendor of bygone eras. The majority of castles have been renovated into five-star hotels in recent years.

   Hotels Made of Ice and Snow:

   The experience of staying in an ice hotel, which is built entirely from snow and ice, is once in a lifetime for most people. They offer comfortable sleeping bags, as well as one-of-a-kind ice sculptures and ice bars.

   The term "glamping" refers to "glamorous camping"

   The term "glamping" refers to an activity that mixes traditional camping with the amenities and luxuries of a hotel stay. Safari tents, yurts, and Airstream trailers are among of the options for overnight accommodations.

   Towers of Light:

   A stay in a lighthouse provides guests with breathtaking vistas of the coastline as well as a novel historical perspective. In many cases, lighthouses offer a setting that is both secluded and intimate.

4. **Specific Categories of Lodging Facilities**

   The Capsule Hotel Concept:

   Capsule hotels are all the rage in Japan and offer compact sleeping pods together with the standard hotel conveniences. They are a good option for lone travelers looking for a handy and reasonably priced somewhere to stay.

   Cathedrals, Abbeys, and Convents:

   There are many monasteries and convents across the world that welcome visitors and provide an environment that is conducive to quiet reflection and contemplation. Prayers and other daily rites are frequently performed with guest participation.

Houses on Wheels:
Tiny houses are characterized by their small size and minimalist design, and they offer residents an alternative way of life that is also environmentally friendly. They are appealing to people who are looking for a simpler way of life.

Hotels that float on water and houseboats:
Floating hotels and houseboats offer a one-of-a-kind experience on the water and are frequently situated in picturesque settings. Guests are welcome to unwind on the deck while taking in the picturesque vistas of the lake.

Hotels in Airstream Trailers:
Airstream hotels are distinguished by their vintage-looking trailers, which provide guests with a one-of-a-kind and nostalgic vacation experience. They frequently offer contemporary conveniences while retaining a classic appearance.

5. **Accommodations with a Particular Theme**

    Hotels with a Focus on Space:
    Guests of space-themed hotels can get a taste of outer space thanks to the hotel's galactic decor and activities that are inspired by astronauts.

    Themed Accommodations Based on Harry Potter:
    Fans of the series are able to fully submerge themselves in the world of the wizards when they stay at hotels with Harry Potter-themed decor and activities.

    Houses Fit for Hobbits:
    Hobbit dwellings, which were inspired by the works of J.R.R. Tolkien, give a stay that is whimsical and warm, similar to that of the Shire.

    Lodges for Safari:
    Travelers have the ability to remain in the middle of animal reserves by booking a stay at a safari lodge, which creates a more immersive safari experience.

    Treetop Accommodations:
    It is common for treetop hotels to provide opulent treehouse accommodations, which give guests the opportunity to sleep among the branches while also enjoying a variety of high-end amenities.

6. **Obstacles and Things to Consider When Arranging Unusual Accommodations**

    Location as well as ease of access:
    It's possible that some one-of-a-kind lodging options are located in inconvenient or unusual areas, which may make them difficult to reach or transport guests to.

    Cost and Discretionary Availability:
    Because unique lodgings typically come at a higher price and may have a smaller capacity, it is critical to reserve in advance if possible.

    Long-term viability:
    It is essential to take into account issues relating to the long-term viability of one-of-a-kind accommodations, in particular in ecologically sensitive regions.

    Security and ease of living:

It is the responsibility of the traveler to verify that the one-of-a-kind lodging meets all safety and comfort requirements.

7. **Predicted Developments in the Hospitality Industry**

Eco-Friendly Lodging:
As more people look for ways to reduce their environmental impact, the demand for eco-friendly lodging will only continue to rise.

Hotels With a Focus on Wellness:
Accommodations with a focus on wellness will provide activities and facilities oriented on health, relaxation, and mindfulness for its guests.

The Digitization of Everything:
With smart rooms and contactless services, the incorporation of technology will play a vital part in the enhancement of the overall experience for the hotel's guests.

Hyper-personalization, also known as:
In the future, more and more lodging establishments will make use of data-driven insights to personalize their guests' experiences by providing individualized facilities and services.

Accommodation is an essential component of a trip, and travelers have a broad variety of options to choose from in order to choose lodging that is suitable for their needs, tastes, and financial constraints. Traditional forms of lodging, such as hotels, motels, resorts, and holiday rentals, offer dependable and comfortable places to spend the night. Travelers have the ability to make unique memories by staying in accommodations that are unusual and out of the ordinary. Some examples of these kinds of accommodations include treehouses, underwater hotels, and castles.

Accommodations that cater to certain hobbies are known as niche accommodations, whereas themed accommodations give experiences that are immersive and whimsical. When selecting a one-of-a-kind place to stay, tourists should take into account factors such as location, accessibility, affordability, sustainability, safety, and comfort. The hospitality sector is continuously undergoing change, and as a result, the future of lodging will be shaped by eco-friendly accommodations, wellness-focused hotels, digital transformation, and hyper-personalization. No matter what you decide, the lodging you select is one of the most important factors in determining how memorable and satisfying a trip will be.

6.2 Quality Standards and Regulations

Maintaining high-quality standards and complying to laws are crucial in the dynamic and competitive hospitality sector. These practices are necessary for providing excellent experiences for guests, establishing trust, and encouraging sustainable growth. In order to provide visitors with stays that are secure, comfortable, and satisfactory, businesses are obligated to adhere to a wide variety of rules, certifications, and regulatory criteria that fall under the umbrella of quality standards and regulations. In this extensive guide, we look into the relevance of quality standards and regulations, the essential components that they cover, the impact that they have on the sector, as well as the problems and opportunities that they bring for hospitality firms.

1. **The Importance of Having Regulations and Standards in Place for Quality**
   The Happiness of Our Guests:
   The establishment of quality standards and rules is an essential component in preserving and boosting the happiness of guests. They make certain that visitors receive the services, conveniences, and experiences that they have come to anticipate and demand.
   Peace of Mind and Protection:
   The observance of legislation relating to safety and security is of the utmost importance for ensuring the protection of employees and guests. The standards for this domain include things like building codes, fire safety, and emergency protocols.
   Credibility and reliability:
   A company's reputation can be improved by adhering to quality standards and regulations, which also helps to develop trust and credibility among customers, business partners, and other stakeholders.
   Advantage in the Market Place:
   Establishments that regularly meet or surpass quality requirements enjoy a competitive advantage in the market. As a result, these establishments are able to attract a greater number of guests and achieve higher occupancy rates.

2. **Essential Components of the Requirements and Standards for Quality**
   Sanitation and Personal Hygiene:
   Guest accommodations, dining establishments, and public areas must adhere to certain hygiene and sanitation standards in order to be considered clean and safe for patron use.
   Services to Guests:
   The provision of fast and responsive customer service, efficient check-in and check-out procedures, and individualized guest experiences are examples of the kind of characteristics that are included in quality standards for guest services.
   Precautions Taken for the Protection of Others:
   The protocols for fire safety, emergency exits, security staff, and surveillance systems are all examples of aspects that are covered by regulations pertaining to safety and security.
   Ability to be reached:
   The provision of accessible rooms, facilities, and services are the primary focuses of the regulations that must be adhered to in order to meet quality standards. This is because accessibility for guests who have disabilities is an essential component of quality standards.

3. **The Effects That Quality Regulations and Standards Have On The Industry**
   Enhanced Experiences for Our Guests:
   Positive experiences for guests are facilitated by high-quality standards and regulations, which in turn lead to greater levels of guest satisfaction and subsequent repeat business.
   Effectiveness in Business Operations:
   When regulations are followed, the operations of a company typically become more streamlined, resulting in increased efficiency and superior resource management.
   Enhancement to One's Reputation:
   Establishments that are able to achieve or surpass quality requirements and regulations build a strong reputation for excellence, which in turn attracts more guests and commercial prospects.
   Protection from Legal Obligations:
   In the event that firms fail to comply with regulations, they put themselves at risk of facing potential liability difficulties, legal challenges, and possibly financial fines and penalties.

4. **Obstacles to Overcome and Opportunities to Seize When Implementing Quality Regulations and Standards**
   The price of conformity:
   Compliance with quality standards and laws frequently includes significant costs, such as training, infrastructure upgrades, and annual maintenance. These expenses can provide a financial burden for firms, particularly more compact organizations.
   Changing Characteristics of the Regulatory Climate:
   The regulatory environment is always shifting, and as a result, fresh standards and prerequisites are being published on a regular basis. It might be difficult to stay on top of these developments and to ensure that compliance is maintained continuously.
   Education and On-the-Job-Training:
   Ongoing education and professional development programs are required in order to guarantee that employees have received adequate training and are knowledgeable regarding quality standards and laws.
   Differentiation in the Market:
   Businesses have the potential to differentiate themselves in the market by adhering to high-quality standards and regulations, which will attract customers who are looking for exceptional service and experiences.

5. **Regulations and Quality Standards that are Generally Accepted in the Hospitality Industry**
   Regulations Regarding Health and Safety:
   These standards address food safety, sanitation, fire safety, and emergency

readiness in order to safeguard the health and safety of both customers and workers.

The Standards for Accessibility:
The provision of equal access for people with disabilities is the primary objective of accessibility standards. This includes making accessible facilities, accommodations, and services available.

Certifications Relating to Quality Management:
Certifications in quality management, such as ISO 9001, reflect an organization's dedication to developing and sustaining efficient quality management systems.

Environmental Standards for Long-Term Sustainability:
Environmental sustainability standards encourage environmentally responsible behaviors like as energy efficiency, waste minimization, and responsible sourcing in order to lessen the negative impact that the industry has on the surrounding environment.

6. **Strategies for the Implementation of Procedures to Ensure Compliance**

   Audits and Inspections Conducted on a Routine Basis
   Audits and inspections should be carried out on a regular basis to help pinpoint areas that could use some work and to verify continued conformity with quality standards and legislation.

   Staff Instruction and Continuing Education:
   The ability of personnel to maintain a current knowledge of industry best practices and regulatory standards is made possible by investments in staff training and development programs.

   The Integration of Technology:
   Streamlining processes and ensuring that quality standards are fulfilled on a continuous basis can both be accomplished with the help of technology in the form of management software and automation technologies.

   Working in Partnership with Various Industry Associations:
   Working together with trade groups and taking part in industry activities and projects can provide beneficial insights into current best practices as well as new trends in quality standards and legislation.

7. **Projected Developments and Changes in Quality Regulations and Standards**

   Monitoring of Compliance with Digital Standards:
   It is anticipated that there will be an increase in the number of instances when monitoring and guaranteeing compliance with quality standards is carried out making use of digital tools and data analytics.

   Regulations for Improved Environmental Impact:

It is anticipated that there will be a rise in the number of sustainability laws imposed on the hospitality industry in order to address environmental issues and promote responsible practices.

The Importance of Being Accessible:

In order to accommodate a wide variety of visitor requirements and to deliver inclusive

experiences, there will be a sustained emphasis placed on the improvement of accessibility standards.

Standardization on a Global Scale:

The global hospitality business is in need of greater consistency and transparency, which can be addressed by efforts directed at the global standardization of quality measurements and laws.

In the hospitality industry, quality standards and regulations play an essential role in assuring the satisfaction of customers, the protection of employees, and the reputation of enterprises. They include a variety of factors that lead to remarkable experiences for guests, such as cleanliness, excellent customer service, a secure environment, and easy accessibility. Although implementing and sustaining these standards presents a number of problems, doing so also presents potential for increasing operational efficiency, differentiating oneself in the market, and enhancing one's reputation.

To remain compliant in a regulatory environment that is in a state of perpetual change, businesses are required to make investments in the training of their employees, regular audits, the integration of technology, and coordination with industry groups. Because the monitoring of digital compliance, sustainability, accessibility, and worldwide standardization will become increasingly important in the future, the hotel industry will need to adapt in order to keep up with the ever-changing requirements imposed by regulatory agencies and guests. In the end, a commitment to quality standards and regulations helps to cultivate an atmosphere in which visitors can trust the establishments they are staying at and have a positive experience throughout their stays. This helps to ensure the long-term success and survival of enterprises in the hospitality industry.

6.3 Accommodation Business Models

Because of shifting consumer preferences, advances in technology, and increased globalization, the hotel business has gone through substantial upheaval over the course of the past several decades. Business models for providing lodging have developed over time to cater to the numerous requirements and preferences of tourists, which has resulted in a wide variety of creative solutions. In this in-depth guide, we investigate a variety of business models for providing lodging, ranging from the time-honored hotel to the innovative platform, and we assess the significance of these models, as well as their essential characteristics, advantages, and disadvantages.

1. **The Importance of the Different Types of Accommodation Businesses**
   Different Travelers Have Different Preferences:
   Travel is now within reach of a wider demographic thanks to the proliferation of accommodation business models that cater to a diverse range of traveler preferences and financial constraints.
   Influence on the Economy:
   The hospitality sector is essential to the development of local as well as international economies, as it is the primary source of new business possibilities, revenue, and employment.
   Both new ideas and intense competition:
   In the hospitality sector, innovation, competition, and improved experiences for customers are all fostered by the constant transformation of room types and layouts.
   Increases in Tourism Around the World:
   Accommodation business models contribute to the development of global tourism by facilitating connection across cultural boundaries and the dissemination of knowledge. The number of people traveling internationally is expected to continue rising.

2. **Conventional Modes of Operation for Accommodation Businesses**
   The Hotels:
   Hotels are a time-tested and widely used model for operating a business that provides lodging. Hotels can range from five-star establishments to more affordable options. They provide a variety of amenities and services, including as dining options, room service, and assistance from a concierge, among other things.
   Hotels: Motels :
   Motels are well-known for the affordability as well as the convenient roadside locations that they offer. They offer the essential conveniences required for short stays and focus mostly on serving travelers who are on the go.
   Hotels and Resorts:
   The purpose of resorts is to provide guests with a holistic holiday experience by providing a variety of amenities, including swimming pools, spas, restaurants, and other recreational opportunities.
   B&B stands for "bed and breakfast"
   Staying in a bed and breakfast, often known as a B&B, typically results in a comfortable and customized experience. Guests may look forward to host-prepared breakfasts and engaging conversation about the surrounding area.
   The Hostel:
   Hostels are places to stay that are easy on the wallet and promote mingling and conversation among their patrons. It is common for younger people to stay in these accommodations because of the dormitory-style rooms and shared amenities.

3. **Creative Alternatives to Traditional Hotel Business Models**
   Rentals for vacations:
   Property owners are able to rent out their homes, apartments, and other holiday properties to travelers by using vacation rentals, which are made available through online platforms such as Airbnb and Vrbo.
   Small, specialized hotels:
   The accommodations at boutique hotels are typically one-of-a-kind, focusing on a particular theme or style, and offer a tailored experience that is geared toward individual preferences.
   Models That Are Hybrid:
   A hybrid model is one that combines elements of conventional hotels with those of short-term rentals, such as apartment-style lodgings with services and amenities similar to those found in hotels.
   Apartments with Room Service:
   The feeling of being at home made possible by serviced apartments makes them an excellent choice for extended stays. They frequently cater to business travelers and provide culinary facilities for their convenience.
   The term "glamping" refers to "glamorous camping"
   Glamping is an outdoor activity that mixes camping with luxury. Tents, yurts, or cabins with exquisite amenities are offered to guests who are looking for an adventurous vacation.

4. **Innovative Alternatives to Traditional Accommodation Business Models**
   Platforms for the Shared Economy:
   Platforms such as Airbnb, HomeAway, and Booking.com give hosts the ability to sell their properties, and they give passengers the ability to book short-term stays in a variety of accommodations. These platforms are upsetting the traditional landscape of the hospitality industry.
   Places to Sleep Without a Host:
   Self-check-in, personalized stays, and hotel-like facilities are available at hostless lodgings such as Sonder and Lyric. These kinds of accommodations do not have hosts living on the premises.
   Hotels in "Pods":
   Pod hotels provide small, modular sleeping areas that are designed to appeal to tourists on a tight budget who place a high value on comfort and solitude.
   Shared Living Quarters:
   Companies that specialize in shared housing arrangements, such as WeLive and Common, provide their tenants with a variety of amenities and services, which helps to cultivate a sense of community among the tenants.
   Stays that are Only Temporary and Pop-Up:
   Stays in temporary accommodations, such as pop-up hotels and mobile lodging

solutions, give guests with an experience that is both distinctive and versatile in unusual settings.
5. **Advantages and Difficulties Associated with Different Accommodation Business Models**

Gains to Obtain:

1. A Wide Variety of Options Travelers have the ability to select a lodging option that is suitable for both their preferences and their financial constraints.
2. **individualized experiences:** Many of the models offer individualized experiences, which increase the level of happiness experienced by guests.
3. **Competitive Pricing:** The variety of available lodgings helps keep prices in a competitive range, which is to the benefit of vacationers.
4. **Contribution to the Growth of the Economy:** The Accommodation Industry helps to sustain and create jobs in the Community.

The Obstacles:

1. **Regulation and Compliance:** Disruptive business strategies might run into regulatory hurdles and compliance problems in certain parts of the world.
2. **Quality Control:** Keeping a product's quality consistent over time can be difficult, especially when it comes to peer-to-peer networks.
3. **Competition:** The widening availability of different types of lodging ratchets up the level of business rivalry.
4. The impact on the economy may cause some existing business models to struggle financially as a result of increased competition from disruptors.

VI. Emerging Patterns in the Business Models for Accommodations
Accommodations that are Kind to the Environment:
This sector will have a higher emphasis on sustainability, which will result in an increase in the number of lodgings and practices that are environmentally friendly.

The Digitization of Everything:
The utilization of digital tools, artificial intelligence, and data analytics will continue to result in improved experiences for customers and more efficiency in business processes.

Providers of Specialty Lodging:
The popularity of lodging concepts that cater to certain interests, such as wellness getaways, is expected to increase.

The Development of Historically Used Models:

In order to maintain their position in the market, traditional business models will continue to develop and change, adopting new ideas and technologies.

Business models for lodging play an important part in the development of the hospitality industry. These models give tourists a variety of options to choose from in order to satisfy their individual requirements and inclinations. Traditional models such as hotels and resorts coexist with innovative and disruptive models such as vacation rentals and hostless lodgings, allowing tourists a broad variety of options to choose from in terms of where they will stay.

These models offer benefits in the forms of variety, personalization, competitive pricing, and expansion of the economy. On the other hand, they also face obstacles connected to issues of regulation, quality control, competitiveness, and the influence of their activities on the economy. Future trends will be driven by sustainability, digital transformation, niche accommodations, and the adaptation of traditional models. This will ensure that accommodation business models continue to be responsive to the ever-changing needs of travelers and continue to foster unforgettable travel experiences.

6.4 The Airbnb Effect

The Airbnb effect, which is a word that was made up to characterize the enormous influence that Airbnb has had on the travel and hospitality sector, has transformed the way that people look for and experience different types of lodging. This cutting-edge platform has been there since 2008, and ever since then, it has been shaking up the conventional hotel business model and giving rise to a phenomena known as the sharing economy.

In this section, we will go deeper into the core of the Airbnb effect, highlighting its impact on passengers, hosts, the industry as a whole, and the ever-changing regulatory landscape.

Travelers Gaining the Upper Hand:

The Airbnb effect has had several significant repercussions, one of the most important of which is the empowerment that it has bestowed upon travelers. Airbnb has revolutionized the way that people think about and plan their vacations by providing a large and varied selection of unique lodging options. These lodging options range from inexpensive shared rooms to amazing, one-of-a-kind properties such as treehouses and castles. Travelers now have the opportunity to explore a world of non-traditional lodging options, freeing them from the constraints of traditional hotel chains.

The local experience:

Airbnb is also responsible for ushering in a shift in travel philosophy, one that places a greater emphasis on local immersion. When guests book accommodations through Airbnb, they frequently get the opportunity to experience a destination from the point of view of a local resident. The platform invites travelers to go beyond the conventional tourist areas and explore the heart and spirit of a city or region by providing them with information about these off-the-beaten-path locations.

Options That Are Friendly to the Wallet:

Airbnb's ability to provide accommodations at lower prices has been one of the company's most significant contributions. When traveling with a family or a large group of friends, many people find that renting a property through Airbnb is more cost-effective than staying in a regular hotel. When compared to booking multiple hotel rooms, renting out a complete house or apartment can frequently prove to be the most cost-effective option.

Inspiring Confidence in Hosts:

On the other hand, Airbnb has brought about significant change in the lives of hosts. Hosts have gained the capacity to create money from their real estate assets by gaining the ability to generate income from their real estate investments by opening their homes, spare rooms, or properties to travelers. They are able to strike a balance between their personal and commercial interests thanks to the flexibility that Airbnb affords them in determining when and how frequently they will welcome visitors.

Individualization in conjunction with Community:

Airbnb encourages a sense of individualization while also fostering a sense of community. Hosts have the ability to modify their listings so that they reflect their individual tastes, personalities, and the cultural backgrounds from which they come.

Through direct interaction with guests, they frequently foster a sense of camaraderie as well as cultural exchange and an atmosphere reminiscent of a home away from home. The personal touches and insights into the surrounding area that hosts provide are highly valued by a significant number of guests.

The Repercussions for the Hospitality Sector:

The hotel business has been irrevocably altered as a result of the Airbnb effect, which reaches well beyond guests and proprietors. The business model of Airbnb ushers in cutthroat competition, which compels conventional hotels and other types of accommodations to make adjustments. In order to provide guests with a higher level of happiness, hotels have had to reinvent themselves by providing unique and unforgettable experiences and embracing technological advancements.

Responses from Regulatory Agencies:

The Airbnb effect has led to regulatory hurdles and a demand for more strict control. Both of these developments are a direct result of Airbnb. In response to the expanding effect of short-term rentals, a number of towns and regions have implemented municipal regulations covering everything from occupancy limits to safety requirements. These regulations cover a variety of aspects related to vacation rentals. Some local governments have taken a hard line in response to concerns such as housing shortages and safety difficulties. As a result, they have instituted stringent fines and punishments for those who do not comply with the regulations.

There is no question that the Airbnb impact has changed the way that we think about traveling and staying in hotels. It gives passengers the ability to select from a variety of one-of-a-kind accommodations and encourages them to engage in local activities, all while providing hosts with the option to generate additional cash. Its disruptive nature has forced regulatory bodies to respond with new rules and regulations as a result of its influence, which in turn has stimulated innovation and competitiveness in the hospitality industry.

As Airbnb continues to develop, one of the company's ongoing challenges is to find a happy medium between empowering customers, providing possibilities for hosts, adjusting to changes in the business, and maintaining regulatory oversight. There is a good chance that the effects of Airbnb will continue, continuously transforming the landscape of travel and encouraging new ways to explore and experience the world.

Chapter 7

Food and Beverage Tourism

Within the larger travel and hospitality sector, a significant subset of the market known as food and beverage tourism, also referred to as culinary tourism, has recently come into its own. It is centered on the investigation and appreciation of various cuisines, culinary traditions, and dining experiences, and it provides tourists with a novel method to become fully immersed in the culture, history, and flavors of a location. In this all-encompassing book, we delve into the complex world of food and beverage tourism, investigating its roots, relevance, numerous forms, impact on local economies, and role in molding the experiences of tourists.

1. **The Beginnings and Development of Tourism Revolving Around Food and Drink**
   The Origins in History:
   Culinary exploration has always played a pivotal role in the process of locating new cultures and civilizations throughout history. Food has always been an essential component of vacationing and exploring new places.
   The Exchange of Cultures:
   The dissemination of culinary customs, ingredients, and methods of preparation from one country or region to another has played a significant role in the development of a wide variety of cuisines as well as the expansion of the food and beverage tourism industry.
   Current Shifts In:
   In recent decades, the expansion of the food and beverage tourism industry has been fueled by a number of factors, including the rise of globalization, the advent of social media, and a greater emphasis on authentic and experiential travel.
2. **The Importance of Tourism in the Food and Beverage Industry**
   Participation in a Culture:
   Food and beverage tourism provide vacationers with a one-of-a-kind opportunity

to get fully immersed in the cultures, traditions, and rituals of the places they visit through the investigation of local cuisines and dining experiences.

Influence on the Economy:

The expansion of the food and beverage tourism industry has had a considerable impact on the economies of destinations, contributing to the growth of local economies, the creation of new jobs, and the promotion of small-scale food enterprises.

Distinguishing Between Destinations:

A destination's ability to display its own gastronomic identity and attract a wide variety of travelers looking for authentic culinary experiences can be greatly enhanced by the development of its culinary offerings, which have emerged as a crucial differentiator in recent years.

3. **Varieties of Tourism Involving Food and Drink**

   Tours & Experiences Focusing on Gastronomy:

   Travelers can get first-hand experiences of local products, cooking techniques, and traditional foods by participating in culinary activities such as guided culinary tours, cooking lessons, and food tastings.

   Food-related celebrations and events:

   Festivals and events that honor local cuisines, beverages, and culinary traditions attract both locals and tourists to a destination so that they can sample the delicacies and participate in the vibrant cultural life of that location.

   Agricultural tourism:

   Travelers are able to get insights into agricultural methods, production processes, and farm-to-table experiences through the participation in agritourism activities such as seeing a farm, sampling wine and cheese, and touring vineyards.

   Food Hikes & Hiking Routes:

   Food trails and routes encourage tourists to embark on gastronomic adventures and discover the gastronomic diversity of a region by showcasing regional specialties, local food, and culinary landmarks.

4. **The Influence That Tourism Involving Food And Drink Has On The Economies Of Local Communities**

   Creating New Jobs:

   The expansion of the food and beverage tourism industry creates job openings in a variety of industries, such as restaurants, local food markets, food production, and hospitality services.

   The Development of Small Businesses:

   As a result of an increase in tourism, local food companies, such as restaurants run by families, artisanal food producers, and street food vendors, profit, which in turn helps to maintain and promote traditional methods of preparing food.

   Protecting Our Cultural Heritage:

   Consumables of every kind Tourism has a positive impact on the preservation of culinary traditions and heritage recipes, as it encourages local communities to teach their children how to cook in the traditional manner and to pass on their recipes to subsequent generations.

5. **The Impact That the Hospitality Industry Has on the Types of Experiences Travelers Have**

   Travel With an Authentic Purpose:
   Travelers now have the opportunity to engage in an immersive and multisensory investigation of a destination's cultural identity and local way of life thanks to the proliferation of culinary experiences as an essential component of experiential travel.

   Interactions Between Societies and Cultures:
   The act of eating together with locals and participating in other gastronomic experiences with them is a great way to build social relationships and cultural exchange, which in turn leads to a deeper understanding and respect of a variety of communities and traditions.

   The Formation of Memories:
   Travelers' overall impressions and recollections of a location are shaped by the restaurants they ate at and the new flavors they discovered, both of which contribute to the formation of treasured memories of the places they visited.

6. **Obstacles to Overcome and Opportunities to Seize in the Food and Beverage Tourism Industry**

   Concerns Regarding the Environment:
   Concerns about sustainability are raised in relation to overconsumption, the impact on the environment, and the depletion of resources as a result of the increased demand for local and exotic ingredients in the food and beverage tourism industry.

   Authenticity with Respect to Culture:
   Despite the growing commercialization and internationalization of the food and beverage tourism industry, it is still difficult to maintain the traditional character of regional cuisines and cooking practices.

   Infrastructure and Availability of Services:
   It is essential to improve infrastructure, transportation, and accessibility to remote culinary locations and local food enterprises if one want to improve the entire experience of food and beverage tourism.

   Developing Your Capabilities:
   It is absolutely necessary to make financial investments in culinary education, training programs, and the skill development of aspiring chefs in local communities in order to maintain and improve the quality of culinary experiences.

7. **The Most Effective Methods and Methodologies for Tourism Involving Food and Drink**

   Working Together and Forming Partnerships:

The creation of comprehensive strategies for food and beverage tourism is facilitated by the formation of collaborative networks involving local food businesses, hospitality establishments, and tourism organizations.

Initiatives for the Cultural Preservation of:

Traditional cooking methods and the heritage of the local food supply can be better protected through the implementation of cultural preservation programs such as heritage food festivals, culinary workshops, and community-led culinary tours.

Gastronomy that is Gentler on the Earth:

The long-term viability of the food and beverage tourism industry can be improved by encouraging activities that contribute to sustainable cuisine. These practices include responsible sourcing, the reduction of food waste, and the support of local farmers and producers.

The Integration of Technology:

By incorporating digital platforms, mobile applications, and online resources into tourist

campaigns for food and beverage, bookings may be made more easily, the visitor experience can be improved, and access can be provided to essential information and advice regarding food preparation.

8. **Upcoming Developments and Breakthroughs in the Food and Beverage Tourism Industry**

Experiencing the Best of Fusion Cuisine:

The convergence of many culinary traditions and the proliferation of global cuisines will provide tourists with opportunities to partake in novel and exciting gastronomic adventures.

Traveling the World Through Your Mouth:

The incorporation of technology such as virtual reality (VR) and augmented reality (AR) into the tourism industry pertaining to food and beverage would make it possible for tourists to virtually visit various culinary destinations and take part in interactive cooking experiences without leaving the convenience of their own homes.

Responsible Tourism in the Culinary Arts:

The emphasis on responsible and ethical approaches to the preparation of food and drink will continue to fuel the creation of environmentally friendly culinary tours, farm-to-table experiences, and zero-waste dining programs.

Exchanges of Culinary Traditions and Other Cultures:

Facilitating cross-cultural learning and fostering a greater appreciation of varied culinary traditions and global food cultures can be accomplished through the implementation of initiatives such as cultural immersion programs, chef collaborations, and culinary exchange programs.

Within the travel and hospitality sector, food and beverage tourism has evolved into a category that is multidimensional and dynamic, offering passengers a rich tapestry of gastronomic experiences, cultural immersion, and economic development chances for local communities.

Not only does it have the potential to produce one-of-a-kind and unforgettable travel experiences, but it also has the ability to protect culinary history and encourage environmentally responsible methods of cuisine. Both of these aspects contribute to its relevance.

The food and beverage tourism business must solve difficulties linked to sustainability, cultural authenticity, and accessibility in order to maintain its growth and innovation. Food and beverage tourism has the potential to thrive and continue to captivate tourists if certain best practices, technological advancements, and the promotion of responsible gastronomy are implemented. This will allow food and beverage tourism to continue to provide travelers with the joy of gastronomic exploration and cultural enrichment on a worldwide scale.

7.1 Culinary Tourism Trends

The subfield of culinary tourism, which is part of the larger industry of travel and hospitality, has been slowly picking up steam in recent years, alluring tourists with the allure of the possibility of great gastronomic experiences. It goes beyond the typical activities of sight-seeing and relaxing at the beach, instead encouraging adventurers to dig into the realm of flavors, ingredients, and culinary customs. In this in-depth guide, we look into the current trends in culinary tourism that are altering the way people travel, eat, and experience new locations. These trends are having a significant impact on all three of these activities. These trends provide food fans and visitors with new perspectives and ways to enjoy their favorite activities even more, ranging from immersive culinary experiences to practices that promote sustainable dining.

1. **Completely Immersive Gastronomic Experiences**
   Cooking Lessons That Are Hands-On:
   Cooking lessons taught by local chefs are a fun and interactive way for tourists to learn about the cuisines of different regions as well as the methods that have been used to prepare them traditionally. These lessons frequently include trips to local markets, during which participants get the opportunity to select fresh ingredients and then learn how to create traditional foods.
   Complementing Food with Wine:
   Food and wine pairing experiences have been increasingly popular in recent years, providing guests with the opportunity to sample mouthwatering pairings and investigate the complexities of flavor. Numerous restaurants and vineyards provide escorted tastings that shed insight on the complementary relationship between food and wine.
   Market Walks and Gastronomic Explorations:

Travelers can completely submerge themselves in the local cuisine culture by participating in market tours and gourmet walks. Exotic ingredients, food vendors on the street, and undiscovered culinary jewels are all things that tourists can learn about from local guides.

2. **Excursions in the World of Street Food**
   Tours of Local Eateries:
   It is becoming more common practice to acknowledge the street food scene as a vital and genuine component of the culinary culture of a particular location. Participating in a guided tour of the greatest local street vendors and stalls, where customers may sample a variety of snacks that are both reasonable and delectable, is an option for tourists who are traveling.
   The Culture of Food Trucks
   The proliferation of food trucks and other mobile vendors has given traditional street cuisine a vivacious and up-to-date spin. Food truck parks, which are locations where a number of different vendors can be found in close proximity to one another, have recently become popular vacation spots for people who are looking for convenient and varied dining options.
   Diversity in Cultural Expression:
   The world's diverse culinary traditions are beautifully woven together in the form of street food. The wide variety of cuisines that are available to tourists in cities all over the world, such as Mexican tacos, Thai street noodles, Indian chaat, and Italian arancini, demonstrates the rich cultural heritage of these places.
3. **Dining from the Farm to the Table**
   Tours of Local Farms:
   Farm tours provide tourists with the opportunity to connect with local food producers, observe environmentally responsible farming techniques, and gain a better understanding of the process by which food moves from the farm to the table. Some farms also provide dining experiences, where visitors can enjoy meals prepared with ingredients that are freshly prepared on the farm itself.
   Menus Prepared With Local Ingredients:
   More and more restaurants are making a concerted effort to source their food locally, promote regional agriculture, and showcase the fruits and vegetables that are in season. Guests get a better sense of the flavors of the area when restaurants use regionally sourced ingredients on their menus.
   Ethical and Environmentally Sound Business Practices:
   Farm-to-table dining trends link with the growing relevance of ethical and sustainable food

   practices, such as organic farming, decreasing food waste, and responsible sourcing, which resonate with environmentally concerned tourists. In addition, farm-to-table dining trends are aligned with the growing popularity of eating locally sourced food.

4. **Multicultural and Fusion Cooking Techniques**
   Crossroads of Culinary Art:
   The coming together of distinct culinary traditions is becoming increasingly common, which has led to the development of novel and surprising flavor combinations. For instance, restaurants serving fusion food might combine the cuisines of Japan and Peru, or they might combine flavors from the Middle East and the Mediterranean.
   Culinary Adventures Around the World:
   Eat sushi in the middle of Paris or have Neapolitan pizza in Bangkok—these are the kinds of global culinary experiences that tourists are looking for in an expanding number of restaurants throughout the world. This movement expands the range of culinary possibilities and promotes an appreciation of other cultures.
   Collaborations and Pop-Ups in the Culinary World:
   The eating scene is made more exciting by the presence of pop-up restaurants and partnerships amongst chefs. In a number of locations, unique eating opportunities that are only available for a limited time and are prepared by visiting chefs and restaurants from other countries are made available.
5. **Methods That Are Less Harmful To The Environment**
   Dining Without Generating Waste:
   Restaurants and other businesses that serve food are increasingly adopting "zero waste" strategies in an effort to lessen their negative impact on the environment. These efforts include reducing the amount of food that is thrown away, using compostable packaging, and organizing recycling initiatives.
   Options that are derived from plants and are vegan:
   The increasing desire for food options that are ethical, health conscious, and sustainable has led to an increase in the number of restaurants offering plant-based and vegan cuisine. A growing number of eateries now provide diners with a comprehensive selection of plant-based options that satisfy their appetites.
   Restaurants That Are Kind to the Environment
   The use of renewable energy, water conservation, and the reduction of single-use plastics are just some of the environmentally responsible activities that eco-friendly restaurants implement. These efforts make dining out at an eco-friendly restaurant a more sustainable experience for tourists.
6. **Gastronomic Tourism and the Use of Social Media**
   Food-Related Vacations:
   The influence of social media is strongly connected to the current trends in the culinary tourism industry. Food and eating experiences that are "Instagrammable" are becoming increasingly important to travelers, who are actively seeking out photogenic and aesthetically pleasing places to eat throughout their travels.
   Influencers in the Culinary World:

The rise of culinary influencers on social media platforms has impacted the preferences of travelers and influenced the restaurants that they choose to frequent. The followers of an influencer hear about the many dining experiences the influencer has had, receive suggestions from the influencer, and are introduced to unusual restaurants.

Online reviews and reservations are available at:
Online resources are becoming increasingly relied upon by travelers in order to identify and book eating options. The dining experience can be made more streamlined with the help of websites and applications like OpenTable, TripAdvisor, and Yelp, which allow access to reviews, ratings, and reservation options.

7. **Festivals of Gastronomic Travel Destinations**
Festivals de Gastronomie Internationales:
The many culinary traditions of the world are brought together under one roof at international food festivals, which celebrate different cuisines from around the world. By trying foods from a variety of nations, vacationers can experience a wide variety of cuisines within the confines of a single location.

Celebrations of the Regional Cuisine:
Many different locations have local cuisine festivals that highlight the delicacies and ingredients that are specific to the locality. These events provide a glimpse into the culinary history of a location and frequently incorporate live cooking demos in addition to other forms of entertainment.

Events Focusing on Gourmet Food:
Travelers who are looking for refined and affluent culinary experiences will find that gourmet cuisine events, such as wine and dine festivals, chocolate festivals, and seafood extravaganzas, are catered to their needs. These events are frequently accompanied by wine tastings and live entertainment.

8. **Intercultural and Gastronomic Cooperation**
Programs for both Food and Homestay:
Some vacationers choose to participate in immersive culinary and homestay programs, which give them the opportunity to live with families from the area and take part in everyday cooking routines. These encounters provide a profound comprehension of culinary customs as well as the dynamics of family life.

Swapping Out the Chefs:
Culinary and chef exchange programs encourage cross-cultural learning because they bring together chefs from a variety of nations who work together, share their knowledge, and showcase a variety of international cuisines to an audience from all over the world.

Vacations centered around Food:
Cooking vacations offer a one-of-a-kind opportunity to discover a new location while picking up essential skills for preparing regional specialties.

The culinary experiences available to tourists range widely, from learning how to make pasta in Italy to mastering the art of rolling sushi in Japan.

9. The Prospects for Tourism Involving Food

The Integration of Technology:
By creating dining experiences that are both interactive and immersive, the incorporation of technology, such as augmented reality (AR) and virtual reality (VR), will contribute to the expansion of the culinary tourism industry.

Gastronomy that is Gentler on the Earth:
As more tourists place an emphasis on making ethical and environmentally responsible food choices, the hospitality industry will continue to be shaped by sustainable gastronomy practices such as responsible sourcing, eco-friendly dining, and attempts to reduce waste.

Authenticity and the Maintenance of Cultural Practices:
Because tourists are more interested in having genuine and culturally significant gastronomic experiences, there will be a greater emphasis placed on the preservation of culinary traditions and legacy recipes.

Wellness in the Kitchen:
The convergence of wellness tourism and gastronomic tourism will become increasingly important as more people look for dining experiences that are in line with their personal health and nutrition objectives.

Trends in culinary tourism are a reflection of the changing desires and preferences of tourists, who increasingly regard food and beverages as essential components of their journeys. This attitude has contributed to the rise of culinary tourism as a distinct subset of the tourism industry. The landscape of culinary tourism is continuously evolving, resulting in an ever-increasing variety of experiences being made available to tourists. These experiences range from immersive cooking workshops to street food adventures and farm-to-table dining. The future of culinary tourism will be as rich in variety and flavor as the meals that it celebrates because to the confluence of flavors from around the world, environmentally responsible practices, and technology advancements. These trends are a reflection of a larger shift toward genuine, immersive, and environmentally responsible travel, in which the pleasure of discovering new cuisines and culinary traditions plays a major role in the process of creating unforgettable travel experiences.

7.2 Restaurants and Local Cuisine

Restaurants are more than just locations to get food to fulfill our hunger; they are also centers of culture, labs for flavor creation, and entryways into the beating heart of a destination. When tourists eat at restaurants in the area, they are embarking on a gourmet adventure that goes beyond the mere consumption of food; rather, it is a window into the history, culture, and identity of the location. In this book, we will investigate the complex link that exists between restaurants and regional food.

Specifically, we will delve into the significance of eating locally, the impact that it has on tourists and communities, and the role that real regional cuisine plays in the formation of culinary tourism.

1. **The Importance of Using Local Ingredients**
   An Experience Rich in Authenticity:
   The original flavors, components, and methods of preparation that are native to a place are reflected in the cuisine that is prepared there. It is the embodiment of a place's culture and legacy, and experiencing it through tasting it delivers an authentic and immersive experience of that place's culture and heritage.
   Assistance to Local Communities:
   Consuming food produced locally helps communities by bolstering the local economy by boosting locally owned companies, farmers, fishers, and craftspeople. It helps to maintain money inside the local economy, contributes to the creation of jobs, and contributes to more sustainable ways of making a living.
   Responsibility Toward the Environment:
   The carbon footprint that is linked with food transportation can be reduced by selecting locally sourced ingredients and eating at restaurants that place a priority on sustainability and environmentally friendly practices. It promotes dining that is ethically responsible and mindful of the environment, which is in line with the concepts of sustainable gastronomy.

2. **The Influence that Travelers Have on the Cuisine of the Area**
   Participation in a Culture:
   Travelers can further immerse themselves in the culture of their destination by trying some of the regional dishes that are popular there. It provides an understanding of the culinary customs, rituals, and stories that have contributed to the formation of the local way of life.
   Life's Most Indelible Moments:
   Experiencing new foods and flavors when traveling frequently contributes to the formation of unforgettable trip memories. When vacationers eat at restaurants in the area, they are sometimes exposed to new cuisine, some of which become cherished mementos of their trips.
   Establishing a Link and Carrying on a Discussion:
   Connecting with locals or fellow visitors over a meal is a great way to start conversations and build relationships. Eating is a kind of communication that is independent of national boundaries and may bring strangers together, and this holds true whether they are gathered around a food cart parked on the sidewalk or at a large table at a local eatery.

3. **The Importance of Maintaining Culinary Authenticity**
   True and Original Ingredients:
   Authentic local food is frequently prepared using local ingredients, which are

used to highlight the terroir and flavors that are specific to a particular location. This authenticity encourages a more profound relationship with the natural world as well as a celebration of the diversity of the food produced locally.

Techniques of the Traditionally Prepared Meal:
The utilization of time-honored cooking methods that have been handed down through the centuries lends a feeling of history to the cuisine of the region. The use of these techniques helps to maintain the authenticity of the food by ensuring that time-honored procedures and recipes are not forgotten.

The Art of Telling Tales Through Food:
The cuisine of a place can tell you a lot about its history. Each meal tells a tale, both about the history of the area and about the cultural influences that have shaped it, as well as about the ingenuity of the local chefs. As they appreciate each bite, patrons become active players in the narrative that is being told.

4. **The Internationalization of Regional Cooking**
   The Fusion Cooking Method:
   Fusion cuisine is a result of globalization; it combines regional flavors with those from other parts of the world to produce dishes that are both unique and interesting.
   This melding of different culinary traditions can be seen in restaurants all around the world, which has resulted in the creation of menus that are varied and appealing.

   The processes of recognition and adaptation:
   Numerous cuisines have attained prominence on a worldwide scale, and restaurants have evolved to satisfy the preferences of diners from all over the world. It is now possible for tourists to locate their preferred regional dishes at a variety of locations around the world, allowing them to experience a flavor familiar to them even while they are away from home.

   Influence from Different Cultures:
   The sharing of culinary knowledge and the resulting cultural influence has resulted in the development of regional cuisines that are distinct and ever evolving. Local dishes have been made more interesting as a result of the introduction of new ingredients, spices, and methods of preparation, which have spread throughout numerous regions.

5. **Regional Food Outside of Restaurants and Cafes**
   The Culture of Street Food:
   The food that is sold on the street is a significant part of the cuisine of the area. Travelers and residents alike can benefit from the quick and inexpensive options provided by street food sellers, which in turn enables them to sample a wider range of the regionally distinctive flavors.

   Festivals and Markets Specializing in Food:
   Food fairs and festivals are the beating hearts of a region's culinary culture since

they highlight the finest products and preparations that can be found in that area. These events are a smorgasbord for the senses, giving visitors a genuine flavor of the gastronomic culture of the destination they are visiting.

Home-Cooked Meals & Stays at Private Homes:
Travelers are able to get a feel for the regional cuisine in a more intimate environment by taking part in home-cooked meals that are offered through homestay programs. An authentic and personal dining experience can be had by sitting down to a home-cooked meal with a local family.

6. **The Importance of Restaurants to the Culinary Tourism Industry**

   Tourism in the Culinary Arts Initiatives:
   The travel business is home to a subfield known as culinary tourism, which is seeing explosive expansion. Numerous locations are working to boost their culinary tourism industries by creating programs that highlight the region's cuisine and restaurants as primary points of interest.

   Dining Experiences That Are Truly Authentic:
   When it comes to offering guests with genuine experiences of local cuisine, restaurants play a crucial role. Travelers will have the chance to experience local cuisine in a way that will stick in their memories thanks to a collaboration between local restaurants, food tours, and culinary events.

   Responsibility and Long-Term Sustainability:
   The world of culinary tourism is becoming increasingly populated with restaurants that practice responsible and sustainable business practices. These businesses place an emphasis on ethical sourcing, environmentally conscious business methods, and community involvement, reflecting the priorities of today's travelers.

7. **Obstacles to Overcome and Potential Benefits**

   Striking a Balance Between Innovation and Tradition:
   Finding a happy medium between innovation and tradition is one of the challenges. Restaurants have a difficult balancing act to do between attempting to maintain the traditional regional food they serve and embracing new forms of culinary innovation and evolution.

   Impact on the Environment and Long-Term Sustainability:
   In accordance with the tenets of sustainable gastronomy, eating establishments have a responsibility to address the environmental impact of their operations by instituting policies and procedures that cut down on waste, encourage responsible sourcing, and reduce their overall carbon footprint.

   Ability to Participate and Accessibility:
   Restaurants should make an effort to be easily accessible and friendly to customers with dietary preferences and restrictions, so ensuring that everyone is able to experience the delights of the food of the region they are located in.

8. **Predictions for the Future**

Cuisine that is hyperlocal:
Restaurants will embrace the usage of ingredients acquired from their immediate surrounds as part of the hyperlocal movement. This will put an emphasis on the flavors that are characteristic of the neighborhood or even of specific urban districts.

The Rise of Digital Dining
Technology will continue to play an important role, with digital platforms connecting tourists with local restaurants. This will allow tourists to find genuine eating experiences and make bookings in an easy manner.

Innovation Center for the Culinary Arts:
Hubs for culinary innovation will evolve into experimental centers, where local chefs and artisans will work together to develop one-of-a-kind meals and push the boundaries of regional cuisine.

Restaurants are more than just places to dine; they also serve as entry points to communities, cultures, and flavors. The soul of a location can be captured through its local cuisine, which is characterized by its use of genuine ingredients, time-honored cooking methods, and anecdotal culinary tales. When tourists eat in neighborhood eateries, they are embarking on a culinary adventure that is simultaneously a celebration of the local culture and a connection with the local community. Local cuisine and the restaurants that offer it are at the core of a location's identity and the memories of individuals who taste its flavors. This is true whether the cuisine is served from a food stall in a market, a family kitchen, or an establishment known for its fine dining.

7.3 Food Festivals and Tours

Festivals and tours focused on food are forms of culinary celebrations that provide a lovely way to investigate the cultural and gastronomic richness of a particular area. These events have acquired appeal on a global scale and are now attended by those who are interested in eating, traveling, and culture. They offer a one-of-a-kind chance to sample delectable cuisine, find out about local ingredients, and immerse oneself in the vibrant culinary history of a particular location.

Food festivals are lively get-togethers that feature a wide variety of dishes and beverages, typically those that are considered to be the signature dishes of a certain region. Food vendors, cooking demos, and even competitions amongst chefs are common features at these festivals. You can indulge in anything from street food to gourmet creations, and it provides an opportunity to sample things that might not be available in other settings.

For instance, the Taste of Chicago in the United States and the Tomato Festival in Spain are both well-known for the delicious food that they offer.

On the other hand, participants on food tours are led by an expert through the most popular restaurants and food shops in a particular location. Travelers will have the opportunity to discover local markets, dine in hidden gems, and engage in conversation with chefs and artisans thanks to these trips. They provide a more immersive experience since in addition to tasting the food, attendees not only learn about its history but also how it is prepared. On culinary excursions, you could participate in activities such as wine tasting in the vineyards of Tuscany, preparing sushi in Tokyo, or experiencing street food in Bangkok.

Food festivals and food tours are both beneficial to the tourism industry of a region since they highlight the culinary traditions of the area while also encouraging a sense of community. These events frequently encourage sustainable practices and lend support to neighborhood farmers and producers, so making a contribution to the conservation of culinary history.

Food festivals and tours can be a gateway to better understanding the cultural, historical, and social aspects of a location, in addition to providing an opportunity to indulge in a variety of exquisite sensations. They offer a glimpse into the heart of a place, as the cuisine of a region frequently reflects the culture of the locals and the style of life they lead.

7.4 Farm-to-Table Initiatives

Farm-to-table initiatives have become a significant and sustainable trend in the food business. As a result, there has been a fundamental shift in the way that we think about the origin of our food and the process by which it is prepared for consumption. This movement emphasizes locally sourced, fresh, and seasonal ingredients while promoting a direct and transparent interaction between farmers and consumers. It has huge repercussions for both our health and the environment, as well as for the communities that stand to gain from this.

The concept of reducing the amount of time that passes between the production of food and its consumption is at the core of the farm-to-table movement. Consumers now have access to food that is grown or manufactured in close proximity, eliminating the need for them to rely on a convoluted network of middlemen and lengthy supply chains. This results in a smaller carbon footprint connected with transportation as a result of the food not having to travel hundreds of miles or more before reaching the customer. Not only does this help reduce emissions of greenhouse gases, but it also encourages the growth of food economies on a regional and local scale.

Freshness and a focus on the seasons are at the heart of farm-to-table efforts. Consumers will be able to eat food at the point where its flavor and nutritional worth are at their highest. Fruits and vegetables typically have a more appetizing flavor and maintain a greater quantity of their vital elements if they are allowed to ripen on the plant where they were grown before being picked and eaten. Both the tongue's taste buds and the body stand to benefit from this circumstance.

In addition, the farm-to-table movement encourages a more profound relationship between people and the food that they consume. People have the opportunity to gain knowledge about farming practices, ethical considerations, and even the difficulties that are faced by local farmers. This information leads to more educated decision-making, promotes environmentally responsible agriculture, and frequently results in a deeper appreciation for the effort that goes into the production of our food.

Farm-to-table efforts, on the other hand, have been a driving factor in the revival of rural communities as well as small-scale agriculture. These projects help develop economic possibilities and contribute to the preservation of farmland by providing support to regional farmers and food producers. As a consequence of this, farm-to-table is not only about food; rather, it is about strengthening communities and guaranteeing a food system that is more robust.

Chapter 8

Transportation and Accessibility

In spite of the fact that I am unable to produce a response of three thousand words, I am able to present a comprehensive summary of the subject. Transportation and ease of access are two factors that significantly contribute to the development of modern society. It is crucial for economic growth, social connectivity, and overall quality of life to have transportation options that are both efficient and effective for moving people and things. Transportation systems, which range from municipal infrastructure to global networks, are the "arteries" of contemporary civilization because they make it possible for the sharing of ideas, resources, and cultural practices. Transportation that is accessible to all members of society not only fosters inclusivity and equal opportunities for all, but it also contributes to the creation of a more sustainable society and the preservation of the environment. Let's dig deeper into this complex issue and see what we can learn.

Infrastructure for Transportation and Travel:

The physical facilities and operational systems that facilitate the movement of people, products, and services are collectively referred to as "transportation infrastructure." This infrastructure consists of various forms of transportation networks, such as roads, trains, airplanes, and canals, as well as public transportation networks. For the purpose of both economic expansion and the consolidation of regional economies, the construction and upkeep of a solid transportation infrastructure are of the utmost importance. Efficient transportation networks lower the costs of carrying goods, make commerce easier, and attract investments; these factors all contribute to accelerated industrial development and the creation of new job possibilities. In addition to improving access to education, healthcare, and other necessary services, transportation networks that have been thoughtfully built also make a positive contribution to the overall well-being of communities.

Transportation in the City:

Transportation is an essential component of daily living in urban settings, and it plays a role in determining how easily cities can be accessed and how well they can be lived in. Congestion in urban areas can be reduced, air quality can be improved, and the overall quality of urban living can be raised when urban transportation networks are well managed. Integrated public transit systems, which may include buses, subways, light rails, and programs for sharing bicycles, encourage environmentally responsible mobility and cut down on dependence on individual automobiles. The incorporation of "smart transportation technologies," such as the monitoring of traffic in real time and the automated collection of fares, contributes to the further improvement of the effectiveness and accessibility of urban transportation networks.

The development of infrastructure that is hospitable to pedestrians and the promotion of alternative modes of transportation both contribute to the creation of urban settings that are healthier and more vibrant.

Connectivity in Rural Areas:

When it comes to linking rural villages with metropolitan areas and regional markets, transportation is one of the most important factors. In rural areas, where there is less access to transportation infrastructure, economic development might be hampered, and social imbalances can become more pronounced. Increasing access to important services like healthcare and education, as well as encouraging agricultural productivity and rural entrepreneurship, are all goals that can be accomplished through the construction and maintenance of rural roads, bridges, and other forms of transportation networks. Innovative mobility solutions, such as community transportation programs and mobile health clinics, have the potential to close the accessibility gap in rural areas that are currently underserved and distant, hence improving the general health of the population living in these areas.

Accessibility for Individuals Who Suffer from Disabilities:

Making public transportation more accessible is a critical step in achieving the goal of providing people with disabilities with equal opportunities and full participation in society. Accessible transportation infrastructure enables those with disabilities to move independently and participate more fully in society. Examples of accessible transportation infrastructure include wheelchair ramps, elevators, and reserved seating sections on public transit. Individuals who have varying requirements for mobility are guaranteed to be able to navigate the transportation system in a dignified and hassle-free manner if the principles of universal design are applied to the construction of transportation facilities and vehicles. Communities may make their environments more welcoming and inclusive for all of their citizens by giving accessibility a higher priority in the planning and design of transportation systems.

Transportation that is Kind to the Environment:

In light of the many environmental problems that exist on a worldwide scale, it is more important than ever to encourage the use of environmentally friendly modes of transportation. The reduction of carbon emissions, the mitigation of environmental contamination, and the preservation of natural resources are the goals of sustainable transportation efforts. The adoption of environmentally friendly transportation technology, such as electric vehicles, hybrid engines, and biofuels, helps to offset the detrimental effects that transportation has on the surrounding environment. Integrated urban planning methods that prioritize compact, mixed-use developments, as well as those that encourage public transit and non-motorized transportation options, contribute further to the achievement of sustainable urban mobility. The development of ecologically responsible transportation networks requires a number of key initiatives, including the promotion of bike-friendly infrastructure, the encouragement of carpooling, and investments in green transportation alternatives.

Connectivity on a Global Scale:

The movement of people, products, and services across international borders is made possible, in large part, by transportation, which acts as the linchpin of global trade and connectivity. The efficient operation of global transportation networks, which include oceanic shipping, air freight, and cross-border trains, makes possible the fluid trading of goods and resources, hence contributing to the growth of economic interdependence and globalization. Collaboration among nations is encouraged through the formation of international transportation partnerships and agreements, which helps to keep the flow of commodities uninterrupted and lowers trade barriers. The optimization of the effectiveness of global transportation networks brought about by the incorporation of cutting-edge logistics and supply chain management systems contributes to the expansion of international commerce and the growth of global value chains.

The Obstacles to Overcome and the Way Forward:

Even if there are a lot of advantages to transportation and accessibility, there are still a lot of obstacles to overcome when it comes to the construction and management of transportation systems. The efficient and equitable movement of people and commodities continues to be significantly hampered by problems like as traffic congestion, inadequate infrastructure upkeep, and unequal access to transportation services. These problems continue to pose substantial impediments. In order to effectively address these difficulties, a comprehensive strategy is required, one that integrates forward-thinking technical solutions, environmentally responsible infrastructure expenditures, and equitable regulatory frameworks. The adoption of up-and-coming technologies in transportation, such as driverless cars, intelligent mobility solutions, and digital transportation platforms, has the potential to completely transform how we think about and make use of transportation in the foreseeable future. We can establish a transportation ecosystem that is more resilient, inclusive, and sustainable if we encourage collaboration across governmental institutions, private industries, and organizations of civil society. This will allow us to address the ever-changing requirements of our globally interconnected world.

8.1 The Role of Transportation in Tourism

Transportation is an essential component of the tourism business since it is the medium that brings tourists to their destinations and provides them with the experiences they want. Without transportation networks that are both effective and easily accessible, tourism would be severely stunted. Travelers would have a difficult time reaching their intended places, which would in turn impair economic development, cultural interaction, and recreational pursuits. During this in-depth examination of the subject, we are going to look into the vital position that transportation plays in the world of tourism. Specifically, we are going to examine its impact on travel patterns, regional development, environmental sustainability, and the experience that travelers have.

Facilitator of Travel :

The provision of transportation is the primary factor that makes travel possible. It makes it possible to move people and products from their points of origin to the destinations of their choosing using a variety of different techniques. This can refer to a variety of types of transportation for visitors, such as flying, driving, taking the train, going on a cruise, or any combination of these. The convenience of these various modes of transportation has a considerable impact on the locations that visitors choose to visit as well as the number of times they go on vacation.

The Capability to Reach Destinations:

Access to locations is facilitated by well-functioning modes of transportation. The tranquil vistas of the countryside, the bustling streets of a major city, or the pristine beaches of a coastal town are all places that visitors may like to discover on their vacation. The inaccessibility of these locations would prevent many people from traveling there, which would reduce the amount of revenue that might be generated from tourism in these regions.

The Engine of the Economy:

The tourism industry is significantly reliant on transportation as a key economic engine. Airports, train stations, bus terminals, and ports all contribute significantly to overall revenue and offer employment possibilities. Transportation companies such as airlines, cruise lines, and others play a significant part in luring travelers to visit a variety of locations across the world. This, in turn, stimulates the local economy by benefiting businesses such as hotels, restaurants, gift stores, and entertainment establishments.

The development of regions:

The growth of a region's infrastructure and services related to transportation can have a substantial impact on that development. It is possible for previously underserved communities to experience a surge in economic development as a result of government investments in the infrastructure of transportation. The creation of new tourism markets, the encouragement of investment, and the advancement of regional development can all be facilitated by the improvement of roads, trains, and airports.

The Exchange of Cultures:

Transportation makes cultural exchange easier to accomplish. People go on vacation in order to immerse themselves in other cultures, languages, and traditions. They can gain a mutual awareness of and admiration for a variety of cultures by going to local museums, participating in local events, and interacting with the community around them. Without access to various modes of transportation, the likelihood of such interactions occurring would be significantly reduced.

Influence on the Environment:

Although transportation is essential to the tourism industry, it is not exempt from having an impact on the surrounding environment. The tourism industry is primarily responsible for the generation of greenhouse gases and the damage of the environment because of the activities that are related to transportation. To lessen the severity of these negative effects on the environment, the industry is making strides toward adopting more environmentally responsible modes of transportation, such as hybrid vehicles and electric buses.

The Development of Infrastructure:

The improvement of existing modes of transportation is a vital component of expanding tourist destinations. Airports are being improved to accommodate increasing numbers of travelers, and new highways and bridges are being built to accommodate the increased volume of traffic. These advancements make it easier to access previously inaccessible locations and inspire more people to travel to new places.

Travelers Have Choices and Are Free to Do What They Want:

Travelers have access to more options when there is a well-developed transportation network. They are free to select the mode of transportation that caters to their individual interests as well as their financial constraints, giving them the opportunity to enjoy the brevity and ease of air travel, the independence afforded by driving, or the breathtaking panoramas afforded by rail travel.

Management of Emergencies:

In the tourism industry, crisis management cannot function without the involvement of transportation. Transportation is essential for the successful evacuation of visitors and the protection of their safety in the event of an emergency such as a natural disaster or a worldwide health crisis. In addition, the providers of transportation are crucial players in the process of delivering aid and relief supplies to areas that have been impacted.

The Improvement of the Tourist Experience:

The travel itself is frequently an important component of the overall tourist experience. There are scenic train routes, scenic drives, and even themed cruises that tourists can enjoy on their vacations. The onboard experience is becoming an increasingly important focal point for transportation services, with an increased emphasis being placed on providing travelers with amenities and services that cater to their comfort and leisure needs.

Provision of Access for a Variety of Groups:

It is crucial to have accessible transportation choices available in order to cater to a wide variety of tourist demographics, including persons of all ages who are traveling, as well as those who have impairments. It is essential for the development of the tourism business to make certain that transportation services are accessible to all people and can meet their needs.

Creativity and technological advancement:

To accommodate the ever-evolving requirements of tourists, the transportation business is always revising its approaches and developing new ones. The process that tourists use to plan and carry out their excursions has been completely transformed as a result of technological advances such as high-speed rail, electric automobiles, and internet platforms for booking and information.

Connectivity on a Global Scale:

In particular, the aviation sector is an essential player in the process of linking countries and continents to one another. Travelers now have easier access to more parts of the world thanks to the network of connection that was created by global airlines, airports, and alliances. The worldwide connectivity that exists today is one of the primary motivating factors behind international travel.

The Obstacles and the Future of Sustainability:

While transportation is vital to the tourism industry, the sector also confronts issues when it comes to sustainability. The environmental impact of transportation, which includes emissions and the consumption of resources, is becoming an increasingly pressing issue. In order to address these problems, more and more attention is being paid to the investigation of sustainable transportation options, such as electric vehicles and modes of travel that use less fuel.

Tourism in Isolated and Rural Areas:

Transportation is absolutely necessary for rural and outlying tourist destinations. Travelers from all over the world come here to experience landscapes that are truly unique and unspoiled. Enhancing transportation connectivity to such destinations might open up new doors for economic development prospects, including those in the fields of agritourism, adventure tourism, and ecotourism.

8.2 Improving Accessibility to Towns

The enhancement of inhabitants' quality of life as well as the promotion of long-term sustainable development are both directly tied to the accessibility of local communities. The term "accessibility" refers to the ease with which one can reach and move around inside a town, taking into consideration aspects such as transportation, infrastructure, and services that enable seamless mobility for all citizens, including those with impairments. Towns have the potential to become more welcoming, vibrant, and conducive to economic growth if they place a higher priority on accessibility. During this in-depth investigation, we will investigate a variety of tactics and initiatives that may be put into action to improve accessibility to towns and to build a community that is more inclusive and environmentally sustainable.

Infrastructure for Transportation and Travel:
Building up a solid transportation infrastructure is absolutely necessary in order to make places more accessible. This comprises the building of well-connected road networks, bridges, and public transit systems, as well as their ongoing maintenance, so that different portions of the town can be reached quickly and easily. A town's accessibility and environmental friendliness are both improved by investments made in contemporary and environmentally responsible modes of transportation, such as pedestrian walkways, bike lanes, and public transportation that is easily accessible.

Systems of Public Transportation:
Providing inhabitants with transportation options that are both economical and convenient requires the establishment of public transit networks that are both efficient and easily accessible. This may involve the introduction of bus routes that cover various portions of the town, as well as the establishment of schedules that are dependable and user-friendly. Additionally, making sure that persons with disabilities, particularly those who use wheelchairs, have access to public transportation is a key step that may be taken to dramatically improve inclusion and accessibility.

Infrastructure that is Friendlier to Pedestrians:
It is vital to develop infrastructure that is friendly to pedestrians if one want to promote accessibility and encourage citizens to engage in the practice of walking inside the municipality. Not only do sidewalks, crosswalks, and well-lit pathways increase pedestrian safety, but they also make it easier and more convenient for people to go around on foot. It is absolutely necessary, in order to construct a town environment that is accessible to people with mobility issues, to plan the streets and walkways taking into consideration the requirements of all pedestrians.

Infrastructure Dedicated to Cycling:
Residents can be encouraged to use bicycles as a viable means of transportation by the establishment of a complete cycling infrastructure. This infrastructure should include bike lanes, bike-sharing programs, and secure parking facilities for bicycles. Cycling advocacy not only helps to alleviate traffic congestion, but it also makes for a more environmentally friendly, healthy, and sustainable urban environment. The establishment of a network of bike routes that are both secure and well-connected inspires a greater number of residents to take up riding as a regular mode of transportation.

Design that is Universal:
The implementation of universal design principles into town planning makes it possible to guarantee that all individuals, regardless of age or ability, have access to the built environment, including public areas. As part of this process, buildings, parks, and other public facilities may be designed with accessible elements like ramps, elevators, and tactile pavement in order to accommodate persons with all types of impairments. The implementation of universal design not only helps to develop

inclusivity, but it also helps to generate a more equal and user-friendly environment for the town's citizens overall.

The Integration of Technology:

Utilizing technology to improve accessibility can considerably contribute to a more enjoyable experience of the town as a whole. The implementation of smart city technologies such as digital navigation systems, real-time transportation information, and mobile applications for transportation services can assist citizens in more effectively planning their journeys and providing access to real-time information regarding available transit alternatives and routes. The incorporation of technology into the town's infrastructure has the potential to both improve traffic flow and make the town more easily accessible as a whole.

Participation in the Community:

It is absolutely necessary to include members of the community in the process of planning and carrying out accessibility initiatives if one want to take into account the requirements and preferences of local citizens. It is possible for town planners and policymakers to identify important accessibility concerns and develop focused solutions by soliciting comments and insights from local inhabitants through the use of methods such as conducting surveys, holding workshops, and holding public forums. The involvement of the community helps to establish a sense of ownership and collective responsibility for the improvement of accessibility, which in turn leads to development projects that are more sustainable and community-centered.

Facilities Open to the Public That Are Reachable:

It is vital, in order to promote inclusion within the community, to make sure that all public facilities, such as government buildings, parks, libraries, and recreational centers, are accessible to all citizens. People who have disabilities are given the opportunity to fully engage in community events and access important services when public buildings are equipped with the required features, such as ramps, elevators, accessible restrooms, and other essential amenities. Building a community that is more welcoming to newcomers and cohesive among its members requires, among other things, making sure that all of the town's inhabitants have unrestricted access to its public amenities.

Collaboration with Neighborhood Organizations:

The accessibility and inclusiveness of the community as a whole can be significantly improved by the coordinated efforts of local companies, which can have a substantial impact on those two aspects of the community. It is possible to ensure that people living in the area with disabilities have equitable access to goods and services by encouraging local companies to construct storefronts, entrances, and facilities that are accessible. Enhancing the entire experience of a town by encouraging and supporting local companies to implement accessibility measures not only contributes to a more welcoming and inclusive local business climate, but it also improves the general quality of life for residents and visitors alike.

Integration of Multiple Modalities:

Improving overall accessibility inside the town necessitates the promotion of multi-modal transportation integration, which comprises the seamless integration of multiple modes of transportation such as buses, trains, bicycles, and pedestrian walkways. This is an essential step toward achieving this goal. By encouraging inhabitants to employ a combination of transportation alternatives, developing transportation hubs that make it easier to transfer between multiple modes of transportation encourages citizens to do so, which in turn reduces residents' reliance on privately owned vehicles and promotes a transportation network that is more environmentally friendly and integrated.

Solutions for Sustainable Transportation:

The implementation of sustainable mobility solutions, such as electric public transit, car-sharing programs, and other environmentally friendly transportation options, can help to the reduction of the town's carbon footprint while simultaneously boosting accessibility for the town's population. Not only does supporting the adoption of environmentally friendly modes of transportation contribute to the promotion of environmental sustainability, but it also helps to improve the general quality of life in a community by providing its citizens with a living environment that is more hygienic and less polluted.

Planning for the Long Term and Establishing Policy Frameworks:

It is absolutely necessary to devise all-encompassing, long-term planning strategies as well as policy frameworks that put an emphasis on accessibility in order to guarantee the growth of an inclusive and sustainable community. Accessibility considerations can be incorporated into urban planning guidelines, zoning rules, and development policies, which can help direct future infrastructure projects and support the establishment of a more accessible and equitable town environment. Accessibility will continue to be a primary concern in the town's growth trajectory if planning efforts are aligned with sustainability goals and community requirements, since this will ensure that accessibility is maintained.

8.3 Sustainable Transportation Solutions

As the negative effects that traditional modes of transportation have on the surrounding environment grow more obvious, it is more important than ever in the modern world to find environmentally friendly alternatives to these techniques. The transportation industry is a major contributor to the emissions of greenhouse gases, the pollution of the air, and the depletion of resources on a global scale. As a consequence of this, there is a growing demand for innovative and ecologically friendly transportation solutions that can lower the carbon footprint of the industry as a whole and support a more sustainable future. This in-depth investigation of sustainable transportation solutions will look into a variety of techniques and technology with the goal of reducing the negative effects that transportation has on the environment while simultaneously promoting economic growth, social equity, and public health.

Transit systems and shared modes of transportation:

Public transportation systems, such as buses, trams, and trains, play a significant part in lowering the total number of individual vehicles on the road. This, in turn, results in a reduction in the amount of congestion on the roads as well as the emissions of greenhouse gases. Investing in public transportation that is both effective and inexpensive will encourage more people to use these services, which will ultimately result in a reduction in overall carbon emissions and an improvement in air quality. Carpooling, ride-sharing, and bike-sharing programs are examples of shared mobility solutions that further contribute to the reduction of the environmental effect of transportation by maximizing the use of automobiles and encouraging more environmentally responsible modes of transportation.

Vehicles that Run on Electricity and Hybrid Power:

There has been substantial progress made toward lowering the carbon footprint of the transportation sector thanks to the introduction of electric and hybrid vehicles. These vehicles emit significantly fewer pollution than conventional automobiles because they are powered by electric motors and batteries rather than internal combustion engines. The widespread adoption of electric and hybrid vehicles, supported by developments in battery technology and charging infrastructure, can considerably contribute to lowering air pollution and dependency on fossil fuels, leading to a more sustainable and cleaner transportation system.

This can be accomplished via the introduction of a cleaner and more environmentally friendly transportation system.

Alternative Combustion Methods:

The research, production, and utilization of alternative fuels, such as biofuels, hydrogen, and natural gas, present a possible answer for minimizing the negative effects that transportation has on the surrounding environment. Biofuels, which are generated from organic matter, have the potential to cut greenhouse gas emissions by a large amount while also promoting energy independence. Hydrogen fuel cells are an environmentally friendly and resourceful replacement for old fossil fuels because they produce only water and heat as byproducts of their energy production. Natural gas, when used as a transportation fuel, produces fewer levels of pollutants compared to conventional gasoline or diesel, making it a cleaner and more sustainable option for powering vehicles. In addition, natural gas may be utilized to generate electricity, making it an attractive alternative to traditional power sources.

Transportation by Physical Activity:

Active transportation choices, such as walking and cycling, contribute not only to a reduction in carbon emissions but also to an improvement in public health and well-being when more people choose to use them. Investing in pedestrian and cycling infrastructure, such as dedicated bike lanes, walkways, and bike-sharing programs, encourages more people to choose non-motorized transportation alternatives for their daily commutes and for their recreational activities. This can be beneficial for the environment. Not only can encouraging active transportation help alleviate traffic congestion, but it also promotes the development of communities that are healthier and more livable.

Innovative Technologies for Transportation:

The incorporation of smart transportation technology, such as intelligent transportation systems, real-time traffic monitoring, and digital networking, has the potential to increase the efficacy of transportation networks while simultaneously lowering their overall energy consumption. These technologies make it possible to control traffic more effectively, encourage more efficient route planning, and improve transportation operations generally. Smart transportation technologies can assist reduce congestion, improve travel times, and cut fuel consumption, all of which will contribute to a more sustainable and streamlined transportation system. These benefits can be achieved through the utilization of data and analytics.

Planning for Cities and the Use of Land:

Strategies for urban planning and land use are inextricably related to environmentally responsible solutions for land transportation. The adoption of compact and mixed-use development patterns that enhance walkability, cut down on urban sprawl, and promote the use of public transit can lead to the adoption of more environmentally friendly modes of transportation. Urban planning projects can reduce the need for long commutes, cut down on emissions related to transportation, and create a more sustainable and integrated urban environment if they are successful in building communities that are well-connected and easily accessible.

Integration of Multiple Modalities:

Creating a network that is smooth and enables for quick transitions between multiple modes of transportation, such as buses, trains, cycling routes, and pedestrian paths, is an essential component of multi-modal transportation integration. Cities and communities can lessen their reliance on privately owned vehicles and encourage the use of transportation systems that are more environmentally friendly and energy efficient if they encourage the use of several modes of transportation and build convenient linkages between the various modes. The integration of various means of transportation offers citizens a variety of travel options, which in turn fosters more sustainable and flexible mobility choice possibilities.

Development of Sustainably Friendly Infrastructure:

It is vital to make investments in the construction of environmentally friendly infrastructure in

order to promote environmentally friendly transportation options. The widespread adoption of sustainable transportation choices is facilitated by the construction of transportation facilities that are energy-efficient and environmentally beneficial. Examples of such facilities include electric vehicle charging stations, bike parking facilities, and green infrastructure. The construction of sustainable infrastructure also includes the utilization of recyclable materials, energy-efficient lighting, and green building methods, all of which contribute to the creation of a transportation network that is both more sustainable and more resilient.

Frameworks for Both Policy and Regulation:

In order to drive systemic change and encourage the adoption of environmentally friendly transportation solutions, it is essential to establish comprehensive policy and regulatory frameworks that emphasize sustainable mobility. It is possible to effectively lead the transportation industry toward a more sustainable and low-carbon future by implementing policies that promote the use of electric vehicles, encourage sustainable urban planning, and incentivise the development of green transportation infrastructure. When it comes to determining the course that sustainable transportation growth will take, the role that policy initiatives such as emissions requirements, carbon pricing mechanisms, and transportation planning guidelines play is essential.

Management of Green Supply Chains and Logistical Operations:

The goals of green logistics and supply chain management are to minimize the negative effects of freight transportation on the surrounding environment while simultaneously increasing the efficiency with which items are transported. When sustainable logistics practices are used, such as route optimization, fuel-efficient transportation, and the use of cars with low emissions, carbon emissions can be greatly reduced, and the ecological footprint of activities related to transportation can be minimized. A transportation system that is more environmentally conscious and sustainable can be contributed to by adopting green supply chain management methods. These strategies encourage the use of environmentally friendly packaging materials, increase the transparency of supply chains, and stimulate the adoption of environmentally friendly transportation solutions.

Integration of Renewable Energy Sources:

The environmental impact of the transportation sector can be mitigated even further by incorporating renewable energy sources, such as solar and wind power, into the infrastructure of the transportation sector. Cities and towns may dramatically lessen their dependency on fossil fuels and reduce their overall carbon footprints if they power their transportation networks with energy that is clean and generated from renewable sources. Integration of renewable energy sources not only bolsters the transition toward a transportation system that is less harmful to the environment, but it also promotes greater energy independence and resilience.

Transformation of Behavior and Education:

It is vital, in order to cultivate a culture of environmentally responsible mobility, to promote behavioral shifts and educational activities that raise knowledge about the benefits of environmentally responsible transportation. It is possible to persuade individuals to adopt more sustainable travel behaviors by educating the public on the environmental and health impacts of transportation, as well as the benefits of choosing sustainable transportation options. Communities can be inspired to adopt more environmentally friendly transportation behaviors and contribute to a more sustainable and resilient transportation ecosystem by participating in and promoting activities such as car-free days, public transportation campaigns, and sustainable commuting challenges. These types of activities include: car-free days; public transportation campaigns; sustainable commuting challenges.

Chapter 9

Economic Diversification through Tourism

The act of broadening a nation's economic base by developing new businesses and sectors is referred to as economic diversification. This helps a nation become less dependent on a single source of income while also producing an economy that is more stable and robust. Because it has the capacity to contribute to a variety of different economic sectors, such as hospitality, transportation, agriculture, and retail, tourism is an extremely useful instrument for the achievement of economic diversification. This all-encompassing study of how economic diversity can be achieved through tourism will dig into the myriad of ways in which tourism can strengthen local economies, create employment opportunities, and foster economic expansion. In addition, it will cover the difficulties that are associated with utilizing tourism as a tool for economic diversification as well as the best practices that are now available.

The Part That Tourism Plays in the Process of Economic Diversification
Several Different Sources of Income:
The local and national economy both benefit from the varied economic streams that tourism brings. The revenue generated by tourism is not confined to a single industry but rather is shared across a wide variety of enterprises. These businesses include those that offer lodging, food and beverage services, transportation services, tour operators, and local handicrafts. This diversification of revenue streams can assist lessen a region's reliance on a single industry, which can help make the economy more strong and less subject to economic downturns in a single sector.

Creating New Jobs:
The hospitality and tourism sector contributes significantly to the nation's labor force. It gives employment opportunities in a variety of industries, ranging from restaurants and hotels to transportation and cultural attractions. Additionally, many of these positions do not require a significant amount of formal education, which makes tourism an approachable and inclusive source of employment for local populations.

The establishment of new jobs within the tourism industry can contribute to the reduction of unemployment and provide families and people with a steady income.

Effects that Reverberate:

The tourism industry creates a domino effect that benefits a diverse range of other industries. For instance, a strong tourism business can help local agriculture by raising demand for fresh produce, meat, and dairy products in restaurants and hotels. This, in turn, can lead to increased production of these goods. In a similar vein, the development and upkeep of tourism infrastructure can be a source of economic stimulation for the real estate and construction industries. These spillover effects extend to services like as banking, insurance, and healthcare, all of which face higher demand as a direct result of the expansion in tourism.

Support for the Preservation of Cultural Heritage:

The protection and dissemination of cultural traditions are both supported and encouraged by tourism. To entice visitors, several locations highlight the cultural significance of their past as well as the natural beauty of their surroundings. The community will have a greater feeling of pride and connection as a result of the preservation and restoration of cultural landmarks and traditions that are made possible as a result of this. Destinations have the ability to develop a unique and alluring character that will attract tourists from all over the world if they choose to highlight and celebrate the cultural history of their location.

The acronym "SMEs" stands for "small and medium-sized enterprises"

The expansion of small and medium-sized businesses (SMEs) can be facilitated by tourism's availability of growth prospects. Local business owners have the opportunity to launch successful ventures in the tourism industry by opening boutique hotels, souvenir stores, and guided tour companies. This makes it possible to have a diverse and thriving business ecosystem, which gives citizens of the area the opportunity to become stakeholders in the tourism industry and benefit from the expansion of that industry.

The Development of Infrastructure:

Infrastructure development, including transportation networks, airports, roads, and utility networks, typically has to be improved in order to accommodate the growth of tourism. Not only do these infrastructural upgrades benefit tourists, but they also improve the general quality of life for locals. Improving infrastructure like roads and utilities, for example, can cut down on travel times, increase access to vital services, and make the surrounding environment more habitable.

Education and Training to Develop Abilities:

The expansion of the tourism business may encourage increased investments in areas such as education and the cultivation of skills. As a result of the growing demand for jobs in the tourism industry, more and more training programs and educational institutions are being set up to equip potential employees with the information and abilities they need.

This, in turn, makes it possible for more local citizens to gain access to high-quality education and training, which eventually boosts their employability.

Exchange of cultures and comprehension across cultural boundaries:

Tourism encourages cultural interaction and mutual comprehension between people of different backgrounds, both of which can result in a variety of economic opportunities. The interaction between tourists and local people has the potential to kickstart the development of cultural exchanges, language learning programs, and initiatives to foster intercultural discussion. These activities have the potential to produce cash and employment possibilities while simultaneously encouraging intercultural understanding and collaboration.

Innovation and entrepreneurial endeavors:

The tourism industry frequently stimulates new business ventures and innovative ideas. It's possible for entrepreneurs to spot unmet needs in the tourism industry and fill them by developing one-of-a-kind activities, accommodations, or services to meet the requirements of travelers. This enterprising mindset has the potential to result in the production of ground-breaking ideas and the expansion of a business climate that is both dynamic and intensely competitive.

The development of regions:

By luring new investment and new infrastructure to parts of a region that were not previously well served, tourism has the potential to propel regional development. It is possible that areas that have natural beauty, historical monuments, or cultural assets that have not been fully exploited could witness a rise in public and private investments, which will contribute to increased economic diversification and an improvement in local living standards.

Concerns and Things to Take Into Account

Seasonal differences:

Visitor counts fluctuate throughout the year in many popular tourist spots, reaching highs and lows at different times of the year. It can be difficult to manage the economic effects of seasonality, as it can be difficult for businesses and communities to function normally during off-peak times. The effects of seasonality can be lessened by offering attractions that are open throughout the year, attracting tourists during shoulder seasons, and diversifying the products that are offered to tourists.

Influence on the Environment:

Tourism has the potential to have negative effects on the environment, including increased energy use, increased waste output, and greater pressure on natural resources. Sustainable tourism activities are important to limit these negative affects and maintain the long-term viability of destinations. These strategies include eco-friendly infrastructure, conservation efforts, and responsible tourism campaigns.

Excessive tourism:

The over-concentration of tourists in certain locations can result in congestion, the damage of the surrounding environment, and the straining of the infrastructure. In order to effectively manage overtourism, proper planning and regulation are required. These measures should aim to disperse tourists more fairly across locations and encourage environmentally responsible tourism activities.

Protecting Our Cultural Heritage:

The expansion of tourism brings with it the possibility of cultural commodification as well as the loss of local traditions and practices. In the process of developing tourism, one of the most important factors to take into account is how to strike a balance between the desire to draw tourists and the requirement to preserve cultural assets. Training in cultural awareness, rules for responsible tourism, and involvement of the local community are some of the strategies that might assist reduce the effects of these problems.

Investments in the Infrastructure:

Significant financial resources are required to be invested in both the creation and maintenance of tourism infrastructure. To ensure that the required infrastructure, which includes transportation, lodging, and cultural attractions, is in place to enable growth in tourism, governments and commercial players must collaborate. This can be a considerable financial burden, and the means for funding must be well planned out and carried out in order to be effective.

Improvements Made to Human Resources:

It can be difficult for businesses in the tourism industry to satisfy the demand for trained labor, particularly in locations that are seeing substantial expansion in tourism. It is imperative that educational and training options be made available to the local workforce in order to ensure that locals have access to jobs in the industry and that the level of service that tourists have come to expect is maintained.

Advertising and public relations:

The ability to successfully sell and promote a location is absolutely necessary in order to draw in tourists. Destinations are required to compete in a worldwide market, which necessitates the implementation of effective marketing strategies as well as investments in branding and promotion. When it comes to the development of successful marketing activities, collaboration between the public and private sectors is frequently required.

Sustainability of Existing Infrastructure:

In the tourism industry, one of the most important considerations is the creation of environmentally friendly infrastructure. This includes buildings that are efficient in their use of energy, as well as options for transportation that are kind to the environment. Although initial expenditures might be necessary, investments in environmentally friendly infrastructure frequently result in lower total costs over time as well as less adverse effects on the natural world.

Participation in the Community:

It is essential to involve the local community in the planning process for tourism in order to guarantee that locals will profit from tourism and have a role in how it will develop. Participation from the local community can also assist in resolving potential disagreements and societal problems brought on by the expansion of tourism.

Peace of Mind and Protection:

It is of the utmost importance for vacation spots to take precautions to protect the personal safety and property of visitors. It is vital to have robust safety measures, emergency response plans, and enough law enforcement in order to defend the reputation of the destination and keep the faith of the tourists who visit there.

Implementing Industry Standards to Maximize Tourism's Contribution to Economic Diversification

Development of Tourism That Is Sustainable:

Implementing eco-friendly methods, safeguarding natural resources, and reducing the environmental impact of tourism activities should all be high on your list of priorities when it comes to the development of sustainable tourism. Encourage local businesses to implement environmentally friendly policies and encourage visitors to engage in responsible tourism practices.

Increase the Variety of Tourist Attractions:

By providing a wide variety of tourism activities, you may increase the size of your visitor pool and lessen the impact that seasonality has on your business. Think about offering cultural, outdoor, gastronomic, and nature-based tourism experiences if you want to appeal to a wide variety of interests.

Put Your Money Into Infrastructure:

Investing in crucial infrastructure such as transportation, lodgings, and attractions is essential to supporting growth in the tourism industry. In order to guarantee the economic viability of future infrastructure expansions, these investments may call for the formation of public-private partnerships, the provision of grants, or the provision of incentives.

Foster the preservation of cultural traditions:

Create plans that will safeguard and maintain cultural heritage while simultaneously boosting tourism. Encourage the participation of local communities in decision-making processes and lend your support to activities that honor and preserve traditional rituals and practices.

Take Steps to Control Over Tourism:

It is important to implement measures for visitor management in order to more equitably distribute tourists and to encourage ethical tourism behaviors. It may be necessary to implement visiting limits, zoning laws, and crowd control measures in order to stop sensitive regions from becoming overcrowded.

Development of the Workforce:

Make investments in educational and vocational training programs in order to cultivate a trained labor force at the local level for the tourism industry. Make it possible for locals to receive high-quality education and training, which will increase their chances of finding work in the relevant industry.

Working Together and Forming Partnerships:
Encourage cooperation between the governmental and private sectors, as well as local communities and the various players involved in the tourism business. Establish destination management groups in order to build unified tourist plans and coordinate the many efforts being made.

Advertising and public relations:
Create successful advertising and public relations efforts in order to increase the number of visitors to the location. Utilize digital marketing, social media, and branding strategies to develop an engaging and powerful identity for the location.

Frameworks for Regulatory Compliance:
Put into place regulatory structures that will encourage tourism behaviors that are both responsible and sustainable. This may include rules for zoning, codes of behavior for tourism operators, and recommendations for environmental impact studies.

Participation in the Community:
Include members of the community in the process of planning and developing tourism. It is important to solicit the opinions of locals, including them in decision-making processes, and guarantee that they will share in the economic benefits of tourism.

Peace of Mind and Protection:
Place a high priority on safety and security measures to safeguard both residents and visitors. Maintaining a safe and welcoming environment requires the creation of emergency response plans, the enforcement of safety standards, and the coordination of efforts with law enforcement agencies.

Tourism has the potential to be a significant economic diversification driver since it offers many revenue streams, the creation of jobs, and chances for both large and small businesses. Destinations have the ability to lessen their reliance on seasonal tourism by increasing the diversity of tourists they attract, diversifying the tourism product, and fostering cultural preservation through investments in sustainable tourism development. To guarantee that tourist expansion is both sustainable and responsible, it is vital to regulate overtourism, engage with local people, and emphasize safety and security. These three things are interconnected and must be done simultaneously.

Because every vacation spot is different, the tactics that are used to diversify the local economy through tourism should be adjusted to the destination's particular set of advantages, disadvantages, and goals. The potential of tourism may be harnessed by regions to develop dynamic and resilient economies that are to the benefit of both the residents of the region as well as visitors to the region if they learn from successful case studies and implement best practices. In the long run, increasing economic diversity through tourism can result in higher living standards, better infrastructure, and an inclusive and bright future for the local communities.

9.1 Tourism and Economic Resilience

It has been known for a very long time that tourism is an important contributor to economic resilience, as it offers potential for growth, diversity, and sustainability in a number of different places all over the world. The ability of a system to endure and recover from external shocks, such as economic downturns, natural disasters, or geopolitical instabilities, is referred to as economic resilience. Within the scope of this in-depth investigation, we will investigate the complex relationship that exists between tourism and economic resiliency. Specifically, we will focus on the many of ways in which tourism may support economies, encourage the creation of jobs, and contribute to the overall stability and adaptability of communities. In addition, we will explore the issues that are connected with utilizing tourism as a means of improving economic resilience, as well as the best practices that are now available.

The Crucial Function of Tourism in Ensuring Economic Durability

Increasing the Variety of Sources of Income:

Tourism helps economies become less susceptible to the effects of shocks from the outside world by diversifying their sources of revenue and reducing their reliance on a single industry. Tourism creates income that is less vulnerable to variations caused by regional or seasonal factors because it draws visitors from a wide variety of geographical regions. The economy is helped to become more stable as a result of this diversity, which also helps to establish a buffer against economic downturns in other industries.

Opportunities for Employment and the Creation of New Jobs:

The hospitality, transportation, retail, and entertainment industries are just few of the fields that benefit from the substantial employment opportunities made available by the tourism industry. Jobs in the tourism industry provide a vital source of income for millions of people all over the world, particularly in parts of the world where there are less chances for other types of work. This consistency in employment contributes to an overall increase in the robustness of local economies and communities.

Improvements Made to the Existing Infrastructure:

The expansion of tourism infrastructure, including airports, hotels, highways, and cultural sites, not only helps the tourism industry expand, but it also has positive effects on the economy as a whole. An improvement in infrastructure makes regions more accessible and connected, which in turn makes commerce and investment easier to carry out and creates conditions that are favorable for the growth of businesses and the introduction of innovative new products and services.

Preservation of Both Cultural Objects and the Natural World:

Many times, tourism acts as a driving force behind the protection of natural habitats as well as cultural traditions. Communities are encouraged to invest in the protection of natural and cultural resources and the sustainable management of such resources because of the need to preserve and highlight the uniqueness of these assets. Destinations can maintain their allure to tourists while also promoting a sense of pride and identity within the local community if they make an effort to preserve their cultural legacy as well as their natural ecosystems.

SMEs, often known as small and medium-sized businesses, were given a boost

Small and medium-sized businesses (SMEs) are given a boost by tourism because it provides company owners with chances to start companies that cater to the requirements of tourists. This, in turn, accelerates the overall rate of economic expansion. Tourism-related activities not only contribute to the overall economic stability of communities but also build a lively and diverse business ecosystem. Beneficiaries of tourism-related activities include local artisans, tour operators, souvenir stores, and hotel services.

Catalyst for the Development of Regional Areas:

Tourism may act as a driving force behind regional development, which is especially important in less-populated or more rural areas. Tourism has the potential to boost economic growth and revive local economies if it is successful in attracting investments in infrastructure, services, and facilities. The establishment of tourism-related facilities frequently results in the launch of ancillary enterprises, which in turn contributes further to the robustness and durability of regional economies.

Encouragement of Intercultural Communication and Comprehension:

Tourism helps to create cultural understanding and exchange, which in turn helps to foster cooperation and mutual respect among populations of varying backgrounds. Interactions between tourists and local inhabitants have the potential to result in the creation of cultural exchange programs, language learning initiatives, and community-based tourism projects, all of which contribute to the social cohesion and economic resilience of the area.

Encouragement of Innovative Activity and Entrepreneurship:

The tourist industry fosters an environment that is conducive to entrepreneurship and innovation because it enables business owners to see and seize possibilities within the tourism market. This enterprising spirit helps to stimulate the development of tourist experiences, goods, and services that are one-of-a-kind and original, and that are tailored to meet the ever-changing requirements and preferences of travelers. The economic resiliency and competitiveness of destinations as a whole can be improved with the help of initiatives that encourage entrepreneurialism and innovative thinking.

Concerns and Things to Take Into Account

Exposure to Stressors from the Outside World:

The tourism business is vulnerable to disruptions from the outside world, such as natural disasters, economic slumps, and geopolitical unrest. It is possible for sudden shifts in travel patterns, global economic conditions, or political climates to have a considerable impact on tourism demand and profits, which can result in economic precariousness for locations that rely largely on tourism revenue.

Variations Caused by Seasons and Recurring Cycles:

There are periods of high demand and periods of low demand throughout the year for many tourist attractions since visitor numbers tend to fluctuate seasonally and cyclically at these locations. Businesses and communities that rely on tourism for their livelihoods may find it difficult to successfully manage these swings and keep a steady flow of money during off-peak seasons.

Degradation of the Environment and of Cultural Practices:

The unbridled growth of tourism can result in the destruction of natural habitats, the commercialization of cultural practices, and the loss of long-held community norms and practices. It is vital, for the purpose of ensuring the long-term sustainability and resilience of destinations, to strike a balance between the requirements for increased tourism and the protection of natural and cultural assets.

Strain on the Infrastructure:

The rapid increase of tourism can put a strain on the existing infrastructure and public services, which can result in traffic congestion, exhausted resources, and a decrease in the overall quality of the experience for tourists. It is essential for maintaining economic resilience to plan and manage the development of infrastructure in a way that satisfies the requirements of a growing tourist population while also protecting the authenticity of the destination's natural and cultural assets.

Disparities in Social and Economic Status:

There is a possibility that the benefits of tourism development will not always be spread fairly among the populations in the area, which can result in social and economic inequities. For the purpose of supporting inclusive and sustainable tourist growth that is to the advantage of the entire community, it is vital to make certain that the local workforce has access to job opportunities, training, and fair compensation.

Examples of Good Practices in the Field of Tourism for the Promotion of Economic Resilience

Planning and Management for a Sustainable Tourism Industry:

Planning and management techniques for sustainable tourism, which strike a balance between economic expansion and environmental and social responsibility, should be given priority. It is important to ensure that the growth of the tourism industry is in line with the long-term goals of sustainability, hence it is important to implement sustainable tourism certifications, environmental impact assessments, and responsible tourism rules.

Diversification of Tourist Attractions and Activities:

In order to combat the impacts of seasonality and attract a wider range of tourists, it is important to encourage the diversification of tourism-related goods and experiences. Make an investment in the creation of cultural, nature-based, and adventure tourist products that highlight the distinctive qualities and sights of the area.

Engagement with the Community and Efforts to Empower Its Members:

Ensure that the views of local communities are heard and that their interests are represented by involving those communities in the process of tourist planning and development. To enable local inhabitants to actively participate in the tourism industry and benefit from its growth, it is important to equip them through the implementation of programs that create capacity, training initiatives, and support for entrepreneurial endeavors.

Investing in the Country's Services and Infrastructure:

To better support the expansion of tourism, investments should be made in the creation of infrastructure and public services that are both sustainable and robust. Investing in transportation networks, utility systems, waste management systems, and cultural amenities should be given high priority in order to improve both the overall experience that visitors have and the quality of life for locals.

The Protection of Heritage and the Encouragement of Cultural Observances:

Put into action measures that will encourage the preservation and conservation of natural assets and cultural heritage. The authentic cultural identity of the destination should be highlighted through community-based tourist activities, cultural festivals, and historical conservation programs. Additionally, visitors should be encouraged to participate in cultural exchanges that are both responsible and meaningful.

Advertising and Promotion in the Tourism Industry:

To increase the number of visitors to the location, it is necessary to devise successful advertising and public relations initiatives that make use of digital marketing, social media, and branding. Work together with public and commercial stakeholders to develop integrated marketing activities that highlight the one-of-a-kind offerings and experiences that are available at the location.

Investing in the Professional Development of Employees:

Investing in education and training programs can help cultivate a local workforce that is knowledgeable and skilled, which is essential for the tourism business. Make it possible for locals to obtain high-quality education and training, so ensuring that they will be well-equipped to obtain jobs in the tourism industry and to provide services that are of the highest possible standard for visitors.

Management of Sustainable Tourism Destinations:

Establish destination management organizations (DMOs) or tourism authorities to coordinate the efforts of the public and commercial sectors, as well as local communities and stakeholders in the tourism industry. DMOs play an essential part in the governance of destinations, the planning of strategic initiatives, and the participation of various stakeholders, all of which contribute to the development of an ecosystem that is cohesive and sustainable for tourism.

Precautions Taken for the Protection of Others:

Place a high priority on safety and security measures to safeguard both residents and visitors. Maintaining a safe and welcoming atmosphere that also improves the entire experience for visitors requires the development and implementation of emergency response plans, the enforcement of safety rules, and close collaboration with law enforcement authorities.

Monitoring and adjusting to conditions:
Maintain a constant vigilance over tourism trends, the comments of visitors, and innovations in the business in order to adapt to ever-shifting conditions. Install a process for collecting and evaluating data so that you can make educated decisions and adapt to changing situations in the market as well as the preferences of individual customers.

The tourism industry acts as a dynamic catalyst for strengthening economic resilience, fostering diversification, and providing support for local communities. Tourism contributes to the steadiness and adaptability of economies in a number of ways, including the generation of a variety of revenue streams, the creation of job opportunities, and the stimulation of the growth of small and medium-sized businesses. It is vital, however, to handle difficulties such as a sensitivity to external shocks, seasonal changes, preservation of the environment and cultural traditions, and social imbalances.

Destinations have the ability to maximize the benefits of tourism while simultaneously reducing

the negative consequences it has on the local environment and community by putting into practice industry best practices. These include the promotion of cultural preservation, community participation, investment in infrastructure, and sustainable tourist planning. Case studies from all across the world demonstrate that tourism may be an effective tool for achieving economic resilience. These studies also show the significance of sustainability, diversification, and adaptation within the tourism industry.

In a world that is always shifting, the ability of communities and regions to be economically resilient is absolutely necessary for their overall well-being. Tourism provides chances for growth, innovation, and sustainable development that are beneficial to both inhabitants and visitors, making it a potential avenue for reaching this resilience and offering a path toward its achievement. Destinations may build robust and thriving economies that are better suited to withstand the effects of external shocks and adapt to changing circumstances if they take advantage of the possibilities offered by tourism. This will ensure a profitable and stable future for everyone.

9.2 Encouraging Entrepreneurship

Fostering innovation, producing new job openings, and propelling economic growth all require a strong emphasis on entrepreneurial activity, which must be actively encouraged. higher productivity, higher competitiveness, and more market diversity can all be attributed to increased levels of entrepreneurial activity, which fuels the development of new ideas, goods, and services. In this in-depth investigation, we will investigate the significance of entrepreneurial activity in driving economic expansion, discuss the advantages of cultivating an entrepreneurial culture, and highlight the various strategies and best practices for encouraging entrepreneurial activity at the local, national, and international levels.

The Role of Entrepreneurship in the Process of Economic Growth and Development

Development of New Ideas and Improvements in Technology:

By stimulating the development of new products, services, and business models, entrepreneurship is a driving force behind innovation and the progress of technological capabilities. Many times, entrepreneurs are the ones to recognize voids in the market and develop products or services to fill those voids. As a result, they propel forward movement and improve the quality of life for both individuals and communities.

Opportunities for Employment and the Creation of New Jobs:

Employment opportunities are generated by entrepreneurial endeavors, and these opportunities contribute to the increase of employment overall, particularly in developing markets and industries. Small and medium-sized firms (SMEs) and startups are key sources of employment because they offer opportunity for individuals of varying skill levels to contribute to the economy while also gaining experience and abilities that are valuable in their own right.

Economic Competitivity and the Diversification of Markets:

Through the cultivation of a dynamic business environment, entrepreneurship contributes to increased economic competitiveness as well as increased market diversity. Startups and small businesses are responsible for the introduction of novel goods and services, the escalation of competitive activity, and the encouragement of established enterprises to innovate and enhance the products and services they provide. This competitive environment, with its dynamic markets, helps to cultivate a culture of continual improvement, which in turn generates economic growth and resiliency.

The Elimination of Poverty and the Promotion of Wealth Creation:

Individuals who engage in entrepreneurial activity are given the opportunity to establish prosperous firms and procure a steady income, which can ultimately lead to the generation of wealth and the reduction of poverty. The success of an entrepreneur can help pull individuals and communities out of poverty, contribute to social mobility, and give marginalized populations the ability to participate in the economic growth of their community.

Growth in Regional Infrastructure and Development of the Region:

Activities related to entrepreneurship help to the expansion of regional infrastructure and development by luring investments, boosting local economies, and encouraging the formation of ecosystems that are beneficial to the growth of businesses. When entrepreneurial endeavors are successful, they frequently result in the construction of supply chains, the development of infrastructure, and the growth of auxiliary enterprises, all of which contribute to the general economic well-being of a region.

The Impact on Culture and Society:

The spirit of invention, resiliency, and community engagement are all fostered by the entrepreneurial spirit, which has a profound impact on both culture and society.

A successful entrepreneur often acts as a role model for others and encourages them to follow their own entrepreneurial dreams. This creates a ripple effect that encourages more entrepreneurial activities and cultivates a culture that values creativity and collaboration.

Advantages of Creating an Environment That Encourages Entrepreneurship
Encouragement of Creative and Innovative Thinking:

Individuals are encouraged to pursue new ideas, take risks that have been well considered, and question the status quo in an entrepreneurial culture, which in turn fosters innovation and creativity. This culture of innovation helps to cultivate a dynamic and forward-thinking company environment, which in turn leads to the development of innovative technology, business models, and ground-breaking solutions to difficult problems.

Strengthening the Capacity for Economic Resilience and Adaptability:

An entrepreneurial culture strengthens economic resiliency and adaptation by encouraging the development of a business ecosystem that is diversified as well as flexible. Economies are able to respond more swiftly to external shocks, market fluctuations, and technological disruptions when entrepreneurs are present because entrepreneurs are skilled at recognizing shifting market dynamics and developing appropriate responses to those changes. The ability of economies to be flexible and resilient contributes to their overall stability and long-term viability.

Investment and Activity in Venture Capital Have Been Encouraged:

An entrepreneurial culture that is healthy and thriving is more likely to attract investment and venture capital activity, which in turn provides entrepreneurs with the financial resources and support they need to expand their firms. The availability of finance from venture capitalists and angel investors allows entrepreneurial businesses to scale up, extend operations, and enter new markets. This, in turn, contributes to the expansion of the economy and the creation of new jobs.

The Cultivation of Gifts and the Advancement of Abilities:

An entrepreneurial culture fosters talent and encourages the development of abilities by giving individuals the chance to gain first-hand experience, learn from their mistakes, and broaden their skill set through a variety of learning opportunities. Entrepreneurs frequently gain a diverse set of talents, including as leadership, problem-solving, and adaptability, which are helpful in a variety of professional and personal undertakings. These qualities can be transferred from one activity to another.

Growth in Industry Accompanied by a Diversified Business Landscape:

A culture that encourages entrepreneurship contributes to the development of a more diverse commercial landscape and fosters the expansion of a number of different industries and market segments.

The existence of new businesses, particularly small and medium-sized businesses (SMEs) and innovative companies, promotes healthy competition, stimulates industry growth, and promotes the establishment of niche markets, so producing an economy that is vibrant and dynamic.

Support for Individual Advancement and Community Integration:

By giving people from all sorts of different communities and backgrounds the chance to follow their own entrepreneurial aspirations, a culture that encourages entrepreneurship helps increase social mobility and fosters an inclusive environment. It is possible for members of underrepresented groups, such as women, minorities, and underserved communities, to gain economic autonomy, take part in the labor force, and contribute to the general prosperity of society through the pursuit of entrepreneurial endeavors.

Encouragement of Entrepreneurship: Methods and Strategies

In order to promote entrepreneurship, it is necessary to put into action a number of different strategies and activities that create an atmosphere that is favorable to business and encourages growth. The following is a list of important tactics that can be used to promote entrepreneurship on various levels:

Education and Training for Professional Development:

Incorporate entrepreneurship education and skill development programs into the curricula of schools, institutions that provide vocational training, and educational institutions that offer higher education. In order for students to be successful in today's rapidly changing and increasingly competitive business scene, they need to be equipped with the information, business acumen, and practical skills essential to undertake entrepreneurial endeavors.

Obtaining Access to Financial Resources and Funding:

Establish financial systems and support structures that enable access to funds, grants, loans, and funding from venture capital for businesses. Establish public-private partnerships, investment funds, and angel investor networks to promote the flow of financial resources to promising startup companies and small and medium-sized enterprises (SMEs). This will allow these companies to expand their operations and become more profitable.

The Difference Between Incubators and Accelerators

Build and promote business incubators and accelerators that offer entrepreneurs mentoring, coaching, and resources to help them begin and build their ventures. These types of programs are essential for the success of new businesses. Incubators and accelerators provide companies with access to co-working spaces, opportunities for networking, help for business development, and market validation. This creates an atmosphere that is favorable for the growth and success of entrepreneurs.

Reforms in the Regulatory System and Support for Policy:

Entrepreneurs would benefit from regulatory reforms and policy support measures that would make it easier for them to register their businesses, obtain licenses, and comply with regulations. Establish a favorable regulatory framework that promotes entrepreneurship, safeguards intellectual property rights, and simplifies the process of conducting business in order to cultivate a thriving ecosystem that is conducive to the growth of small and medium-sized businesses (SMEs).

Partnerships between the public sector and the private sector:

Encourage public-private partnerships and collaboration in order to allow the sharing of information, the pooling of resources, and the trading of best practices between government agencies, industry groups, and stakeholders in the private sector. Create an entrepreneurial ecosystem that is coherent and synergistic by engaging in cross-sector collaboration to identify and address the needs and concerns of entrepreneurs.

Programs for Professional Networking and Mentoring:

Establish networking and mentorship programs that connect budding entrepreneurs with experienced industry professionals, company leaders, and mentors who are able to provide guidance, advice, and support for the aspiring entrepreneurs. Help entrepreneurs develop useful relationships by facilitating networking events, workshops, and mentoring programs that provide them the opportunity to learn from experienced professionals, gain access to valuable ideas and resources, and learn from other entrepreneurs.

Technology and the Innovation of Digital Media:

Encourage technological progress and digital innovation by providing financial backing for the

establishment of "tech hubs," "innovation centers," and "digital ecosystems" that inspire businesspeople to develop and implement digital solutions. Give start-up companies access to the digital infrastructure, tools, and platforms they need to create and grow their businesses using the power of technology.

Access to Markets and the Promotion of Exports:

Market access and export promotion measures should be facilitated to assist business owners in expanding their operations beyond the scope of local markets. In order to stimulate international commerce and export operations, business owners should be provided with access to market research, export incentives, trade agreements, and global value chains. This will enable business owners to expand their client base and enter new markets.

Entrepreneurship that Welcomes Everyone and Diversity:

Encourage inclusive entrepreneurship and diversity by making it possible for people from different walks of life, such as women, minorities, and underserved communities, to take part in the development of the entrepreneurial ecosystem. Create programs that help encourage the participation of people from these groups in the entrepreneurial world while addressing the specific problems they confront.

Clusters of Research and Innovative Activity:

It is important to establish research and innovation clusters that will boost research and development. These clusters should bring together industrial partners, academic institutions, and research centers. Encourage business owners to work together with research institutes, gain access to cutting-edge research, and come up with innovative solutions that will fuel economic growth and industry improvements.

Initiatives Taken on a Global Scale to Encourage Entrepreneurship

There are a great many programs and organizations all over the world that are devoted to fostering an entrepreneurial spirit and assisting in the expansion of new businesses and smaller businesses. Global collaboration, the provision of resources, and the promotion of entrepreneurial ecosystems are the three primary goals of these efforts. The following are examples of notable worldwide initiatives:

GEN stands for the Global Entrepreneurship Network

GEN is a global platform that encourages entrepreneurship by easing the process of working together and exchanging information amongst business owners, investors, government officials, and other groups that provide support. The Global Entrepreneurship Network (GEN) is responsible for organizing Global Entrepreneurship Week and provides information, initiatives, and events in an effort to boost entrepreneurial engagement.

The Sustainable Development Goals (SDGs) of the United Nations are as follows:

The United Nations has recognized the importance of entrepreneurship in promoting sustainable and equitable economic growth, hence it has included economic development and entrepreneurship as part of its Sustainable Development Goals (SDGs). Goal 8, which is titled "Decent Work and Economic Growth," places an emphasis on the encouragement of entrepreneurialism, the creation of new jobs, and economic autonomy.

The Startup Countries:

The global network known as Startup Nations provides assistance to organizations and governments in the process of formulating policies and programs designed to encourage entrepreneurial ecosystems. The network works together to produce policy suggestions, discuss research findings, and collaborate on best practices to encourage entrepreneurial activity.

(YBI) stands for Youth Business International

Young Business International (YBI) is a worldwide network with the mission of encouraging and assisting young people from underprivileged backgrounds who are interested in starting their own businesses. Young business owners can get assistance in starting their companies, as well as training and access to capital, from member organizations of the Young Entrepreneurs' Business Initiative (YBI).

The World Economic Forum, abbreviated as WEF:

The mission of the Entrepreneurship and Innovation team at the WEF is to encourage and support entrepreneurial endeavors all over the world. In order to establish strategies and initiatives that encourage innovation and entrepreneurship, the WEF collaborates with corporate leaders, policymakers, and entrepreneurs to develop these strategies and initiatives.

Concerns and Things to Take Into Account

Access to Financial Resources:

Access to finance is still a big obstacle for many aspiring business owners, particularly in economies that are still new and still developing. It is absolutely necessary for the success of entrepreneurs to ensure that they have access to a variety of different forms of funding such as venture capital, angel investments, and microfinance.

Obstacles Created by Regulations:

The presence of regulatory obstacles and administrative burdens can be detrimental to entrepreneurial endeavors. It is vital, in order to create a favorable climate for business, to simplify the processes of business registration, licensing, and compliance, as well as to address any regulatory impediments that may exist.

Competencies and Education:

The ability to be an entrepreneur needs a varied range of skills, and many people who aspire to be entrepreneurs may lack the knowledge and training necessary.

It is essential, in order to provide individuals with the resources they need to be successful as entrepreneurs, to make entrepreneurship education, training programs, and chances for skill development accessible to them.

Access to the Market:

It can be difficult for entrepreneurs to break into new markets, whether those new markets are domestic or worldwide. Entrepreneurs can reach a wider consumer base and achieve sustainable growth with the assistance of market access and export promotion projects that receive financial support.

Both diversity and inclusivity are important:

It is crucial to promote inclusivity and diversity in the realm of entrepreneurship in order to ensure that people from all walks of life have the opportunity to pursue entrepreneurial pursuits. It is essential, in order to cultivate an entrepreneurial ecosystem that is inclusive, to remove the obstacles that are faced by marginalized groups, such as women and members of underrepresented groups.

Promote the health of ecosystems:

There is a wide disparity between the regions in terms of the availability of support ecosystems such as incubators, accelerators, mentorship programs, and possibilities for networking. For the sake of fostering entrepreneurial spirit, it is essential to broaden and strengthen these support structures.

It is essential to promote entrepreneurial activity in order to generate innovation, the creation of new jobs, and overall economic growth. Entrepreneurship is an extremely important factor in generating economic growth, fostering resilience, and finding solutions to difficult problems that face society. Communities, regions, and even entire nations have the capacity to harness the power of entrepreneurship and create economies that are dynamic and prosperous if they create a culture that encourages entrepreneurship and put into action tactics that support and nurture entrepreneurs.

Entrepreneurship is, and will continue to be, a potent engine for the forward movement of constructive change in the globe. The development of an entrepreneurial ecosystem and the encouragement of the goals of individuals and small enterprises can result in creative solutions, possibilities for employment, and a future that is more equitable and prosperous for all people. It's important to remember that fostering an entrepreneurial spirit isn't only about boosting the economy; it's also about giving people the tools they need to pursue their ambitions, have an influence that matters, and make a positive contribution to the overall health of society.

9.3 Supporting Artisan and Craft Industries

The artisanal and craft sectors each play an important part in the process of retaining cultural legacy, encouraging creative expression, and propelling economic expansion. These sectors include the production of a diverse selection of handmade goods, ranging from textiles and pottery to jewelry and carpentry, both in terms of their historical significance and their modern relevance. The artisan and craft industries offer several benefits, both cultural and economic, therefore it is beneficial to support these businesses.

The Maintenance of the Cultural Heritage:

The artisanal and craft industries of a region are frequently strongly entwined with the cultural history of that place. They contribute to the preservation of traditional methods of handicrafting, designs, and techniques that have been passed down through the years. These types of businesses help to preserve a community's history and identity, so guaranteeing that its cultural practices are passed down from generation to generation. We are able to preserve the intangible cultural legacy that gives each community its individual character by investing in artisanal and craft enterprises.

Encouragement of the Free Expression of Creativity:

The artisan and craft industries serve as a forum for the expression of creative ideas and new product development. In order to produce one-of-a-kind works of art, artisans and craftsmen frequently combine contemporary design principles with more conventional production techniques. This synthesis of antiquity and modernity inspires inventiveness and enables craftspeople to convey their cultural identities in fresh and engaging ways by providing them with the opportunity to express both.

Economic Expansion and the Generation of New Jobs:

The artisanal and craft industries both contribute to the expansion of the economy by bringing in cash and offering new employment opportunities. These kinds of businesses are absolutely necessary for the survival of many communities, particularly in more remote and economically depressed areas of the world. Artisans and craftsmen frequently run their own small companies or cooperatives, which helps to stimulate the economy of their communities and provides individuals and communities with sustainable means of subsistence.

Practices that are Friendly to the Environment and Lasting:

A great number of artisan and craft sectors place an emphasis on eco-friendly and sustainable business practices. Craftspeople frequently make use of components that are derived from their immediate environment and are made of natural or organic resources. This emphasis on sustainability is in line with modern worries about the environment and strikes a chord with customers looking for products that are created in an ethical and environmentally responsible manner.

Increasing Intercultural Communication:

The sharing of the stories and traditions that are behind each handmade product is one way that the artisan and craft industries encourage cultural exchange. Customers are not simply purchasing an item; rather, they are establishing a connection with the heritage and way of life of the craftspeople. This communication helps to overcome cultural divides, promotes mutual understanding, and acknowledges and appreciates the vast diversity that exists among people.

Providing Assistance to the Artisan and Craft Industries:

Options Available to Consumers We, as consumers, have the ability to choose whether or not to support the artisan and craft sectors by purchasing handcrafted goods, either locally or through groups that promote fair trade. When we purchase items made by hand, we are helping to ensure the continued existence of the people who made them.

Market Access: Market access can be facilitated for artisans by governments and organizations by establishing platforms (such as craft fairs, e-commerce sites, or physical markets) where craftsmen can present and sell their items to a wider audience. Examples of these platforms include craft fairs and physical marketplaces.

Education and Training: Providing educational opportunities and training programs can assist craftsmen in improving their abilities, increasing the variety of products they offer, and gaining access to markets in more efficient ways. These opportunities can be made available through the combined efforts of several organizations and communities of artisans.

Protection of Intellectual Property Putting in place safeguards to maintain traditional designs and techniques and ensuring that artists are paid fairly for their products can be accomplished through the implementation of intellectual property protection measures.

Supporting fair trade groups that connect local artists with global marketplaces can assist local craftspeople in obtaining fair pricing for their wares and accessing resources for the creation of goods in a manner that is environmentally responsible.

Preserving Cultural Heritage Through cooperative efforts on the part of governments, organizations, and individual craftspeople, we may be able to ensure the survival of our cultural traditions and art forms. This comprises the documentation of traditional knowledge as well as the provision of resources for projects aimed at cultural preservation.

9.4 Other Economic Spin-offs

The creation of new jobs is one of the most important results that flow from an economic stimulus package. The expansion of an industry or a company usually results in the creation of new employment opportunities all throughout the supply chain. For instance, a new manufacturing plant not only creates jobs for people directly, but it also makes it more likely that jobs will be created in the fields of transportation, logistics, and a variety of service industries.

The growth of an economy almost always results in a rise in the amount of money collected as taxes by the various governments. The growth of successful firms and the increased incomes of individuals leads to an increase in tax collections, which in turn enables governments to pay improvements in public services and infrastructure.

Investing in Education and Training: A thriving economy is an excellent catalyst for expanding one's financial holdings in educational and vocational programs. It is vital to have trained labor in order to maintain economic expansion, which has led to the development of initiatives that aim to increase the quality and relevance of education and training programs.

Increased investments in research and development (R&D) are one potential outcome of economic spin-offs, along with innovation and research and development. When the economy is doing well, firms and governments typically spend more money on research and development (R&D), which, in turn, supports technical improvements and innovation.

Better Roads, Bridges, and Public transit: An increase in the economy often leads to improvements in the nation's roadways, bridges, and public transit systems. The investment in new infrastructure not only contributes to the growth of the economy, but it also raises the standard of living for the populace as a whole.

Community Development: The expansion of the economy can pave the way for community development efforts, such as the establishment of public spaces, cultural venues, and recreational facilities, among other things. These investments provide a positive contribution to the well-being of local communities and bring in additional economic activity.

Investment from Overseas: An expanding economy has the potential to attract Foreign Direct Investment (FDI), which occurs when investors look for business possibilities in an environment that is both stable and successful. Foreign direct investment (FDI) has the potential to transfer capital, technology, and knowledge into the country that is receiving it.

Environmental Stewardship The creation of new economic opportunities often results in an increased emphasis on environmental stewardship. When economies expand, there is typically a corresponding increase in interest in sustainable development, alternative energy sources, and conservation initiatives, all of which can have positive effects on the environment in the long run.

The many facets of economic expansion are interwoven with the direct and indirect economic repercussions that result from those repercussions. They underscore the significance of a balanced and sustainable approach to development while illustrating the interdependence of many economic, social, and environmental aspects.

Chapter 10

Measuring Success and Future Trends

The level of success achieved in any industry or field is not solely judged by financial measurements; rather, it is also defined by the field's impact on society and the environment, as well as its ability to be maintained throughout time. In our fast changing environment, the criteria that determine what constitutes success are always being refined and expanded. Understanding how to quantify performance and forecast future trends is essential for continued progress and development across a wide variety of fields, including but not limited to technology, healthcare, education, and business. Let's dig into how success is now assessed in a variety of industries, and then investigate the burgeoning trends that are influencing the future of those industries.

The Technology Industry:

Success is often judged in the technology industry by a number of important factors including user engagement, market acceptance, revenue growth, and innovativeness. Businesses frequently evaluate their level of success based on the rate of technological breakthroughs they are able to accomplish, the scalability of their solutions, and their capacity to meet the ever-changing demands of their customers. Additionally, in this industry, the success of technological products and services can be measured in large part by how well customers are satisfied with the product and how secure their data is.

Appearing trends point to an emphasis in the future on artificial intelligence (AI), machine learning, and automation, all of which are poised to change numerous industries. When we look into the future, we can see that these trends are already appearing. In addition, the implementation of blockchain technology, the development of quantum computing, and the expansion of the Internet of Things (IoT) are anticipated to be the primary drivers of the subsequent wave of technological innovation. The capacity to harness new technologies in order to achieve equitable and sustainable growth will become an increasingly important factor in determining success.

The Healthcare Industry:

Patient outcomes, the efficiency of treatment methods, and the effectiveness of healthcare delivery systems are the conventional yardsticks by which success in the healthcare industry is traditionally judged. Indicators of vital importance include mortality rates, the degree to which patients are satisfied with their care, and the ease with which they may get medical services. Success is gradually being redefined to include the promotion of total well-being, the reduction of healthcare inequities, and the incorporation of customized medicine as a result of the introduction of digital health solutions, the incorporation of telemedicine, and the rising focus on preventive care. This gradual redefinition of success is occurring as a result of the increasing focus on preventative care.

The adoption of precision medicine, the utilization of big data analytics for predictive healthcare, and the implementation of innovative healthcare technologies such as virtual reality (VR) and augmented reality (AR) for medical training and patient care are anticipated to be the primary drivers of future trends in the healthcare industry. Looking further into the future, we can anticipate that these trends will continue to dominate the industry. In addition, the priority placed on integrated and comprehensive treatment models within the healthcare industry is likely to have a significant impact on the sector's future prosperity.

The Education Industry:

Success in the field of education has traditionally been judged by academic performance, rates of graduation, and the employability of graduates. However, modern educational techniques place an emphasis on a wider range of criteria, such as the capacity to think critically and creatively as well as the flexibility to adapt to a global environment that is always shifting. Students need to develop their social and emotional abilities in addition to their digital literacy if they are going to be successful in today's school system, which places a premium on instilling a "growth mindset" in its students.

When we look to the future, we can see that future trends in education indicate toward the introduction of gamification and interactive content into educational curricula, as well as the employment of adaptive learning technology and immersive learning experiences. In addition, the proliferation of online education platforms, the growth of competency-based learning, and the increased emphasis on personalized learning journeys are expected to play significant roles in determining the level of success that the education industry achieves in the years to come.

Commercial Activity:

It is normal practice in the world of business to gauge success based on financial performance, market share, and the level of customer happiness achieved. When assessing the success of a company, key performance indicators (KPIs) like revenue growth, profitability, and brand awareness play an essential part.

However, modern business practices are placing a greater emphasis on corporate social responsibility (also known as CSR), ethical business conduct, and the generation of a good impact on society as well as the environment.

When we look into the future, we see that there will be a growing emphasis placed on sustainable business models, the incorporation of green practices, and the application of circular economy principles. Additionally, the rise of social entrepreneurship, the implementation of inclusive business strategies, and the incorporation of diversity and inclusion initiatives are anticipated to be the defining characteristics of the success of enterprises in the future.

10.1 Key Performance Indicators for Tourism

The tourism sector is a substantial contributor to the economy of the entire world. It encompasses a diverse array of activities, ranging from travel and hospitality to cultural experiences and outdoor activities. Understanding and accurately assessing one's performance inside one's organization, whether it be a destination, a business, or an organization functioning within the tourism industry, is crucial for both growth and long-term sustainability. The use of key performance indicators, or KPIs, is essential to accurately gauging the success of tourism-related endeavors and achieving both short- and long-term objectives, as well as gaining valuable insights for ongoing enhancement. In this piece, we will discuss the notion of key performance indicators (KPIs) in the tourist business, as well as their importance and many crucial KPIs that are used to evaluate various elements of the industry.

Having a Solid Understanding of the Key Performance Indicators (KPIs) Within the Tourism Industry

KPIs, also known as key performance indicators, are quantitative measurements that can be used to evaluate the efficiency, productivity, and success of a company, a particular endeavor, or an entire sector. In the context of the tourism business, key performance indicators (KPIs) offer helpful insights into a variety of areas, such as destination management, hospitality, transportation, marketing, and the level of satisfaction experienced by tourists. By monitoring these indicators, stakeholders will be able to make decisions based on accurate information, effectively manage resources, and improve the tourism experience as a whole.

The Value of Key Performance Indicators in Tourism

Using Key Performance Indicators (KPIs) as Benchmarks Key performance indicators serve as benchmarks for monitoring the success of tourism-related initiatives. These measures, whether they pertain to the occupancy rate of a hotel, the number of visitors to a place, or the revenue of a tour operator, assist stakeholders in determining whether or not their objectives are being reached.

Enhancement of Performance: Key Performance Indicators (KPIs) provide insights into areas that need to be improved. Tourism businesses and destinations can apply methods to improve their product lines and customer service by first evaluating data to see where their operations fall short and then identifying problem areas.

Allocating Resources It is essential to effectively allocate resources in the hospitality and

tourism business. KPIs enable stakeholders to more effectively manage their budgets, human resources, and marketing efforts by concentrating their attention on those aspects of the business that produce the best outcomes.

Advantage in the Competition Keeping track of Key Performance Indicators (KPIs) assists firms to maintain their competitive edge. By comparing their own performance to that of their rivals, a company can determine its strengths and weaknesses, which paves the way for strategic adjustments that can either keep it ahead of the competition or give it an advantage over it.

Visitor Satisfaction: In the end, ensuring that visitors have a positive experience is one of the most important focuses of those working in the tourism sector. KPIs that are related to the comments and ratings left by customers can assist organizations in better comprehending the experiences of their customers and implementing any modifications that are required.

Tourism's Most Important Key Performance Indicators

This Key Performance Indicator (KPI) is used in the Hospitality Industry to measure the percentage of available rooms or accommodation units that are occupied within a given time frame. It is a primary determinant for hotels, resorts, and other types of lodging facilities. A higher occupancy rate is indicative of increased revenue as well as better usage of available resources.

ADR, which stands for "average daily rate," is a term used in the hospitality industry to refer to the average amount of money made from each room or housing unit. In the hospitality business, it contributes to the analysis of pricing strategies and the generating of income.

Revenue per Available Room, also known as RevPAR, is a metric used in the hospitality industry to evaluate a hotel's overall performance. This metric takes into account both the occupancy rate and the average daily rate. It is an indication of how successfully a hotel is renting out its available rooms and bringing in income.

Customer Satisfaction Score in the Hospitality Industry: Measuring customer satisfaction through questionnaires or online reviews is an effective way to evaluate the quality of the service that is being offered. Higher levels of customer satisfaction almost always result in additional recurring business and favorable word-of-mouth marketing.

This key performance indicator (KPI) relates to the hospitality industry and displays the typical number of nights that guests remain at a location. A lengthier stay often results in higher expenditure, which has a multiplied effect on the economy of the host community.

The number of tourists who arrive at a destination is an essential key performance indicator (KPI) for tourism boards and organizations that manage destinations. It is a reflection of a location's popularity as well as its overall appeal.

This key performance indicator (KPI) is used in destination management to evaluate how well one destination performs in comparison to others in terms of attracting tourists. It is helpful in identifying chances to expand market share through the implementation of marketing strategies and the development of infrastructure.

Economic Impact (Destination Management): It is vital to measure the economic impact of tourism to a region's GDP in order to evaluate the relevance of the industry and advocate for its continued growth and viability.

Load Factor in the Transportation Industry (Transportation Sector): In the transportation industry, load factors are monitored by airlines and other transportation providers to determine how well they are utilizing available capacity. Operations are more productive when they have a high load factor.

Website Traffic and Conversion Rate (Marketing and Promotion): The number of website visitors and their conversion rate (the percentage of website visitors who convert into bookings or inquiries) are crucial measures of the efficiency of an organization's online marketing activities. This is especially true for enterprises that are directly or indirectly tied to tourism.

Assessing tourist feedback and online reviews helps comprehend the visitor experience, identify areas for development, and manage the reputation of destinations and enterprises, all of which are important aspects of the customer experience.

KPIs linked to environmental effect, such as carbon footprint reduction, water conservation, and community participation, are becoming increasingly essential as sustainability becomes a big concern in the tourism industry. Sustainability Metrics (Environmental and Community effect): As sustainability becomes a key concern in the tourism industry, KPIs related to environmental impact.

KPIs for the Tourism Industry: What the Future Holds

Metrics Relating to Sustainable Tourism Key performance indicators (KPIs) relating to sustainable practices, carbon neutrality, and responsible tourism will become more prominent as more tourists look for environmentally beneficial and ethical vacation options.

Metrics for Digital Transformation As the impact of digital technology on the travel and tourist sector continues to expand, key performance indicators (KPIs) pertaining to online presence, e-commerce, and the efficiency of digital marketing will become increasingly important.

KPIs that are based on experiences: Because visitors are increasingly placing a higher value on one-of-a-kind experiences, KPIs that are tied to the variety and quality of experiences that are provided by destinations and enterprises will become more common.

Data Analytics and AI-Driven Metrics: The utilization of data analytics and artificial intelligence for real-time monitoring and predicting key performance indicators will play a crucial role in the improvement of decision-making and the personalization of the visitor experience.

Metrics Relating to Health and Safety In a world in which a pandemic has ended, key performance indicators (KPIs) relating to health and safety, such as requirements for hygiene and emergency response readiness, will be essential for maintaining traveler confidence.

In the tourist sector, Key Performance Indicators (KPIs) are vital instruments for gauging the level of one's success. As this dynamic industry continues to undergo change, stakeholders are required to modify their key performance indicators (KPIs) to account for shifting customer preferences, developing trends, and widespread issues. The tourism sector may strive for continual improvement and long-term sustainability by monitoring the appropriate indicators and making decisions based on the data collected. This will allow the industry to provide outstanding experiences for tourists while also making a beneficial contribution to the economy of the world as a whole and the communities it serves.

10.2 The Importance of Data and Analytics

In today's world, information is being produced at a rate that has never been seen before. Every action that we carry out, regardless of whether it is done online or offline, leaves a digital imprint that may be gathered, evaluated, and converted into insightful new understandings. The introduction of big data and the development of tools for sophisticated analytics have radically changed the way in which individuals, corporations, and organizations make decisions. This article investigates the significance of data and analytics, as well as their function in a variety of industries and the revolutionary effect they have on the ways in which we comprehend, plan, and execute our endeavors to achieve success.

A Wealth of Insights Can Be Obtained From the Data Revolution

The exponential rise of data and our capacity to gather, store, and process it is one of the defining characteristics of the data revolution. This explosion of data is the result of the growth of data from a variety of sources, including as social media, e-commerce transactions, devices connected to the Internet of Things (IoT), sensors, and other sources. The proliferation of data, which is frequently referred to as "big data," has ushered in a new era in which companies have access to massive volumes of information to inform their decision-making processes. In this new era, organizations are able to make more informed decisions.

In the World of Business and Trade

The landscape of business has been significantly altered as a result of the proliferation of data and analytical tools. The amount of precision with which companies are now able to study the behavior of their customers, monitor their sales, and anticipate changes in the market was previously inconceivable. The ability to make decisions based on collected data gives businesses the ability to improve the quality of client interactions, manage their supply chains, and build more targeted marketing campaigns.

E-commerce behemoths such as Amazon, for instance, employ data analytics to deliver personalized product recommendations to customers based on the customers' previous purchases and browsing behavior. This not only boosts revenue but also the overall happiness of the company's clients.

Within the Fields of Healthcare and Medicine

Data and analytics are extremely important in the healthcare industry, playing a part in everything from the diagnosis and treatment planning of patients to the discovery of new drugs and the monitoring of diseases. Electronic health records, also known as EHRs, are capable of storing significant amounts of patient information. This data can then be examined in order to recognize patterns and trends, which ultimately results in more precise diagnoses and improved treatment strategies.

In addition, the integration of data from wearable health devices and the internet of things makes it possible to remotely monitor patients, which paves the way for earlier intervention and improved health management. The use of predictive analytics can assist healthcare providers in more effectively allocating resources, predicting illness outbreaks, and bettering the outcomes for their patients.

Regarding Instruction and Online Learning

Data and analytics have brought about a revolution in education by making it possible to customize each student's educational experience. Data is used by educational institutions and online learning platforms to monitor student performance, determine subject areas in which students may be having difficulty, and customize lessons to meet the specific requirements of individual students.

For instance, adaptive learning platforms make use of data to modify the level of difficulty of questions and information based on a student's success. This results in a learning path that is more tailored to the student's needs and is more efficient.

When it comes to the Government and Other Public Services

Various levels of government make use of data to enhance public services and to make better policy decisions. For example, transportation authorities can examine data on traffic flow in order to improve traffic flow and lessen the impact of congestion. Data can be used by public health officials to monitor the spread of diseases and appropriately distribute resources when an emergency occurs.

In addition, data and analytics play a crucial role in the creation of smart cities. In these cities, data collected by sensors and Internet of Things (IoT) devices assists municipal governments in managing resources, enhancing the quality of life for inhabitants, and improving infrastructure.

The Importance of Analytics in the Process of Developing Insights from Data

Data, despite the fact that it is valuable, is devoid of significance in the absence of the tools and procedures necessary to analyze it and generate insights from it. The process of analyzing data in order to identify patterns, trends, and correlations and, eventually, insights that can be put into action is referred to as analytics. This analytical competence is what enables firms to properly leverage the power that data can provide.

The query "What happened?" is answered by this sort of analytics, which is called descriptive analytics. It entails looking at historical records in order to gain an understanding of past happenings and patterns.

Organizations are able to better comprehend their current position and acquire an overall perspective of their performance with the assistance of descriptive analytics.

Diagnostic Analytics: Diagnostic analytics takes one step further by answering the question, "Why did it happen?" Diagnostic analytics can be thought of as the "why" in the previous sentence. It investigates the reasons that certain historical events or patterns occurred. Organizations are able to make better educated judgments about how to handle issues and enhance future results if they first determine the underlying causes of certain outcomes and then analyze the relationships between those causes and the outcomes.

The focus of predictive analytics is shifted to the future, and the question, "What is likely to happen?" is attempted to be answered. This form of analytics looks at past data in order to develop forecasts about what might happen in the future. It is helpful for making decisions in advance and determining whether or not there may be prospective opportunities or risks.

The most advanced type of analytics is called prescriptive analytics, and it is characterized by the combination of data, analysis, and simulation in order to prescribe particular courses of action. It provides the response to the inquiry, "What should we do?" This kind of analytics is extremely helpful in pointing decision-makers in the direction of the most effective solutions, whether they work in business, healthcare, or any other field.

The Revolutionary Effects That Data and Analytics Have Had
Better Capacity for Making Decisions:

Decision-making that is driven by data results in better, more well-informed choices. It is helpful in the corporate world for the development of products, marketing strategies, and the allocation of resources. For individuals, it helps in making educated decisions regarding their personal lives and their finances.

For instance, financial firms employ predictive analytics to evaluate the risk of extending credit to individuals and to decide whether or not individuals are eligible for loans or credit cards; this results in more precise decisions regarding lending.

Improvements in Both Productivity and Efficiency:

Analytics may detect inefficiencies in processes and operations, which enables businesses to simplify workflows, cut costs, and make better use of their resources.

In the manufacturing industry, for example, data analytics can help identify the maintenance needs of various pieces of machinery, which helps save downtime and ensure constant production.

Personalized expression:

The capability of analyzing enormous quantities of data enables a level of personalization that has not been seen before. Businesses are able to personalize the experiences they provide to customers by catering their goods and services to the tastes of specific individuals.

Streaming services such as Netflix make personalized content recommendations to users by analyzing their watching habits and preferences using data collected from the users' devices.

Innovation as well as the Development of New Business Models:

The analysis of data can lead to the discovery of new business models and prospects. Using data, businesses are coming up with new ideas for products and services, satisfying customers' requirements that were previously unfulfilled.

For example, Uber has revolutionized the taxi and transportation sector by utilizing data analytics to provide on-demand rides based on real-time data. This has led to significant cost savings for customers.

Healthcare, as well as the Management of Illness:

Data and analytics have produced tremendous improvements in the healthcare industry, particularly in the areas of disease prediction, diagnosis, and treatment. The accuracy of diagnostic choices can be improved with the use of machine learning algorithms, which can examine medical images, recognize patterns in patient data, and more.

For instance, IBM's Watson software makes use of natural language processing and machine learning to analyze massive volumes of medical literature and patient data in order to provide medical professionals with assistance in the diagnosis of difficult medical diseases.

Maintenance that is Predicted:

The application of data analytics has revolutionized maintenance procedures, particularly in sectors that are heavily dependent on machinery. Downtime may be cut, equipment lifespans can be extended, and maintenance schedules can be made more efficient if businesses monitor their equipment and predict when repair will be required.

Predictive maintenance is used by airlines, for example, to maintain the safety and reliability of their aircraft by predicting when individual components will require replacement or repair.

Sustainability in Relation to the Environment:

The use of data analytics is becoming increasingly important in the process of identifying and addressing environmental problems. It makes it possible to improve activities aimed at resource management and conservation, such as optimizing energy use, minimizing waste, and managing water resources, among other things.

The implementation of smart grids, which make use of data analytics to control and optimize energy distribution, is absolutely necessary for both the conservation of energy and the reduction of emissions of greenhouse gases.

Data and Analytics: Obstacles to Overcome and Things to Consider

Privacy and protection of sensitive data:

Concerns regarding an individual's right to privacy and safety are raised when personal data are gathered and used. policies such as the General Data Protection Regulation (GDPR) and the California Consumer Privacy Act (CCPA) have been enacted to protect the data rights of individuals. In order to avoid legal and reputational concerns, businesses must comply with these policies.

The Quality and Integrity of the Data:

It is essential that the data be accurate and of high quality. Incomplete or inaccurate data can result in inaccurate analysis, which in turn might lead to conclusions that are not optimal. In order for businesses to guarantee the accuracy of their data, they need to make investments in data quality management.

Bias in the Data and Fairness:

Data that has been tainted by bias might contribute to the maintenance of unfair or discriminatory policies. It is absolutely necessary to overcome prejudice when collecting and analyzing data in order to guarantee justice and equity in the decision-making process.

For instance, recruiting algorithms that are dependent on previous data have the potential to unintentionally perpetuate gender or racial prejudices in the recruitment process if they are not carefully built and maintained.

The Ethics of Data:

Both the collecting of data and its interpretation need to be guided by ethical considerations. When using data to make decisions that affect individuals' lives, such as in the healthcare industry, the criminal justice system, or the loan industry, there is the potential for ethical problems to occur.

Ethical artificial intelligence frameworks and oversight organizations help ensure the appropriate and ethical use of data.

It is impossible to adequately convey the significance of data and analytics in the modern world. Individuals and organizations in a wide variety of industries now have the ability to make educated decisions, improve operational efficiency, and propel innovation because to the abundance of data and the sophisticated analytical tools and techniques that are available to them. As we move forward in our efforts to harness the revolutionary power of data and analytics, it is absolutely essential that we address concerns pertaining to privacy, data security, data quality, bias, and ethics. If we accomplish this, we will be able to release the full power of data and analytics, which will allow us to create a world that is more effective, equitable, and innovative.

10.3 Emerging Trends in Tourism Economics

The tourism industry is an essential part of the world's economy because of the considerable contributions it makes to the fields of employment, revenue generation, and cultural interaction. The study of tourism economics has developed significantly over the years, incorporating a wide variety of elements that have an impact on travel patterns, consumer behavior, and the selection of destinations. The field of tourism economics is undergoing significant upheaval as a consequence of the ongoing transformations taking place in the world. These trends, which are being driven by technological breakthroughs, altering consumer preferences, and global events, are essential to comprehending the future course that the tourist industry will take and the ramifications that this will have for the economy.

The rise of digital technology and online platforms

The growing prevalence of digital technology in the travel industry has brought about a sea change in the ways in which vacationers plan, book, and experience their travels. Consumers now have access to a plethora of options and rates that are comparable thanks to the proliferation of online platforms and travel aggregators as essential components of the booking process. This digital shift has led to greater price transparency, which has made the market more competitive and pushed traditional travel agents' profit margins lower.

In addition, the proliferation of online platforms that facilitate the sharing economy, such as Airbnb and HomeAway, has caused a disruption in the hospitality industry.

As a result, vacationers now have access to a wider variety of lodging options, and homeowners have fresh opportunities to increase their income. These digital platforms have had a considerable influence on the economics of tourism, which has changed the dynamics of the market and posed a challenge to traditional business models used in the industry.

Tourism that is Both Sustainable and Responsible

There is a growing desire for tourism that is both environmentally conscious and responsible as people become more knowledgeable about environmental issues and sustainable practices. More and more tourists are looking for accommodations that are friendly to the environment, participating in activities that aid in the advancement of local conservation efforts, and patronizing companies that can demonstrate a commitment to minimizing their negative effects on the environment. This pattern has had an impact on the formulation of legislation and initiatives pertaining to sustainable tourism, which have in turn encouraged locations as well as enterprises to adopt ecologically friendly methods and to foster community involvement.

Through the promotion of genuine and moral travel experiences, sustainable tourism not only helps to protect natural resources and cultural heritage, but it also results in economic advantages for the communities in which it operates. As the momentum of this trend continues to grow, it is anticipated that it will cause changes in the behavior of consumers and have an influence on the development of new tourism products and services that place an emphasis on sustainability and responsible practices.

Travel That Is Both Personalized and Experiential

Travelers in the modern day are looking for more individualized and immersive experiences during their trips, experiences that are catered to their own interests and preferences. The need for genuine cultural encounters, regional food, and off-the-beaten-path sites has resulted in a change away from the old model of mass tourism and toward a model of travel that is more individualized and experiential.

In order to satisfy this desire, travel destinations and businesses that cater to tourists are expanding their product lines and producing bespoke experiences that offer distinctive insights into the customs and rituals of the places they visit. This tendency has substantial repercussions for the economy since it fosters the establishment of small-scale businesses, supports cultural interaction and community-based tourist initiatives, and fosters the creation of specialty tourism products.

Tourism Dedicated to Health and Wellness

The increased attention paid to health and wellbeing on a global scale has played a role in the growth of a new industry known as health and wellness tourism.

This type of tourism involves tourists seeking out locations and activities that encourage relaxation, renewal, and overall well-being. This movement involves a variety of facets, such as wellness-focused resorts, spa retreats, yoga and meditation retreats, and medical tourism, in which individuals travel outside of their own country to receive specialized medical treatments.

New opportunities have been made available to places as a result of the growth of the health and wellness tourism industry. These destinations may now diversify their tourism offers, profit on their natural resources, and attract high-spending travelers looking for immersive and life-changing experiences. This pattern has also driven the incorporation of wellness services into mainstream tourism, which has led to the development of travel packages with an emphasis on wellness as well as the construction of infrastructure and facilities related to wellbeing.

Management of Emergencies and Developing Resilience

The tourism business is extremely susceptible to disruptions and crises originating from the outside world, such as the occurrence of natural disasters, political unrest, and pandemics on a worldwide scale. In particular, the COVID-19 pandemic brought to light the significance of crisis management and resilience in the tourism industry. At this time, locations and businesses are reassessing their risk management strategies, diversifying their revenue streams, and putting in place solid contingency plans in order to lessen the effect of potential future crises.

As a result of this pattern, it has become abundantly clear that there is a pressing requirement for more coordination among the various stakeholders, the establishment of policies that are malleable and adaptable, and investments in both technology and infrastructure in order to guarantee the sustainability and resiliency of the tourism industry. The importance of crisis management and the ability to bounce back quickly from setbacks has emerged as a core pillar of the tourism industry as countries and cities struggle to win back the trust of tourists and adjust to an ever-shifting threat landscape.

Tourism centered on Culture and Heritage

The number of tourists interested in visiting historical sites, cultural monuments, and traditional activities has contributed to the rise in popularity of cultural and heritage tourism. This movement has resulted in the renaissance of historic cities, the protection of cultural heritage places, and the development of cultural understanding and interchange. Destinations are capitalizing on their one-of-a-kind cultural assets in order to entice tourists with the promise of genuine and all-encompassing cultural experiences. In doing so, they are helping to ensure the continuation of local customs and contributing to the growth of cultural tourism infrastructure.

The promotion of local economies, the creation of employment opportunities, and the support of community development programs are all significant contributions that may be made by cultural and heritage tourism.

This trend is projected to promote investments in cultural tourism programs and encourage collaboration between tourist stakeholders and local communities. As travelers increasingly value cultural immersion and the preservation of history, this trend is also predicted to encourage cultural tourism.

Increasing the Variety of Tourist Attractions

The extension of the tourism season and the attraction of a more diverse group of tourists are two goals that can be accomplished by locations that make an effort to diversify the kinds of visitors they cater to. Destinations are broadening the types of tourism they provide in addition to the classic sun-and-beach vacation. Some of the newer types of tourism include adventure tourism, ecotourism, culinary tourism, and sports tourism. Destinations have the ability to accommodate to the ever-changing interests and preferences of tourists, promote year-round visitation, and boost economic growth in a variety of sectors by diversifying the tourism products that they offer. These sectors include retail, transportation, and the hotel industries.

This pattern has encouraged the development of niche tourism markets, the enhancement of tourism infrastructure, and the collaboration between the public and private sectors in order to create innovative and competitive tourism products that differentiate destinations and contribute to the long-term economic sustainability of those destinations.

10.4 Preparing for Future Challenges

The world is characterized by continuous transformation, and the future is rife with unpredictability. Individuals, businesses, and communities all need to be ready to take on a variety of difficulties in order to thrive in today's world, which is marked by rapid technology breakthroughs, shifting global dynamics, and unanticipated catastrophes like as the COVID-19 epidemic. Constructing resiliency and flexibility in order to confidently traverse the unknown is a necessary step in the preparation process for the future. In this article, we will discuss the significance of being well-prepared for upcoming obstacles, important tactics for building resilience, and the ways in which individuals and organizations may adopt a proactive mindset in order to succeed in a world that is always evolving.

The Crucial Role of Being Well-Prepared for Upcoming Obstacles

Keeping an Eye Out for Change:

Recognizing that change is unavoidable is the first step in getting ready for it, despite the fact that upcoming problems are frequently hard to forecast. Individuals and organizations are able to adopt a proactive approach to meet future uncertainties if they acknowledge the potential of disruption and comprehend that issues will come.

The Art of Building Resistance:

Building resilience, or the capacity to tolerate and adapt to adversity, is an important part of getting ready for the difficulties that lie ahead. Not only does resilience assist individuals and organizations in bouncing back from failure, but it also positions them to succeed in spite of the challenges they face.

Taking Advantage of Opportunities:

The only thing that can be gained from a challenge is a new opportunity for development, innovation, or transformation. Challenges are not always a bad thing. Those who make preparations for the difficulties that lie ahead are in a better position to identify and grab opportunities that may present themselves during times of upheaval.

Improving One's Capacity to Decide:

Having a plan in place to tackle upcoming obstacles makes decision-making easier. Even in the face of unpredictability, individuals and organizations are able to effectively manage risks by making educated decisions when they adopt a proactive mentality.

Adjusting Oneself to the Changing Global Dynamics:

The globe is becoming more interconnected, and as a result, individuals and organizations are being impacted in a variety of different ways by global events and trends. To adequately prepare for future issues, one must first have a grasp of, and then adapt to, the global dynamics.

Important steps to do in order to be resilient and adaptable

Learning New Things and Improving Your Skills Constantly:

The capacity for education and adjustment becomes increasingly important in a world that is always shifting. To ensure continued success in their chosen industries, both individuals and businesses must make lifelong education, the acquisition of new skills, and the updating of existing ones a top priority. Adopting what has been defined as a "growth mindset" by psychologist Carol Dweck inspires a passion for education and a readiness to view adversity as an opportunity for personal advancement.

Planning for Various Outcomes and Managing Risk:

The process of visualizing a number of different possible futures and devising tactics for each of those possibilities is called scenario planning. This strategy enables individuals as well as organizations to plan ahead for a variety of issues and get ready for them, thereby lowering the impact of unanticipated occurrences.

The process of detecting potential risks, determining their likelihood and impact, then developing and putting into action strategies to either reduce or respond to those risks is what's involved in effective risk management. The ability to recognize and manage risk effectively are essential components of resilience.

The importance of both diversification and redundancy:

Increasing resiliency can be accomplished by diversifying one's resources, investments, and methods. This may entail, for individuals, diversifying their sources of income or investing in the development of a wide range of abilities. The supply networks, client bases, and revenue streams of organizations are all susceptible to diversification.

Increasing a system's or process's adaptability can also be accomplished by incorporating redundancy. This may involve having backup plans, duplicate data storage, or staff who are cross-trained so that they can cover for one another in the event that they are absent.

Preparedness for Emergencies and Response to Emergencies:

The formulation of well-defined contingency preparation and response plans is absolutely

necessary in order to effectively meet unforeseen situations. In the event of an emergency, these plans should detail the roles, duties, communication tactics, and resource distribution that will be implemented.

Invention and Creative Problem Solving:

Adaptability can be increased by fostering a culture that values innovation and creativity. People and businesses should be on the lookout for creative solutions to existing problems, should welcome change, and should be open to experimenting with new methods.

Wellness in Relation to Emotional and Psychological Aspects:

The ability to bounce back from adversity is dependent not just on circumstances in one's environment, but also on one's own emotional and mental health. Taking care of oneself, learning how to deal with stress, and growing one's emotional intelligence are all vital components of resilience. Enhancing an organization's resilience can be accomplished by building a pleasant working environment, offering assistance for employees' mental health, and promoting employee well-being.

Adopting a Mindset That Is More Proactive

A Look Ahead and Some Planning:

Being proactive entails keeping an eye on the future, being aware of potential obstacles, and formulating solutions accordingly. In order for people to attain their aims, they need to define goals, organize their work into priorities, and devise action plans. In a similar vein, businesses ought to have strategic plans that account for both short-term and long-term objectives, as well as incorporate contingency plans for dealing with potential obstacles.

Building Relationships and Working Together:

Increasing flexibility can be accomplished by cultivating a relationship web that is both supportive and cooperative. Individuals are better able to access resources, knowledge, and opportunities as a result of networking, and businesses are better able to interact with partners and industry peers to share expertise and address common difficulties.

Ability to Adapt and Move With Ease:

A proactive mentality is characterized by the individual's ability to respond to challenges with agility and flexibility. When it is deemed necessary, individuals and organizations should be willing to adapt their strategy, change their direction, or pivot.

Generosity of spirit:

Being resourceful is making the most of the resources you have at your disposal. It is important for people to develop the ability to make do with what they have, while businesses should strive to maximize their utilization of assets, human resources, and technology.

Initiative and a sense of self-motivation:

To have a proactive mentality, it is necessary to have the ability to self-motivate and to take the initiative. Setting and achieving objectives should be a motivating factor for individuals, and organizations have the ability to encourage a culture of employee ownership and initiative within their workforce.

Constant Introspection and Efforts at Betterment:

Individuals and organizations can better discover areas in which they can grow by engaging in periodic acts of self-evaluation and reflection. Adopting a proactive mentality entails making a commitment to one's own never-ending expansion and improvement.

The Part That Modern Technology Plays in Getting Ready for Upcoming Obstacles

Data analytics and predictive modeling: the two go hand in hand

Individuals and businesses are able to make decisions that are informed by data thanks to the use of predictive modeling and data analytics. They are able to anticipate issues, make choices that are proactive, and optimize operations through the analysis of trends and patterns in the data.

Working from a distance and collaborating digitally:

The ability to work remotely and collaborate digitally was essential during the COVID-19 epidemic, and technology made both of these things possible. With the help of technologies like video conferencing, remote work tools, and cloud-based project management platforms, businesses are able to respond more swiftly to unforeseen disruptions.

Automation and the use of artificial intelligence:

Both artificial intelligence (AI) and automation have the potential to increase productivity while simultaneously lowering the rate of human errors. Automation, for example, can make production processes more efficient in the manufacturing industry. Chatbots driven by artificial intelligence can provide assistance around the clock in customer support.

Instruments for Resilience-Based Planning and Monitoring:

There is a wide variety of tools that can help businesses prepare for resilience and monitor possible hazards, and there are also platforms that can do this monitoring. The planning of scenarios, the assessment of risks, and the management of crises are all areas in which these tools might be helpful.

Protecting Information and Preventing Cyberattacks:

In a world that is becoming increasingly digital, cybersecurity is absolutely necessary. The ability of an organization to withstand prospective assaults is improved when robust cybersecurity measures are implemented to protect its data and infrastructure from being compromised by cybercriminals.

Innovative Problem-Solving and Market-Shifting:

Technology encourages innovation while also causing disruption in conventional industries, which results in the creation of new opportunities. Individuals and businesses alike can improve their ability to compete and adapt to changing circumstances by embracing innovative technology and undergoing digital transformation.

In a world that is always evolving, it is critical for individuals, organizations, and communities to develop strategies to meet the challenges that lie ahead. Both resilience and adaptability are essential qualities that equip us to overcome unforeseen challenges, make the most of opportunities, and successfully traverse the complexities of the future. We may better prepare ourselves to meet the unknown with confidence, purpose, and a dedication to continuously growing and improving by adopting a proactive mentality, implementing essential techniques for resilience, and embracing technology as an enabler. This will allow us to better tackle the unexpected. As we look into the future, we realize that our collective success and well-being will be heavily dependent on our capacity to both anticipate and successfully navigate upcoming obstacles.

www.ingramcontent.com/pod-product-compliance
Lightning Source LLC
LaVergne TN
LVHW011938070526
838202LV00054B/4702